GREENS CONCISE SCOTS LAW

PI

CW01498694

Kenneth Miller, LL.B., LL.M., PhD.
Senior Lecturer in Law, University of Strathclyde

and

Peter Robson, LL.B., PhD.
Solicitor, Reader in Law, University of Strathclyde

W. GREEN/Sweet & Maxwell
EDINBURGH
1991

First published 1991

© 1991
W. GREEN & SON LTD.

ISBN 0 414 00959 2

A catalogue record for this book
is available from the British Library

Printed in Great Britain by
Thomson Litho

PROPERTY

OGNI ELICA GIRA

PREFACE

This book is intended as an introduction to the Scots law of property. It seeks to outline the basic principles, to explain them and where possible to provide a context for their application. The aim is to produce a clear and concise statement of the law as it applies to property rights generally. Thus the book not only covers those legal concepts which have been regarded traditionally as being part of property law but also deals with the recent statutory developments which both extend and restrict property rights. It examines the common law rules which define property, which regulate ownership rights in moveable property and which create the basic framework of land law in Scotland and also considers the common law and statutory rules pertaining to leases, the statutory regulation of housing and the rights of spouses and cohabitees in matrimonial homes.

The work is aimed principally at law students and is intended to meet the need for a basic textbook which covers the broad principles of Scottish property law. However, the authors have become aware over the years that other groups of students also require access to basic information on the wide scope of Scots property law. Thus the book is also aimed at students attending housing courses or studying land economy at the Scottish universities, polytechnics and colleges. It should also be of value to anyone in Scotland who is seeking membership of the Institute of Housing.

Peter Nicholson at Greens on his many visits to Strathclyde, encouraged us to write this book. Thanks Peter. We are also most grateful to Kenneth Norrie who read the complete book in manuscript and who made numerous helpful suggestions for improvement, most of which have been adopted in the final text. Special thanks are due to Jane Hutton, Denise Greenlees, Cathy Smith, Catherine Whitters, Ruth Anderson, Liz McCallum, Irene Williamson, Elaine Smith, Jean Clark and Helen Pratt.

We would also like to put on record our gratitude to our colleagues at this Law School whose patience with Rolf Harris and the Everly Brothers shows no sign of wearying. Thanks must also go to Rosemary Campbell, the Editorial Manager at Greens, who did an excellent job making sure that our manuscript saw light of day as a book. We are grateful to Ian Bryce who is responsible for the Tables

vii

of Cases and Statutes and the Index. We would like to thank our wives, Margaret and Andrina whose interest in our work remains constant. Finally, thanks too for Love Street and Roker. Sadly the cover could not cope with these or Parkhead. We have compromised in Hampden and Dens.

We have tried to state the law as at May 31, 1991. Any errors or omissions remain those of the other authors.

Kenny Miller and Peter Robson
Glasgow
July 1991.

CONTENTS

TABLE OF CASES

TABLE OF STATUTES

Chapter 1

THE NATURE OF OWNERSHIP OF PROPERTY

1. Introduction

This chapter is intended to consider some of the basic questions in property which will recur throughout much of this book. One critical issue which must be confronted is to explore what is meant in law by "property." As far as common parlance is concerned the word property can either be used to mean a person's ownership of some thing, or, alternatively, to refer to a thing which is actually capable of ownership. Our first task is to discover whether the law acknowledges this particular dichotomy. It is then necessary to consider what rights are given in law to those who possess property. In this regard, we shall also consider the forms of property ownership which are recognised in Scots law.[1]

2. The Meaning of Property

It is also true that in legal terms the word "property" is capable of use in a number of different senses. The law recognises the concept of property either in the sense that it is synonymous with ownership or as describing the things which are capable of creating a right of ownership.

(a) Property as Ownership

The first sense in which the word property is used in Scots law is consistent with the notion of ownership, *i.e.* to talk of someone's

---

[1] For reasons of space we discuss what Charles Reich described as new property rights only in relation to housing in Chap. 12—*The New Property* (1964) 73 Yale L.J. 733. For income support see A. Ogus and E. Barendt, *The Law of Social Security* (3rd ed., 1988).

property is to imply that they own the thing. This ownership can be absolute in the sense of ownership of a house based on the recording of a valid title in the Land Registers of Scotland or in the General Register of Sasines. Alternatively it may be limited as, for example, in the case of the restricted rights of ownership enjoyed by a liferenter who obtains the benefits of the income accruing from a thing but has no rights to the capital. However, as we shall discover, even absolute rights of ownership such as those acquired through registration may be subject to qualification. For example, one's right of property may be qualified by the existence of a "servitude" over one's land in favour of a neighbour.

(b) **Property as the Thing Owned**

The word property is also used to denote the subjects of ownership, *i.e.* the things over which a right of property is enjoyed. In this case Scots law makes a number of divisions, generally based on the divisions which Roman law applies to the word *res*. This can be defined as anything that is the subject of a right and would apply to anything that could form part of a person's property. In Roman law the original division of things was between those things which were the subjects of divine law and those which were not.[2] The former were the property of no person, whereas the latter were usually the property of someone.

A more elaborate division was made by the Emperor Justinian.[3] He divided property into things that could and things that could not be the object of property. There were four types of *res* which could not be the object of ownership:

    res communes—for example, the air or the sea, which were by the law of nature common to all humanity;

    res publicae—for example, public roads and all rivers and parks: since these things were dedicated to public use they could not fall into the ownership of an individual;

    res universitatis—for example, baths or theatres which were held by a municipality for the use of people in general; and

    res nullius—things that did not have an owner, such as wild animals or unoccupied land.

This type of division has generally been followed in Scots law. Thus, just as in Roman law, there are certain things which are incapable of

---

[2] Gaius, *Inst.* ii. 2.
[3] See generally Just., *Inst.* ii. 1 *et seq.*

private ownership such as the sea, air or water flowing in a stream (although the latter two can be appropriated to the ownership of someone, for example, by using air to pump up tyres or by obtaining water for drinking purposes). There are also certain things which are reserved for the use of the public as part of the *regalia*. The Crown's rights of ownership take two forms. First, there is the *regalia majora* which consists of those rights which are vested in the Crown as custodian of the public interest and which cannot be alienated to any subject. The other type of Crown property right is the *regalia minora* which are rights which are held by the Crown as absolute proprietor, but which can be conveyed to subjects. Examples of the *regalia* include the Crown's rights in the sea and the foreshore, navigable rivers, ferries, ports and harbours and roads. In addition certain basic minerals such as gold, coal, gas and oil have in the past been deemed sufficiently important to belong to the community.[4] Equally, as we shall discover, wild animals have no owners until such time as they are appropriated and taken into the possession of the person who becomes their owner. Apart from the above, almost everything else is capable of private ownership under Scots law, except where statute declares otherwise.

It must be noted that the things which the law considers capable of ownership are not limited to concrete, tangible things but include intangible, metaphysical things such as the right to be repaid a debt and rights arising from contract. Such rights are considered items of incorporeal property and are discussed in Chapter 2 below.

(c) Rights Implied by Property

The term property can also be used in law to denote the unlimited right to the use, enjoyment and disposal of a thing. This would be unlimited in the sense that there are no restraints placed on the thing by the operation of the law or under the terms of any contract.[5] As Lord Halsbury L.C. stated in *Glasgow Corporation* v. *McEwan* (1899) 2 F. (H.L.) 25:

> "A person who is entitled to exclude anyone else, and who is himself entitled to enjoy and possess a thing must be in any ordinary sense of the term, the proprietor."

However, the proprietor, as well as having rights of exclusion,

---

[4] These issues are discussed in more detail in Chap. 7 below.

[5] Erskine, *Inst.*, II,ii,1.

enjoyment and possession in relation to the thing, must also have a right to dispose of it. If this right is missing then the "proprietor" does not have complete rights of ownership. As we shall see, it is not unusual in Scots law for the right of possession and the right of disposal to be separated (as, for example, in the case of landlord and tenant). Where a person does possess the sum of all the rights over the thing (or *res* from Roman law) they are said to have the *dominium*. In certain circumstances property may, however, be owned jointly or in common with others and this places further restrictions on the rights of the owner (see below in this chapter).

(d) Forms of Property Ownership

There are various ways in which property can be owned. The most straightforward is simple undivided ownership. This arises where one person has complete rights of exclusion, enjoyment, possession and disposal of property. Traditionally in Scotland heritable property (*i.e.* land) was taken in the name of men. More complex forms of ownership have been developed in Scots law, particularly where the *res* is to be owned by a number of different people. However, this is an area where some of the legal concepts are undeveloped and confused.[6] More recently, changes in the status of women and their involvement in the waged economy have meant that property is usually taken in the joint names of both parties. This is generally done through the mechanism known as joint property. In addition there are relationships where property is owned by two or more people but where they have the right to insist on the dissolution of the relationship and with it the related property rights. This is known as common property. Finally certain special property rights exist as a result of the common interest which individuals have to preserve the structure or amenity of their property. This is best illustrated by the rules governing the mainte- nance of various parts of tenement buildings.

(i) Simple property

Where an individual owns property there are two major con- siderations which need to be taken into account. Does the property owner have legal capacity to deal with the property? For example, in the case of pupil children (boys below 14, girls below 12) whilst

---

[6] See Kenneth G. C. Reid, "Common Property: Clarification and Confusion," 1985 S.L.T. (News) 57; "Common Interest" (1983) 28 J.L.S. 428 and "The Law of Tenement" (1983) 28 J.L.S. 472; "The Law of the Tenement" (1990) 35 J.L.S. 368.

title to land may be taken in their names any dealings in the property would need the consent of their tutor. There may also be limitations placed on the enjoyment of the property stemming from legal or conventional restrictions.[7]

(ii) **Joint property**
Property held jointly arises in two major ways. It makes its appearance chiefly in matters of heritage, but moveables may also be owned jointly or in common.[8] It arises in heritage where the title deed or lease is taken in joint names with a survivorship clause. Alternatively it may stem from the relationship between the parties such as partnership or trusteeship. In the case of joint property, two rules are central to the concept:

    (a) the owners of the property have no separate estates, but only one estate vested in them *pro indiviso*, not merely in respect of possession, but also in respect of the right of the property; and

    (b) the right of one owner transfers on that person's death to the other/s, and cannot be alienated or disposed of either to another living person or on death.

A typical example of this form of property is ownership by trustees, club members or partners.[9] The land is possessed undivided and the owners have a single title to the property. All the parties have an equal interest in the property which passes to the survivor/s. The most frequent modern example one might encounter is a joint tenancy. Local authorities from the mid-1970s have changed their allocation practices and have offered tenancies to husbands and wives in joint names. Initially this was to protect wives against arbitrary marital eviction. The Matrimonial Homes (Family Protection) (Scotland) Act 1981 now supplements this conventional protection with legislative occupancy rights (see Chapter 11 below).

(iii) **Common property**
Common property is distinct from joint property. Here the property does not pass on to the other owners on the death of one proprietor but rather there exist separate property rights in the property which is possessed undivided. Two rules are central to common property:

---

[7] See generally, Chaps. 3, 4 and 8 below.

[8] See generally, Chaps. 3 and 4.

[9] See Lord President Cooper in *Magistrates of Banff* v. *Ruthin Castle Ltd.*, 1944 S.L.T. 373 at p. 388. *Cf.* the decision of the 2nd Division in *Murray* v. *Johnstone* (1896) 23 R. 981 as far as clubs are concerned.

(a) each proprietor has a title to their own share which they may sell or transfer by their own act;
(b) on the death of one of the owners, their share will pass under their will or be distributed according to the rules of intestate succession.

Thus, although the property is possessed undivided, each separate owner has their own separate title to some portion of the undivided whole, which they are at liberty to sell and which they can leave in their will or otherwise be distributed on death in accordance with the rules of intestate succession. This form of ownership was more important in the days prior to 1964 where there still existed the phenomenon of "heirs portioner." An heir portioner existed where there was no male. All the females of the same degree held the property equally. Today it is not so common, although it does exist in the case of some tenement property.

Management

As regards management of common property, the principle operates that in common property the position of the one prohibiting takes precedence.[10] Thus in an action regarding any alteration in a common subject, the person opposing an alteration is favoured above the person desiring to give effect to it. In other words, the person prohibiting has a virtual right of veto. An example would be one co-proprietor preventing others from removing tenants unless better rents or better security are offered.

However, this maxim can be overcome in circumstances where necessity demands it. Thus in *Deans* v. *Woolfson*,[11] for example, where an outside stair of tenement property common to two proprietors was destroyed it was held that one proprietor was entitled to rebuild the common stair notwithstanding the veto of his co-owner. The maxim did not apply to such a necessary restoration as was proposed.

Division

So long as the situation of common property exists no owner has title to any identifiable part of the property, but any party may at any time call for division of the property by agreement or if no agreement can be reached, an action for division can be brought.[12] If the property is, in fact, indivisible, there can be an application for the sale of the property and division of the realised value. Where

---

[10] Covered by the brocard "*In re communi melior est conditio prohibentis.*"
[11] 1922 S.C. 221.
[12] *Upper Crathes Fishings Ltd.* v. *Barclay*, 1989 S.C.L.R. 560 (division of fishings).

the property owned in common is a matrimonial home in terms of the Matrimonial Homes (Family Protection) (Scotland) Act 1981 the court's permission must be sought for such a division and sale.[13] In exercising its powers the court must have regard to all the circumstances of the case, and in particular to the conduct of the parties, their needs and resources, the needs of any child of the family, any business use of the home and whether the spouse seeking the sale decree has offered suitable alternative accommodation.[14] Merely offering half the property price has been deemed inadequate,[15] as also has refusing permission for a sale where the aim was simply to improve the divorce settlement.[16]

(iv) Common interest

Bell defined common interest as:

> "A species of right differing from common property takes place among the owners of subjects possessed in separate portions, but still united by their common interest."[17]

An example of this form of ownership exists in lochs or non-navigable rivers where, because of the parties' common interest in the water, riparian proprietors can take action to prevent unauthorised intrusion on their water. It can also apply to light and air. In *Donald & Sons* v. *Esslemont & Macintosh*[18] three proprietors who owned property in the same street as another proprietor were held to have a title to object to the erection of a bridge by this third party which would have linked the properties which he owned on both sides of the street. Their title was based, *inter alia*, on the fact that as members of the community they had a common interest not merely in the surface of the street but in the space above it. It was held that the proposed bridge would be an appropriation of part of that space for private use.

Law of tenement

The most striking example of common interest is as regards the law of tenement. Here we are talking about flatted dwellings on two or more storeys, owned by separate proprietors who, as well as

---

[13] s. 19.
[14] s. 19; discussed more fully in Chap. 12 below.
[15] *Hall* v. *Hall*, 1987 S.L.T.(Sh.Ct.) 15.
[16] *O'Neill* v. *O'Neill*, 1987 S.L.T.(Sh.Ct.) 26.
[17] *Princ.*, § 1086.
[18] 1923 S.C. 122. See also *Thom* v. *Hetherington*, 1988 S.L.T. 724 (common interest in a garden wall).

owning certain parts of the tenement in common property, have a common interest in the preservation of the fabric of the entire tenement.

Normally nowadays the rights and obligations of the owners of flats in tenements are generally determined from their title deeds and the proportion of contributions for repairs are laid down by rateable value, equally, or some other formula. However, in the absence of such provisions the common or customary law of tenement will apply.[19]

(a) *Roof*

The roof and the space beneath it[20] is the property of the owner of the highest storey. Top storey owners must make sure they do nothing to impair its efficacy as a shelter from the weather. They must ensure that it is properly maintained in order to provide this shelter to all the proprietors in the tenement. The lower proprietors have a common interest in the roof which entitles them to enforce the obligation of maintenance, etc., on the topmost proprietor.

(b) *Solum*

The solum area, which includes the court and back green, belongs to the ground floor proprietors, subject to a right of common interest in the upper proprietors, entitling them to resist any injurious alteration (*e.g.* support, or the building of anything which would encroach upon their light and air).[21]

(c) *Walls*

The owners of each flat have sole property in their own internal walls and ownership of that portion of the external walls which bounds their flat. However, the other proprietors have a common interest to prevent damage to the stability of the building. In the case of internal walls between flats there is a right of common property vested in all those persons whose property abuts the wall,[22]

---

[19] The state of the law of tenement in Scotland is currently being considered by the Scottish Law Commission. See D.P. No. 91, *Law of Tenement* (December 1990). See also Kenneth G. C. Reid, "The Law of the Tenement: New Thoughts on Old Law" (1983) 28 J.L.S. 472.

[20] *Taylor* v. *Dunlop* (1872) 11 M. 25.

[21] See generally, *Johnston* v. *White* (1877) 4 R. 721.

[22] Rankine, *Landownership* (4th ed.), p. 667. Kenneth Reid has argued that this is not a sensible rule and that it would be better to make each proprietor sole owner to the halfway point with a right of common interest over the other half—"The Law of the Tenement" (1983) 28 J.L.S. 472 at p. 474. There is sheriff court authority to the effect that in the case of a mutual wall each proprietor has a right of property *ad medium filum*. See *Gill* v. *Mitchell*, 1980 S.L.T.(Sh.Ct.) 48.

and other proprietors have a common interest to prevent significant harm to the wall.

(d) *Gables*

Initially, it was held that the proprietors of the flats adjoining common gables had a common property in the totality of the gable.[23] However, it is now clear that each proprietor is the sole owner of the gable *ad medium filum* with a common interest in the other half.[24] This latter view was confirmed by the Second Division in *Trades House of Glasgow* v. *Ferguson*,[25] where it was held that the proprietor of property with a common gable was responsible to the other proprietor for half the cost of demolition of the wall caused by loss of support. The loss of support came about when the neighbouring proprietor demolished the top three stories of his tenement and roofed it above the first floor.

(e) *Floors and ceilings*

The floor and roof of each flat are divided by a notional line drawn through the mid-line of the joists. In this case neither party is entitled to weaken the floor or ceiling or to expose them to unusual danger of fire. The duties involved here only amount to the proprietors of the lower flats providing support for the proprietors of the upper flats. The upper proprietors in turn must provide cover for the lower flats. This duty is in no sense absolute. In *Thomson* v. *St Cuthbert's Co-operative Association Ltd.*[26] the Court of Session was asked to consider whether a ground floor proprietor was liable, without specific proof of negligence, for damage done to an upper flat as a result of the fracture of a cast-iron supporting beam situated within the ground floor. It was held that the law of tenement did not impose absolute duties of mutual support or protection on the proprietors of tenement flats. In order for liability to be established, negligence on the part of the ground floor proprietors had to be proved. This decision was followed in the sheriff court case of *Kerr* v. *McGreevy*.[27] In this case the proprietor of the lower flat had

---

[23] *Law* v. *Monteith* (1855) 18 D. 125; *Rodger* v. *Russell* (1873) 11 M. 671.

[24] See, *e.g. Robertson* v. *Scott* (1886) 13 R. 1127.

[25] 1979 S.L.T. 187.

[26] 1958 S.C. 380. The law of nuisance may also provide a cause of action for loss of support—*Lord Advocate* v. *Reo Stakis Organisation Ltd.*, 1981 S.C. 104. However, where the proprietor is seeking damages for loss of support under the law of nuisance, some averments of fault must also be made. See the decision of the House of Lords in *R.H.M. Bakeries (Scotland) Ltd.* v. *Strathclyde Regional Council*, 1985 S.L.T. 214.

[27] 1970 S.L.T.(Sh.Ct.) 7.

damaged an upper flat when carrying out alterations authorised under warrant of the dean of guild court. The upper proprietor sought compensation for the damage caused, averring in effect that the lower proprietor owed him an absolute duty. Sheriff Macvicar held that negligence had to be established before a case would lie against the lower proprietor. It was the view of the sheriff that it had to be shown that the lower proprietor had breached a duty of reasonable care which he owed towards the upper proprietor. Since no breach of such duty was averred the action was dismissed.

(f) *Common passages and stairs*

There is no doubt that these are held in common property by all the proprietors in the tenement. However, it is unclear on what basis such property rights are distributed. Rankine argued that ownership should only vest in those proprietors who required to use the passages and stairs for access.[28] More recently, Reid has suggested that the best solution is to accept that each proprietor co-owns the entire passage and stair in equal shares.[29] Neither position is supported by any judicial authority.

The interest in the other flats which owners of flats in tenement property have, does not arise from the creation of a series of servitudes, but exists by virtue of being incidents of ownership of tenement property. The rights themselves really stem from the common interest which each proprietor of a tenement flat possesses. As Lord Dunedin explained in *Smith* v. *Giuliani*[30]:

"each proprietor of a flat is proprietor of it, but along with his proprietorship there is linked the common interest in the walls or roof, as the case may be, of the other proprietors and this common interest is not a right of servitude nor of common property, but is a right of a proprietary character."

---

[28] *Landownership* (4th ed.), p. 677. See also J. G. S. Cameron, "The Law of the Tenement," I Conv.R. 105 and 248 and II, 102 at p. 105.

[29] "The Law of the Tenement" (1983) 28 J.L.S. 472 at pp. 475–476.

[30] 1925 S.C.(H.L.) 45.

CHAPTER 2

CLASSIFICATION OF PROPERTY RIGHTS

THERE are a number of different ways in which property can be classified. Scots law makes no distinction between personal property for use and property for profit.[1] The law in Scotland protects property whether its basis is in work, creativity or stemming from mere inheritance. The various classifications of the subjects of property which do exist in Scots law serve both to explain the nature of different kinds of property as well as having a clear practical function:

1. Heritable and moveable property;
2. Corporeal and incorporeal property; and
3. Fungible and non-fungible property.

1. HERITABLE AND MOVEABLE PROPERTY

The most important division made by Scots law is into property which is heritable and property which is moveable. This classification follows the old Scots law of intestate succession, whereby property which was connected with the land went to the heir-at-law (the eldest son), and has attracted criticism as being misleading.[2] The classifications are broadly that heritable property covers land and its pertinents together with all rights in and connected with the land, whilst moveable property entails that which by its nature and use is capable of motion or being moved and rights connected with such property. Items may be heritable or moveable according to their nature, by conversion from moveable property to heritage or by the fixing of moveable property to heritage—the law of fixtures (see below at Chapter six).

(a) **By Nature**

Lands and buildings are clearly heritable. So also are stones and

---

[1] Thorstein Veblen, *The Theory of the Leisure Class* (1925).
[2] Gloag and Henderson at p. 611; T. B. Smith at p. 907; W. Gordon at p. 3.

minerals and trees[3] so long as they remain part of the ground. Cut timber, for example, is clearly moveable. The natural fruits of the land, such as grass,[4] which requires no constant cultivation, are also heritable until severed. However, there are problems as regards the exact classification of industrial fruits. Erskine argued that "those annual fruits which require yearly seed and industry as wheat, barley etc. are accounted moveable even before separation, from the moment they are sown or planted."[5] This view would ensure that an agricultural tenant would have no difficulty in removing industrial crops which he has sown since, they are classified as items of moveable property. In *Chalmer's Tr.* v. *Dick's Tr.*,[6] however, a tenant's right of severance was regarded more as a privilege than as an actual property right. Here Lord Low argued that an industrial crop "until separation is not moveable property of the tenant ... the crop is *pars soli*, but the law recognises the right of the tenant who has sown it, to separate it from the soil, unless he has contracted not to do so."

(b) **By Destination**

It is also possible for moveable property to be regarded as part of the heritage in cases of succession, by application of the fiction of conversion. This concept treats money which is required to complete a building which remains unfinished at the date of a person's death as heritage. The amount of money which is required to complete the building will be calculated on the basis of the plans which the deceased has adopted. It operates on the basis of an intention by the deceased to benefit the heritage at the expense of the moveable estate.[7] However, the concept has a wider application because it also operates in the case of a collection of building

---

[3] *Paul* v. *Cuthbertson* (1840) 2 D. 1286. On the other hand, in *Begbie* v. *Boyd* (1837) 16 S. 232 trees in a nursery garden were held to be moveable.

[4] At one time hay was considered to be a natural crop and so was treated in the same way as grass: see *Sinclair* v. *Dalrymple* (1744) Mor. 5421. However, it would now seem that hay must be treated in the same way as other industrial crops and may, therefore, be classified as moveable: see *Lyall* v. *Cooper* (1832) 11 S. 96.

[5] ii. 2, 4. Approved by the Whole Court, albeit *obiter*, in *Paul* v. *Cuthbertson* (1840) 2 D. 1286.

[6] 1909 S.C. 761. But see also *McKinley* v. *Hutchinson's Trs.*, 1935 S.L.T. 62.

[7] See *Malloch* v. *McLean* (1867) 5 M. 335, where Lord Ormidale held that the portion of the deceased's estate which was required to complete his house, in accordance with the plans, was, by destination, heritable. This decision has been criticised by Lord President Clyde in *Fairlie's Trs.* v. *Fairlie's C.B.* 1932 S.C. 216, who argued that it should have rested on the notion that the money required was a personal debt of the deceased.

materials piled on the ground which are ready to be added to the construction.[8] In such a case these items would also be regarded as heritable. It should be stressed that this concept applies only to the law of succession and has no operation in any other part of Scots property law.

(c) By Accession

This principle ensures that an item of property which is moveable in nature and which becomes affixed to heritage can lose its identity as a moveable and become part of the heritable property.[9]

Importance of Heritable/Moveable Classification

The heritable/moveable division emerges in a variety of contexts— the most important being succession, diligence and as regards the sale and lease of heritage. In all of these situations it is important to know whether an item is classified as heritable or moveable.

(i) Succession

Prior to 1964, although the heritable property of an intestate passed to male descendants, widows enjoyed a liferent of part of the heritable property of their deceased husband—called *terce*.[10] This right was superseded under the present rules of intestate succession as laid down in the Succession (Scotland) Act 1964,[11] by prior rights. Prior rights entitle the surviving spouse to a house up to the value of £65,000, furniture and plenishings up to a value of £12,000 and a financial sum from the remaining estate of £21,000 if there are any surviving children and £35,000 if the intestate dies without surviving children.

Whilst it is possible to defeat prior rights by making a will, there are also legal rights from the moveable property which exist irrespective of any will which may have been made. The surviving spouse is entitled to one-third of the moveables and the children also receive one-third—these shares are increased to one-half if

---

[8] *Johnston* v. *Dobie* (1783) Mor. 5443.

[9] The rules which apply to such a change of classification are discussed in more detail below in Chap. 6 at pp. 45–50.

[10] The equivalent right for widowers was a liferent of a proportion of moveables called *courtesy*.

[11] ss. 8, 9. See D. R. Macdonald, *An Introduction to the Scots Law of Succession* (1990) Chap. 4.

there are no surviving children/spouse. Accordingly any person who wishes to ensure that the surviving spouse or children are to receive nothing on their death can only do so at present in Scotland by ensuring that their property is tied up in heritage.

(ii) **Diligence**

Where a creditor is seeking recompense for debts, it is important to know the type of property upon which the debt is based in order that the appropriate action can be brought. There are special forms of diligence which can only be used in relation to heritable property—inhibition and adjudication.[12] These allow the heritable creditor valuable rights over other creditors by providing a high degree of security and ultimately the right to acquire the heritable property. The appropriate legal procedure in relation to corporeal moveable property is through the process of poinding, whereby the goods of the debtor are ascertained and valued and may be sold under warrant of the court.[13]

(iii) **Sale and lease**

The heritable/moveable distinction is also important in the case of the sale of heritable property, as the moveables in the house do not form part of the sale. The seller is entitled to take any moveable property away subject to contractual variation. In the absence of express agreement there may be disputes over what exactly is moveable. Similarly tenants have rights over items of moveables which they have brought on to the property and which have become part of the heritage under the rules governing fixtures. In certain circumstances these may be removed by the tenant.[14]

2. CORPOREAL AND INCORPOREAL PROPERTY

A further classification can be made between these kinds of property. This stems from the Latin *corpus*—body:
  corporeal—tangible and visible, *e.g.* a car; and
  incorporeal—intangible and invisible, comprising rights such as a patent or goodwill.
  Combining these two forms of classification, any type of property in Scotland can be categorised into one of four groups:

---

[12] G. L. Gretton, *The Law of Inhibition and Adjudication* (1987).
[13] G. Maher and D. Cusine, *The Law and Practice of Diligence* (1990), esp. Chap. 9.
[14] These issues are discussed below in Chap. 6 at pp. 49–50.

(i) corporeal heritable property, *e.g.* land or houses;
(ii) incorporeal heritable property, *e.g.* leases and servitudes;
(iii) corporeal moveable property, *e.g.* bicycle or television; and
(iv) incorporeal moveable property, *e.g.* copyrights or trademarks.

3. FUNGIBLE AND NON-FUNGIBLE PROPERTY

There is an additional division which can be made by classifying property as either fungible or non-fungible. A fungible is something which is destroyed by being used—such as money, grain or coal—and can be replaced by equal quantities of the same quality. A non-fungible—such as a work of art—is not destroyed in use, has a specific individual value and cannot be replaced by a similar thing.[15] This classification is important where liferent is involved, since the normal rule is that this involves the enjoyment of property without destroying or encroaching upon the substance of the property.[16]

---

[15] Erskine, *Inst.*, III,i,18, also mentions a horse in this context.
[16] See Chap. 11 at pp. 167–170.

CHAPTER 3

CORPOREAL MOVEABLE PROPERTY

1. NATURE

CORPOREAL moveable property consists of those tangible items which, as we have noted, are capable of motion and are not connected with land or buildings. Animals, cars, clothes and money in cash are all typical instances of corporeal moveable property.[1]

2. ACQUISITION

As we have noted, possession of property gives certain privileges to the possessor.[2] However, it does not by itself confer ownership, although it may set up such a presumption. In order to obtain ownership a person must utilise one of the undernoted mechanisms. There are various distinct ways in which moveable property may be obtained, the majority of which are unique to moveable property, although accession does also operate in relation to heritable property.

(a) Occupation

This is the most primitive way of acquiring property. Moveables which have never been owned by any person become the property of the person who appropriates them, so long as that person has the intention of becoming owner. Accordingly, any wild creatures such as animals, birds or fish or even shells or pebbles can be acquired by the first person to take possession of them—*quod nullius est fit primi occupantis*.[3] Once confined such items remain the property of the

---

[1] See Chap. 2 above.
[2] See Chap. 1 above.
[3] Stair, II,i,33; Erskine, II,i,10; Bell, *Prin.*, §§ 1287ff.

person who exercises control over them and to remove them would be theft. The above items are only capable of acquisition through occupation so long as they have never been the property of anyone—known as *res nullius*. Since there is no property right in a *res nullius* until it has been acquired, apart from under statute, it cannot be theft for someone to shoot or otherwise acquire a wild animal which is on the land of another. However, upon the escape of a wild animal these property rights will be lost when the owner ceases to pursue the creature in order to regain possession.[4] It should be noted that there are certain categories of wild animal such as royal birds and salmon which belong to the Crown so that rights of property cannot be acquired by occupation. Domestic animals, or marked animals as well as those creatures with a homing instinct such as bees, pigeons (and hunting birds) remain the property of their owners even when they stray. Complicated issues of proof of original ownership of domestic animals have arisen, particularly with cats shuttling between two sets of "owners" unbeknown to the other parties.

Occupation is not available for property already in the ownership of another. Thus lost property is not covered by the *quod nullius* maxim. The general rule is that the owners of lost articles still retains possession in them so long as they have the necessary intention of keeping possession or *animus possidendi*. It may be that under Scots common law lost, abandoned or ownerless property goes to the Crown under the maxim *quod nullius est fit domini regis*.[5] There are very few Scottish cases on this issue,[6] and it has not attracted the same level of controversy as it has in England.[7] The present law on finding in Scotland is governed by Part VI of the Civic Government (Scotland) Act 1982, which requires the finder of lost or abandoned property to take reasonable care of it and without unreasonable delay to deliver it or report the find to a police officer.[8] It is clear that no right to claim ownership of the lost article is created by the act of finding alone, although in the event of the property not being claimed the chief constable has the discretion to give the article to the finder.[9] There is no doubt that the Crown can

---

[4] *Ibid.*

[5] See Erskine, II,i,12; Bell, § 1290.

[6] See, *e.g. Corpn. of Glasgow* v. *Northcote* (1921) 38 Sh.Ct. Rep. 76 and *Dawson* v. *Muir* (1851) 13 D. 843.

[7] *Cf. Bridges* v. *Hawkesworth* (1851) 21 L.J.Q.B. 75 and *South Staffordshire Water Co.* v. *Sharman* [1896] 2 Q.B. 44. See also *Hannah* v. *Peel* [1945] K.B. 509 and *Parker* v. *British Airways Board* [1982] Q.B. 1004.

[8] s. 67(1).

[9] ss. 73 and 70(1)(*b*).

claim ownership of treasure trove in Scotland, so that any treasure hidden under the ground would fall to the Crown and not to the occupier of the land.[10] Equally, Erskine claims that stray cattle that have been abandoned by their owner do not belong to the finder but pass to the Crown as escheat or forfeited goods.[11] Legislation covers certain items, such as wrecks which require the appointment of receivers of wrecks by the Department of Trade.[12]

(b) Accession

In this instance a person is given ownership of a new thing through his ownership of the original item which has an intimate association with the secondary property[13]—*accessorium sequitur principale*. Thus the owner of an animal also acquires ownership of her offspring[14] and the owner of a fund of money is entitled to the interest.[15] The former is an example of natural accession because it involves a natural increase in quantity. On the same principle, property can be acquired through the operation of natural forces on land. This could apply where a river gradually alters its course so that new land is exposed or where soil is gradually brought down by a stream and deposited on the banks. The other form of accession involves industrial accession, whereby the increase comes about because of some person's industry. There are a number of other forms of industrial accession to which we shall now turn. It should be noted that the legal rules applied in this area lack certainty and consistency, so that in some cases it may be difficult to ascertain the true state of the law.[16]

[10] Stair, II,i,5; Erskine, II,i,12; *L.A.* v. *University of Aberdeen*, 1963 S.C. 533 where the 2nd Division preferred to apply the *quod nullius est fit domini regis* maxim as regards the ownership of the "St Ninian's Isle Treasure" rather than the law that once applied in Shetland.

[11] Erskine, II,i,12.

[12] Under the Merchant Shipping Act 1894, s. 566, the Department of Trade is given the power to appoint receivers of wreck. The receiver must take possession of any wreck and give notice of this fact so that the owner can claim delivery (ss. 520, 521). It is an offence to fail to notify the receiver of the existence of a wreck (s. 518) and ownership of unclaimed wrecks is vested in the Crown (s. 523).

[13] Stair, II,i,34; Erskine, II,i,14–15.

[14] Stair, II,i,34; *Lamb* v. *Grant* (1874) 11 S.L.R. 672.

[15] *Gillespies* v. *Marshall* (1802) Mor. App I, "Accessorium" No. 2.

[16] See on this point the statement of Lord Ardmillan in *Wylie and Lochhead* v. *Mitchell* (1870) 8 M. 552 at p. 561.

(c) **Specification**

The essence of *specificatio* is that where separate items have been brought together to form a new subject in such a way that the original elements cannot be returned to their previous state, ownership of this new subject will vest in its creator. This will apply even although the creator did not contribute any of the materials that were used in the process.[17] If a new subject is created its owner is required to restore to the former owner of the separate items a like quantity and quality, or failing that the price of the material. A good example of the application of specification is *International Banking Corporation* v. *Ferguson, Shaw & Sons*,[18] where cotton seed oil and other substances had been mixed together to make a lard compound. In an action for damages by the previous owners of the oil, the Second Division held that on the basis of *specificatio* a new species of property had been created and that the makers of this new product had ownership in it and were, therefore, required to compensate the pursuers for the value of the oil which had been used.

It has been argued that the concept of specification is based on equity and so can only apply where the maker has acted *bona fide*.[19] However, the view has been criticised as inaccurate in a later case.[20] The Scottish courts have applied strictly the requirement that in the making of the new product the other ingredients must be destroyed. Thus specification will not apply when the front part of one car is welded to the rear part of another car since such a car could be cut into two once more.[21] Equally, market forces alone cannot create a new species for the purposes of *specificatio*, so that when work is carried out on a product in order to make it ready for sale the concept will not apply.[22] The important issue is that there must be change in the property which involves the disappearance of the original articles.[23]

[17] Stair, II,i,41; Erskine, II,i,16–17; Bell, § 1298(1).

[18] 1910 S.C. 182.

[19] *per* Lord President Clyde in *McDonald* v. *Provan (of Scotland Street) Ltd.*, 1960 S.L.T. 231 at p. 232.

[20] See *North-West Securities Ltd.* v. *Barrhead Coachworks Ltd.*, 1976 S.L.T. 99, *per* Lord McDonald.

[21] *McDonald* v. *Provan (of Scotland Street) Ltd.*, *supra* at p. 231.

[22] See the decision of the 2nd Division in *Armour* v. *Thyssen Edelstahlwerke A.G.*, 1989 S.L.T. 182, reversed on other grounds by the House of Lords at 1990 S.L.T. 891.

[23] *per* Lord McDonald in *North-West Securities Ltd.* v. *Barrhead Coachworks Ltd.*, 1976 S.L.T. 99, rejecting the view that *specificatio* could also operate through the application of consumer credit legislation as expressed by Sheriff Principal

(d) **Confusion and commixtion**

Confusion is the term applied when liquids come together, commixtion applies to solids. In both cases there is undoubtedly an overlap with *specificatio*. Where commodities are mixed together and become inseparable, their ownership will be determined by different rules depending on the character of the commodities. If they are of the same kind, the mixer does not become the owner of the product. Instead, the shares are owned in common and are *pro indiviso* according to the quantity and value of the original contribution.[24] However, the mixer of the items will acquire ownership if the substances are different and the process involves the creation of a new item of property with no possibility of restoring the original substances to their owners. If the substances are capable of being returned, then ownership remains with the original owners. Where two parties agree to produce a new object and contribute work or material towards this end, the new item will be held in common property corresponding to the value of the contributions.[25]

(e) **Other forms of accession**

(i) *Contexture.* A typical example of this would arise when materials belonging to one person are worked into cloth or some other manufactured product which belongs to another. If separation cannot take place ownership of the item belongs to the manufacturer, who will be required to compensate the other for its value and may also be required to make reparation for any damage caused.[26] (ii) *Adjunction.* This would apply where a person paints or writes on the property of another. In the case of a painting, if it is made on the walls of someone's house the picture will become the property of the houseowner. Where it is painted on canvas it will belong to the artist, although the owner of the canvas must be recompensed for its value.[27]

Walker in *F. C. Finance Ltd.* v. *Langtry Investment Co. Ltd.*, 1973 S.L.T.(Sh.Ct.) 11.

[24] Bell, § 1298; Stair, II,i,37; Erskine, II,i,17.
[25] *Wylie & Lochhead* v. *Mitchell* (1870) 8 M. 552.
[26] Stair, II,i,39.
[27] *Ibid.*; Erskine, II,i,15.

3. TRANSFER

Under this head we are only considering cases where the transfer is made during the grantor's lifetime (*inter vivos*)—there are different rules which apply in the case of transfers after death (*mortis causa*).[28] Under Scots law no proper transfer of ownership in corporeal moveable property can be achieved by agreement alone. No real right can be created by an agreement for transfer alone, although writing is commonly used in complicated transactions. However, such writing does not effect a transfer of ownership: it merely creates a personal obligation to deliver the thing. The critical element is for there to be actual delivery.[29] As Lord President Inglis said in *Clark* v. *West Calder Oil Co.*[30]:

"A mere assignation of corporeal moveables *retenta possessione* [with retention of possession] is nothing whatever but a personal obligation."

Moreover it is also vital for the owner to have an intention to or to consent to the transmission and delivery of the thing. Property in the subject will not pass unless these two elements are established. However, it would be legitimate for the parties in a contract of sale of moveables to specify that ownership of the goods will not pass until the full purchase price is paid. In such a case, even although there has been delivery, title will not pass until the purchaser has paid the final instalment.[31] The old traditional Scottish rules have also been affected by the provisions of the Sale of Goods Act 1979. Where the provisions of this Act apply the rule is that the passing of property does not depend upon the delivery of the subject, but upon the force of the contract and the intentions of the parties.

British ships
There is a major exception to the these rules about the transfer of moveables as far as British ships are concerned. All British ships must be registered.[32] British ships must be wholly owned by British subjects or corporate bodies established under the laws of Her Majesty's dominions and having their principal place of business

---

[28] D. R. Macdonald, *An Introduction to the Scots Law of Succession* (1990).
[29] Under the brocard "*Traditionibus non nudis pactis dominia rerum transferuntur.*"
[30] (1882) 9 R. 1017 at p. 1024.
[31] *per* Lord Keith of Kinkel in *Armour* v. *Thyssen*, 1990 S.L.T. 891 at p. 893.
[32] Merchant Shipping Act 1894, Pt. I (as amended). The Act does not apply to river boats and coasters less than 13.7 metres in length and certain Canadian boats.

there. The register is evidence of title to the ship rather than proof of possession. The Merchant Shipping Acts also lay down a special procedure which must be complied with involving entry in the register of the details of the ship and those with a share. The property of a ship is divisible into 64 shares and these shares cannot be subdivided. Nor can there be more than 64 owners registered at the same time. Sea fishing boats are owned in 16 shares by at most 16 individuals, and operate under the same régime. Transfer of the whole or of a share is by bill of sale. The registrar must enter in the register the name of the transferee and endorse the bill of sale to this effect. Until this occurs, former owners remain in a position to dispose of the ship or their shares. Contracts for sale themselves do not need to be in writing provided that the registration procedure with bill of sale is adhered to.[33]

---

[33] *McConnochie* v. *Geddes*, 1918 S.C. 391.

CHAPTER 4

INCORPOREAL MOVEABLE PROPERTY

1. NATURE OF INCORPOREAL MOVEABLES

INCORPOREAL moveable property covers such things as rights to debts, rights to shares in moveable property, insurance policies. The constitution and operation of these matters are the subject-matter of mercantile or commercial law, and here we will limit ourselves to a brief comment on the acquisition and transfer of the property rights involved. In addition there are special protections afforded to those intangible rights which arise from creativity in the artistic, scientific or business spheres. We will look separately at the general principles of acquisition and transfer of property covering all incorporeal moveables, then at the specific protections available for patents, copyrights and trademarks.

2. ACQUISITION AND TRANSFER OF OWNERSHIP

In such cases it is obviously impossible to transfer ownership by means of physical delivery. There must be some form of writing which constitutes the transfer. In this branch of the law the deed of transfer is known as an assignation. Unless there is a statutory rule laying down the form of assignation to be adopted—which there very often is—incorporeal moveables can be transferred by any form of writing.[1] This can be very simple in form. In *Brownlee* v. *Robb*[2] it was held to be sufficient, in an assignation of a life policy where all the deed said was: "I, J.R., hand over my life policy to my daughter." The person who grants the assignation is known as the cedent, and the person to whom it is granted is called the assignee.

---

[1] *Carter* v. *McIntosh* (1862) 24 D. 925.
[2] 1907 S.C. 1302.

23

(a) **Assignation**

The basic rule is that the holder of an incorporeal right has title to transfer ownership whenever he or she wishes. Such transfer is effected by assignation so long as the deed of transfer is in writing. There are, however, certain incorporeal moveables which cannot be transferred at all. This is the case where the right is personal to the owner by virtue of the legal concept of *delectus personae* (the choice of a person to the exclusion of all others). So in the case of employment, for example, there can be no assignation of the contract of employment. The contract only exists between the original parties who actually made it. Nor could there be an assignation of an alimentary provision, since the essence of this is personal to the holder,[3] nor of certain leases.[4]

An incomplete assignation will not entail any transfer of rights, as where an assignee of a lease died before the assignation in his favour was intimated to the landlord.[5] The right of the assignee is completed in a question with the cedent by delivery of the assignation. This gives the assignee an effective right, although there will have to be intimation to the debtor to ensure a right against third parties. Whilst the cedent by assigning the incorporeal rights guarantees that these exist, this does not mean they will be effectual. Thus there can be no complaint by the assignee of a debt if the debtor turns out to be insolvent.[6] Debt collection agencies deal with this possibility through discounting such rights.

(b) **Intimation**

As already noted, mere delivery alone only deals with the rights as between cedent and assignee. As far as making the assignee's rights good against third parties is concerned, there must be intimation to those parties. Such intimation completes the assignee's rights. Formal intimation may be made in any of the ways specified in the Transmission of Moveable Property (Scotland) Act 1862, which provides that this may be by—

> (i) a notary public delivering a certified copy of the assignation to the third party with the certificate of intimation of

---

[3] Erskine, III,v,2.
[4] See Chap. 9 below.
[5] *Smith* v. *Riddell* (1886) 14 R. 95.
[6] Erskine, II,iii,25.

the notary constituting sufficient evidence of the intimation;

(ii) the holder of the assignation or by any person authorised by him transmitting a certified copy by post to the third party and a written acknowledgment by that person is sufficient evidence of such intimation having been duly made.[7]

There are, in addition, other forms of notice or acknowledgment which the law regards as equivalents of intimation—probative acknowledgment by the debtor of the assignee's right; citation in an action by the assignee against the debtor; a charge or citation on any diligence against the debtor; production of the assignation in court in an action between them.

Registration of assignation in the Books of Council and Session will not suffice, as these are for preservation and diligence and not for publication,[8] nor is reference to the oath of the debtor enough.

(c) **Effect of assignation**

Provided there is power or consent to assign, the assignee steps into the cedent's shoes and succeeds to the cedent's rights and obligations. Thus every right competent to the cedent is competent to the assignee and the assignee acquires the right to sue or defend a legal action to the same extent as the cedent.[9] However, the assignee cannot obtain any higher right by the assignation than that possessed by the cedent. Thus if the rights of the cedent are flawed it is just as lawful to raise these objections against the assignee unless there is personal bar.[10] Ineffectual assignations have been held to cover loss of a settlement on remarriage,[11] an insurance policy where the original policyholder had made untrue statements as to his health and drinking habits.[12] However, the above rules do not apply to latent claims. An assignee who takes in good faith and for value is not affected by latent trusts or equitable claims affecting the right of the cedent. Such claims undoubtedly affect the rights of the cedent, but do not affect an onerous assignee. This point was

---

[7] s. 2.

[8] *Tod's Trs.* v. *Wilson* (1869) 7 M. 1100; *Cameron's Trs.* v. *Cameron*, 1907 S.C. 407.

[9] These rights are expressed in the Latin maxim "*Assignatus utitur jure auctoris.*"

[10] *Scottish Equitable Life Ass. Soc.* v. *Buist* (1877) 4 R. 1076 at p. 1081; affd. (1878) 5 R.(H.L.) 64.

[11] *Johnstone-Beattie* v. *Dalziel* (1868) 6 M. 333.

[12] *Scottish Widows' Fund* v. *Buist* (1876) 3 R. 1078.

established in *Redfearn* v. *Somervail*,[13] where a man who was apparently the owner of a share in a private company assigned this in security for a private loan. In fact the share in the private company was held as trustee for the firm of which he was a partner. The creditor took the share in the honest belief that he was the true owner and intimated his right. In a competition between the assignee's creditor and the trustee's firm the assignee's claim was upheld. This was on the basis that the dispute was not between the debtor in the obligation and the assignee, but between the assignee and a beneficiary under a trust whose claim was collateral to the transaction which had transferred the share.

3. INTELLECTUAL PROPERTY

(a) Copyright

(i) Nature of copyright

The present law on copyright in the United Kingdom is regulated by the Copyright, Designs and Patents Act 1988. Copyright is a property right which applies to three kinds of work: (a) original literary, dramatic, musical or artistic works; (b) sound recordings, films, broadcasts or cable programmes; and (c) the typographical arrangement of published editions.[14] Such a right comes into being automatically without any formality as soon as the relevant work is created, and restricts to the owner of the work the right to do certain acts in the United Kingdom which are discussed below.[15] However, in the case of literary, dramatic or musical works copyright does not subsist unless and until it is recorded in writing or otherwise.[16] The phrase "literary work" is defined broadly because it covers not only any work, other than a dramatic or musical work, which is written, spoken or sung; but also included in the definition are a table of compilation and a computer program (*sic*).[17] "Artistic work" means

---

[13] (1813) 5 Pat.App. 707.

[14] See generally, s. 1(1)(*a*)–(*c*). As far as a typographical arrangement of published editions is concerned, it is clear that this is intended to cover the way in which the words or symbols are laid out. See s. 8. See generally Hector L. MacQueen, *Copyright, Competition and Industrial Design* (1989).

[15] s. 2.

[16] s. 3(2).

[17] s. 3(1). "Dramatic work includes a work of dance or mime and a musical work is a work consisting of music excluding any words or action intended to be sung, spoken or performed with the music."

a graphic work, photograph, sculpture or collage, irrespective of artistic quality, a work of architecture and a work of artistic craftsmanship.[18]

The material need not be novel nor the work original; the test is whether the work originates from the author rather than being simply copied from another. Owners of copyright have the exclusive right to do the following acts in the United Kingdom.[19] These are to copy the work[20]; to issue copies of the work to the public[21]; to perform, show or play the work in public[22]; to broadcast the work or include it in a cable programme service[23]; and to make an adaptation of the work or do any of the above matters in relation to an adaptation.[24] A wide definition of copying is provided in the legislation. In the case of literary, dramatic, musical or artistic works, copying involves reproducing the work in any material form (including storage by electronic means).[25] It is made clear that a still photograph might infringe copyright in a film.[26] The protection against copying any typographical arrangement of a published work means making a facsimile copy of the arrangement.[27] This definition is wide enough to include not only photocopying but also transmissions by means of "FAX" machines.

There are, however, certain acts which may be done in relation to copyright works which do not involve any infringement.[28] The various permitted acts must be construed independently of each other.[29] There is a defence of "fair dealing" so far as research, private study, criticism, review and news reporting are concerned.[30] In the case of education, copyright in a literary, dramatic, musical or artistic work is not infringed so long as it is done in the course of or preparation for instruction, provided the copying is done by a teacher or student and is not by means of a reprographic process.[31] However, there are special licence arrangements which enable educational establishments to make reprographic copies from

---

[18] s. 4(1).
[19] s. 16(1)(*a*)–(*e*).
[20] s. 17.
[21] s. 18.
[22] s. 19.
[23] s. 20.
[24] s. 21.
[25] s. 17(2).
[26] s. 17(4).
[27] s. 17(5).
[28] See generally, s. 28 and Chap. III.
[29] s. 28(4).
[30] ss. 29 and 30.
[31] s. 32(1).

published literary, dramatic or musical works without infringing copyright.[32] There are also a variety of acts exceptionally permitted within educational establishments[33]; and a range of special rights in relation to copyright material available to those involved in libraries and archives[34] as well as in public administration.[35]

The 1988 Act also introduced a right in the author of a copyright literary, dramatic, musical or artistic work to be identified as author and for the director of a copyright film to be identified as director.[36] Rights arising from such identification are known as "moral rights" and include the right to object to false attribution of work,[37] the right to privacy of certain photographs and films,[38] and the right to object to derogatory treatment of one's work.[39] A person will only infringe the right of identification if the author or director has asserted his right in due manner.[40] There are exceptions where no right to identification can be asserted. These arise in the case of computer programs (*sic*), the design of a typeface and any computer-generated work[41] as well as where the copyright vests in the employer.[42] There are also a variety of actions which do not infringe the moral right,[43] including the reporting of current events, incidental inclusion in an artistic work, sound recording, etc., as well as examination questions, parliamentary and judicial proceedings and Royal Commissions.

(ii) Extent of copyright

Copyright in literary, dramatic, musical or artistic works expires at the end of 50 years from the end of the calendar year in which the author died.[44] As far as sound recordings and films are concerned copyright lasts for 50 years from the end of the calendar year in

---

[32] s. 36.

[33] See s. 34 (performing, playing or showing work in the course of activities of an educational establishment) and s. 35 (recording by educational establishments of broadcasts and cable programmes).

[34] See ss. 37–44.

[35] Copyright is not infringed by anything done for the purposes of parliamentary or judicial proceedings or the proceedings of a Royal Commission or statutory inquiry—ss. 45 and 46.

[36] Chap. IV.

[37] s. 84.

[38] s. 85.

[39] s. 80.

[40] s. 78.

[41] s. 79(2).

[42] s. 79(3).

[43] s. 79(4) and (5).

[44] s. 12(1).

which it was made or, if the date is later, 50 years from the end of year when it is released.[45] A sound recording or film is "released" when it is first published, broadcast or included in a cable programme service or in the case of a film or film sound-track the film is first shown in public.[46] As for broadcasts and cable programmes, the copyright in these expires at the end of 50 years from the end of the calendar year in which the broadcast was made or the programme was included in a cable programme service.[47] Copyright in a typographical arrangement of a published edition expires at the end of 25 years from the end of the year in which the edition was first published.[48]

(iii) Ownership of copyright

The Act makes it clear that the author is the creator of the work[49] and declares that such a person is the first owner of the copyright.[50] The copyright of works produced by employees in the course of their employment belongs in the first place to the employer, subject to any agreement to the contrary.[51]

(iv) Transfer of copyright and moral rights

Copyright is transmissible by assignation, by will or by operation of law as moveable property.[52] An assignation is not effective unless it is in writing signed by or on behalf of the assignor.[53] Moral rights are not assignable[54] although they may be transmitted on death by will or on intestacy.[55]

(v) Remedies for infringement of copyright

An infringement of copyright is actionable by the copyright owner[56] in the Court of Session. In any action for infringement of copyright the owner may seek relief by way of damages, interdict,

---

[45] s. 13(1).
[46] s. 13(2).
[47] s. 14(1).
[48] s. 15.
[49] s. 9(1). For the rules for identifying the author in the case of sound recording, film, broadcast, cable programme or typographical arrangement of a published edition see s. 9(2)(*a*)–(*d*).
[50] s. 11(1).
[51] s. 11(2).
[52] ss. 90 and 177.
[53] s. 90(3).
[54] s. 94.
[55] s. 95.
[56] s. 96.

count, reckoning and payment.[57] Owners also have the right to apply to the court for an order that the infringing copy be delivered up to them.[58] There are also limited rights to seize infringing copies and other articles.[59]

(b) **Patents**

(i) **Nature of a patent**

A patent is a monopoly right given to inventors to prevent others from making or using their inventions. The law regulating patents is to be found primarily in the Patents Act 1977. This Act protects inventors from infringement of their patent rights, and sets out a procedure by which applications for a patent can be dealt with by the Patent Office. Unlike copyrights, where protection is provided by copyright law as soon as the work is created, an invention will only be protected through the existence of a patent once the inventor has sought and obtained such a right. A patent may be granted only for an invention if the following conditions are satisfied. First, the invention must be new,[60] and an invention is new if it does not form part of the state of the art.[61] The state of the art comprises all matter (whether a product, a process, information about either or anything else) which has at any time before the date of the application been made available to the public by written or oral description, by use or in any other way.[62] Second, it must involve an inventive step,[63] and an inventive step is something which is not obvious to a person skilled in the art, having regard to any matter which forms part of the state of the art.[64] Third, it must be capable of industrial application[65] by being made or used in any kind of industry, including agriculture.[66] Lastly, it must not otherwise be excluded by the Act.[67]

The Act does not define an invention, although it does make it clear that certain things cannot be the subject of a patent application. These include (a) a discovery, scientific theory or mathemati-

[57] s. 96(2).
[58] s. 99.
[59] s. 100.
[60] Patents Act 1977, s. 1(1)(*a*).
[61] s. 2(1).
[62] s. 2(2).
[63] s. 1(1)(*b*).
[64] s. 3.
[65] s. 1(1)(*c*).
[66] s. 4(1).
[67] Patents Act 1977, s. 1(1)(*a*)–(*d*).

cal method; (b) a literary, dramatic, musical or artistic work or any other aesthetic creation whatsoever (a matter for copyright law); (c) a scheme, rule or method for performing a mental act, playing a game or doing business, or a computer program (*sic*); and (d) the presentation of information.[68] Further, a patent cannot be granted for an invention the publication or exploitation of which would be generally expected to encourage offensive, immoral or anti-social behaviour or for any variety of animal or plant or any essentially biological process for the production of animals or plants, not being a microbiological process or the product of such a process.[69]

(ii) Application for a patent

As far as the Patents Act is concerned, the act of making an invention confers no rights upon the inventor. The onus is upon the inventors, or a person acting on their behalf, to apply to the Patent Office for patent rights. Any such application must contain a request for the grant of a patent, a specification containing a description of the invention in a manner which is clear enough and complete enough for the invention to be performed by a person skilled in the art, a statement of claim and any drawing where appropriate and an abstract.[70] The date of filing of a patent application is crucial, because it sets a priority date giving that inventor precedence over any similar applications by others which are submitted at a later date.[71] The details of the application must be published and advertised in the journal of the Patent Office.[72]

Thereafter, the inventor may request that the Patent Office appoint an examiner to conduct a preliminary examination and search to ensure that the application complies with all the formal requirements of the Act—*i.e.* is it accompanied by a specification and claim and an abstract?[73] If the applicant wishes the application process to continue, a request must be made for a substantive examination which is the critical stage in the award of a patent. It is at this stage that the examiner will determine the substantive issues pertaining to the patent application—that is, whether the invention is novel, involves an inventive step, is capable of industrial application and is not otherwise excluded by the Act—and will report on these matters to the Comptroller-General.[74] If the examiner reports

[68] s. 1(2)(*a*)–(*d*).
[69] s. 1(3).
[70] s. 14(2) and (3).
[71] See generally, s. 5.
[72] s. 16(1).
[73] s. 17.
[74] s. 18.

that the application complies with the requirements of the Act, the Comptroller will grant the applicant a patent.

(iii) The effect of a patent

The Act declares that a patent shall remain in force for 20 years.[75] However, patent rights are not normally awarded for such a period. Protection is usually awarded for an initial period of four years, with further annual applications required thereafter in order to retain patent rights. Any patent and any right in or under it is incorporeal moveable property.[76] As such it is capable of being assigned to third parties and being used as security so long as the transaction is probative or holograph of the parties.[77] A licence may also be granted by a proprietor of a patent for the working of the invention by others.[78]

The basic right conferred on the inventor by the patent is a right to take action against any person who infringes its terms either directly or indirectly. Direct infringement arises when a person, without the consent of the proprietor of the patent, makes, disposes of, offers to dispose of, uses or imports a product or keeps it for disposal or some other purpose.[79] A similar prohibition applies to a patented process.[80] Patent rights are also infringed directly if someone uses the process or offers it for use when they know, or it is obvious to a reasonable person in the circumstances, that its use is without the consent of the proprietor.[81] There is an indirect infringement if a person, while the patent is in force and without the proprietor's consent, supplies or offers to supply a person with the means, of putting the invention into effect being an essential element of the invention.[82]

(iv) Remedies for infringement

Proprietors of patents have the right to seek interdict in the Court of Session to prevent the defender infringing the patent and a declarator that the patent is valid and has been infringed. They can also obtain damages in respect of infringements or an account of

---

[75] s. 25(1).
[76] s. 31(2).
[77] s. 31(3) and (6).
[78] s. 31(4).
[79] s. 60(1)(*a*).
[80] s. 60(1)(*c*).
[81] s. 70(1)(*b*).
[82] s. 60(2).

profits and an order requiring the defender to deliver up or destroy any products which entail an infringement of the patent.[83]

(c) Trade Marks

At common law a person has no property right in a trade name,[84] although there may be circumstances where a person may have a cause of action for passing-off if another person uses that name fraudulently or to cause avoidable confusion. Essentially, in such a case the person who argues that the trade name has been infringed would have to establish that the name has become so associated with that person's particular goods that they are regarded in the market as theirs.[85] However, there is also statutory regulation of trade marks. The Trade Marks Act 1938 authorises the Comptroller-General to maintain a register of trade marks[86] and to enter:

(a) all registered trade marks with the names and addresses of their proprietors;
(b) notifications of assignations and transfers;
(c) the names and addresses of all registered users;
(d) disclaimers, conditions and limitations; and
(e) other matters as may be prescribed.[87]

A person who wishes the protection of the Act may register a trade mark in respect of particular goods or classes of goods with the Comptroller.[88] The registration of a trade mark is for a period of seven years, although it may be renewed from time to time.[89] Registration as proprietor of a trade mark in respect of any goods gives that person the exclusive right to the use of that trade mark in relation to those goods and entitles the proprietor to prevent others

---

[83] s. 61(1).

[84] See the judgment of Lord President Dunedin in *Charles P. Kinnell & Co. Ltd.* v. *A. Ballantine & Sons*, 1910 S.C. 246 at p. 251.

[85] See generally, W. J. Stewart, *An Introduction to the Scots Law of Delict* (1989), paras. 3.11–3.13.

[86] A trade mark is defined by s. 68(1) as a mark used or proposed to be used in relation to goods for the purpose of indicating a connection in the course of trade between the goods and a person having the right to use the mark. The Trade Marks (Amendment) Act 1984 extended the powers of the Comptroller to cover a service mark. This is a mark used or proposed to be used in relation to services for the purpose of indicating that a particular person is connected, in the course of business, with the provision of those services—s. 1(7).

[87] Trade Marks Act 1938, s. 1(1).

[88] s. 3.

[89] s. 20(10).

using the trade mark or implying that they have a right to use it.[90] A registered trade mark can be assigned to others and may be transmitted in connection with the sale of the goodwill of a business or in other cases.[91] There is also provision to enable a person other than the proprietor of the trade mark to be registered as a "registered user" of the mark.[92] It is an offence to represent an unregistered trade mark as being registered.[93]

[90] s. 4(1).
[91] s. 22.
[92] s. 29.
[93] s. 60.

CHAPTER 5

FORMS OF LANDOWNERSHIP IN SCOTLAND

1. Feudal Landholding in Scotland

(a) Origins and Development

As the White Paper *Land Tenure in Scotland: a Plan for Reform* (Cmnd. 4099) stated in 1969:

"Most land in Scotland is held today on a system of tenure which has its origin in medieval times. This system is feudal tenure which, in its practical operation in the latter half of the present century, is far removed from its beginnings in a feudal society. A feature of that society was the practice whereby a landowning nobleman would grant to a loyal follower the right to a piece of land in return for service: this service would commonly take the form of an obligation to arm and to fight in wars in which the overlord became engaged."

This form of tenure first appeared in Scotland around the time of the twelfth century. It was developed under English influence, particularly during the reign of David I (1124–53) of Scotland. It depends on an hierarchical structure, with the monarch as ultimate lord. Each landholder appeared in this hierarchical chain and was known as a vassal or feuar, which meant that he was required to pay certain homage to his lord and ultimately the monarch because of his position as "paramount superior."

In the beginning the system of feudal tenure in Scotland developed through the King granting tracts of land to his supporters for the assistance they had given him in wars, etc. In return for this grant, the grantee paid homage and service to the King. This homage symbolised the relationship of "lord" and man, and the idea of service formed the basis for the legal classification of the

35

tenure.[1] Moreover, it also ensured that the grantee's title was conditional and not absolute, since the grantor retained an interest in the land.

The whole system was based on a personal grant of land to the King's servant. As a result of the personal nature of the relationship, when feudal tenure was in its infancy, the land was recallable during the grantee's life. This gradually changed to recall on the grantee's death, until ultimately the law developed to permit the land to pass to the grantee's heir. A further aspect of the personal nature of the relationship was that the feudal system forbade the substitution of another for the original grantee. This was on the basis that since the grant was in theory personal, the superior was entitled to insist on retaining the vassal in the chain. If the vassal wished to dispose of his land then he could subinfeudate, *i.e.* become the lord of the next individual by adding a further link to the chain. This contrasts with the English law, where subinfeudation was forbidden by the statute *Quia Emptores* of 1290. In any case, in later times in Scotland, substitution tended to be more prevalent than subinfeudation. However, even when there was substitution of a new vassal for a previous owner, given the pervasive and personal nature of the feudal system the superior had to approve this substitution of vassals. This was called "entry" and entailed either the superior offering a fresh feudal grant to the new vassal or confirming the continuance of the original feudal grant which had been made to the old vassal. Nowadays obtaining a duly recorded or registered title to the property also ensures entry.[2]

In later times grants of land were sold in return for both a purchase price and a fixed annual payment to the superior known as the feuduty. Following changes introduced by the Land Tenure Reform (Scotland) Act 1974, where the deed has been executed after September 1, 1974 there can be no fixed annual payment. In addition, where there has been a sale of land after this date the feuduty (so long as it is allocated) must be redeemed before the sale can go ahead. There is also provision for voluntary redemption of feuduty by a proprietor serving notice on the superior at any term of Whitsunday or Martinmas. The fact that there is no feuduty, however, in no way affects the feudal relationship. The superior/feuar relationship still continues, and the superior is still entitled to place certain restrictions on the use of the land in the deed.

---

[1] For a discussion of the older forms of feudal tenure see W. M. Gordon, *Scottish Land Law* (1989), paras. 2–07 to 2–18.

[2] This process was rationalised by the Titles to Land Consolidation (Scotland) Act 1868, and is a matter which really relates to conveyancing.

(b) **Feudal Relationship Today**

Let us look at a situation where a landowner, X, who owns an estate directly from the Crown, decides to sell part of it to a building company for housing development. Traditionally along with this sale price there would have been charged a feuduty, since the concept of the feudal chain necessitated the existence of a feuduty. However, as we have seen, in any sale after September 1, 1974 no feuduty may be charged. The builder, Y, will then proceed to build a housing estate, and, on completion each house will be sold to buyers A, B, C, D. In the course of these transactions we have built up a chain as shown below.

Feudal Relationships

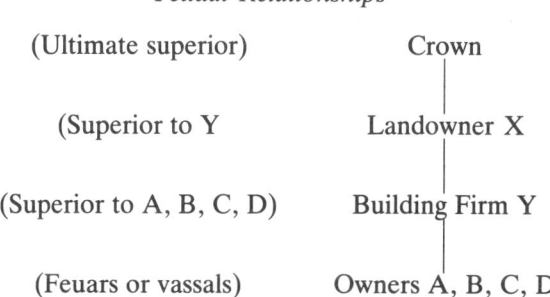

(Ultimate superior)	Crown
(Superior to Y)	Landowner X
(Superior to A, B, C, D)	Building Firm Y
(Feuars or vassals)	Owners A, B, C, D

This chain can extend for as long as the land will bear it.

(c) **Rights and Relationships of Superiors and Feuars**

It is unlikely that the sellers in each of the transactions described above will just hand over their land without laying down certain stipulations in the feudal grant. Thus, X may well stipulate in the sale to Y that Y is to build only houses, and not a shopping plaza, etc. There may even be retention of certain of the property rights associated with the land, such as the right to own and work minerals. Similarly, when Y conveys the houses to A, B, C and D there might well be a stipulation that no garages are to be permitted in the gardens of the houses, or that no house may be used as an office or pub. The nature of the feudal relationship, therefore, permits the superior to lay down certain restrictions called "real conditions or real burdens" on the use of the property.[3]

---

[3] See Chap. 8.

In each of these transactions certain rights have been assigned in return for the performance of a number of duties, principally (before 1974) the payment of feuduty. Thus although A, B, C and D acquire ownership of the property through the sale, Y has not completely given up the entire interest in the property. Y still has an interest to ensure that the restrictions contained in the feudal grant are obeyed, and (where relevant) that any feuduty is paid timeously. Indeed, should any feuar fall down in their obligations the superior has the right to repossess the property. The superior can seek a "declarator of irritancy," which grants the right to repossess the property, although this means foregoing all arrears of feuduty.

The above discussion should make it clear that under the feudal system ownership of the land is actually divided between the superior and the feuar. The feuar in practical terms is the owner of the property, but the superior continues to own a less tangible right, *viz.* the right to enforce the feuing conditions and (in the old days) the right to collect feuduty. Consequently, although the feuar acquires most of the rights to the property under the sale (known as the *"dominium utile"*), some rights are retained by the superior (known as the *"dominium directum"*).

Dominium directum empowers the superior to enforce the conditions of the grant.

Dominium utile gives the vassal exclusive right of possession and enjoyment of the land so long as the conditions laid down are respected.

Dominium plenum is the totality of all rights under the feudal relationship, *i.e.* the combination of both of the above rights.

(d) How a Feudal Grant Is Effected

An original feudal grant could be effected by one of three writs— feu charter, feu disposition and feu contract. The first two deeds are unilateral and are signed only by the grantor. Apart from that, there was very little difference between the three types of deed. More important, in the modern context, is the question of infeftment. Before a person is entitled to exercise feudal rights that person must be infeft. In the old days this involved "delivery of the sasine," where there was a symbolic delivery of the land through a ceremony conducted on the property. Later, infeftment took place once the instrument of sasine was recorded in the land registers. The conveyancing reforms of the nineteenth century[4] permitted the recording of the feudal grant or deed of transfer in the land registers. Since the Land Registration (Scotland) Act 1979, registration of title will suffice in order to create an effective feudal right. As we shall see, it is the registration of title which creates a real right over the property vested in the feuar.

(e) **Reform**

The Scottish Law Commission in their *Fourth Programme of Law Reform* published in April 1990[5] have indicated that their first objective in relation to property law is to consider land tenure law reform with a view to the completion of statutory reform of land tenure. Work on the first discussion paper in the proposed series on the topic of land tenure reform was reported to be well advanced in November 1989, and the Law Commission indicated that a discussion paper proposing the abolition of feudal tenure and its replacement by a system of absolute ownership would be forthcoming in due course.[6]

2. OTHER FORMS OF LANDOWNERSHIP IN SCOTLAND

There are three other forms of landholding in Scotland. These are allodial landholding, contracts of ground annual and long leases.

(a) **Allodial Land**

Although most of the land in Scotland is held under feudal tenure, there are alternative forms of landholding which probably account for about 20 per cent of the total. The most important of these is allodial land. The basic distinction between allodial and feudal land is that allodial landholding does not rely on the doctrine of "universal derivative tenure." There is no derivation of rights through the feudal chain back to the sovereign. Thus allodial property is property which is owned absolutely without acknowledgment of any superior owner.

---

[4] See in this regard the Titles to Land (Scotland) Act 1858 and the Titles to Land Consolidation (Scotland) Act 1868.

[5] Scot. Law Com. No. 126, dated April 25, 1990.

[6] 24th Annual Report 1988–89 (Scot. Law Com. No. 123), Nov. 1989. Due to the wide scope of the topic the Law Commission has had to delay publication of this paper. See 25th Annual Report 1989–90 (Scot. Law Com. No. 128), Nov. 1990.

There are five types of allodial land, as follows:

(a) *The property of the Crown*—the paramount superior can clearly have no superior. Moreover, since all land held under feudal tenure can ultimately be derived back to the Crown, the Crown is entitled to the superiority when no other superior can be ascertained. However, this form of landholding not only encompasses Crown superiorities but covers Crown lands as well. Thus land which has never been feued out or which has been returned to the Crown also falls under this head.

(b) *The property of the Prince of Scotland* which was settled on the eldest son of the sovereign by Act of Parliament in 1469.[7]

(c) *Churches, churchyards, manses and glebes* were exempted from the annexation of Church property after the Reformation.[8] In any case Scots common law recognised that parish churches and churchyards were held by the heritors of the parish under allodial title.[9] By the Church of Scotland (Property and Endowments) Act 1925, churches and manses became the property of and vested in the General Trustees of the Church of Scotland[10] and churchyards were transferred to parish councils.[11] A glebe is that portion of land and other heritable rights which a parish minister is entitled to in addition to his stipend, and its exact ownership is subject to regulations made by the Scottish Ecclesiastical Commissioners.[12]

(d) *Udal land*, which is the land once held under Norse law in Orkney and Shetland, where the owner does not owe any obligations or duties to a superior landholder.

Erskine stated that udal land is held by natural possession and might be proved by witness without there being any title in writing.[13] This anomalous form of tenure arose from the fact that Orkney and Shetland were transferred by Christian I of Denmark to Scotland in 1468, in security for the unpaid part of his daughter Margaret's dowry to James III of Scotland. The islands were formally annexed to the Scottish Crown in 1472 when the balance remained unpaid. The Act 1567 c. 48 declared that neither Orkney nor Shetland should be subject to the common law of Scotland but should continue to have their

---

[7] c. 3 For a discussion as to whether these lands are genuinely allodial see W. M. Gordon, *Scottish Land Law* (1989), para. 3–17.

[8] Act 1587 c. 29.

[9] Stair, II,iii,4; Erskine, II,iii,8.

[10] s. 28.

[11] s. 32.

[12] s. 30 .

[13] *Inst.*, II,iii,18.

own laws. Gradually municipal law has been extended to cover Orkney and Shetland. To this extent, there has been a conflict between the udal law of Orkney and Shetland and the municipal law of Scotland, with the municipal law generally winning the day. However, in *Lord Advocate* v. *Balfour*[14] it was declared that the Crown is not deemed to have been the original proprietor in the islands and so could not claim ownership of salmon fishings.

In *Lord Advocate* v. *University of Aberdeen*[15] the doctrine "*quod nullius est fit domini regis*" ("that which is the property of nobody, belongs to our lord the King"), which is feudal in origin, was applied to give ownership of the "St Ninian's Isle Treasure" to the Crown. To this extent, there is some doubt as to the exact status of udal rights to land.[16]

(e) *Lands compulsorily purchased.* When lands are compulsorily purchased under various statutes, no relationship between the purchaser and the superior of the land is created. The feudal chain is therefore severed, and the lands become allodial. This power to purchase lands compulsorily is conferred by a number of statutes, both general and local. The main types of procedure used under this system are regulated by the Lands Clauses Consolidation (Scotland) Act 1845. The effect of this and subsequent Acts was to destroy the superior-vassal relationship, although the superior could retain the right to recover feuduty by a personal action.

However, feu duties are treated as having been redeemed when land has been compulsorily acquired, and consequently the superiors lose their personal action for feuduty.[17] Since the superior/feuar relationship is destroyed a direct relationship with the Crown and the purchaser is created free from all intermediate superiorities. There is no provision in the forms of statutory conveyance for the insertion of any stipulations as to land use and in effect the superior loses all rights over the land.

---

[14] 1907 S.C. 1360.

[15] 1963 S.C. 533.

[16] For a more detailed discussion of udal law, see *Stair Memorial Encyclopaedia of the Laws of Scotland*, Vol. 24.

[17] s. 6(1) of the Land Tenure Reform (Scotland) Act 1974.

(b) **Contracts of Ground Annual**

The second form of non-feudal tenure arises under a contract whereby a stipulated annual payment is due perpetually from the lands and secured as a real burden over them. This contract of ground annual does not create a feudal relationship between the parties, but merely a personal obligation on the owner to pay the ground annual with the ground being used as security. It is, therefore, the contract and the security which it creates which oblige the purchaser to pay the ground annual. Payment does not depend on the nature of the relationship between the seller and the purchaser.

The reason for the existence of the contract of ground annual was that prior to 1874, when the Conveyancing (Scotland) Act was enacted, the right to sub-feu was prohibited in lands held under burgage tenure (a particular form of tenure found in towns).[18] The relationship which the contract of ground annual constructs is more of the nature of creditor and debtor than superior and feuar. The Land Tenure Reform (Scotland) Act 1974 prohibits the payment of ground annuals in deeds executed after September 1, 1974. There is also provision in the Act[19] for both the voluntary and compulsory redemption of ground annuals.

(c) **Long Leases**

The Registration of Leases Act 1857 provided that leases of over 31 years' duration, which had been recorded in the General Register of Sasines, were to be effectual against singular successors of the lessor even though the lessee had not entered into possession. The Land Tenure Reform (Scotland) Act 1974 reduced the period of duration to 20 years. Thus the 1857 Act provided an alternative method of acquiring occupation of land without resorting to the concept of feudalism, and it was often used as a basis for transferring land rights when there was a prohibition on subinfeudation

Once recorded, a long lease permits occupiers the same sort of enjoyment of their property as they would be given under the terms of a feudal grant. There are now two[20] requirements which must be

---

[18] s. 25 .

[19] ss. 4 and 5.

[20] Formerly the subjects let could not exceed 50 acres (except in the case of mines). This was repealed by the Land Tenure Reform (Scotland) Act 1974, s. 18 and Sched. 6, para. 5.

fulfilled before a long lease can be recorded. First, the deed executing the transfer must be probative, and, second, the period of the lease must be at least 20 years.

The Long Leases (Scotland) Act 1954 permitted the tenant of certain long leases to obtain a permanent "feu right" of the property on certain conditions, provided that the process was started within five years of the introduction of the 1954 Act.

CHAPTER 6

ACQUISITION AND DISPOSAL OF HERITAGE

1. ACQUISITION OF HERITABLE PROPERTY

THERE are three ways in which heritable property can be acquired. It may be acquired originally by occupation, by accession or derivatively by title. Original occupation may be relevant as far as non-feudal land is concerned,[1] but cannot apply so far as the feudal system is concerned, since, as was noted in Chapter 5, all heritage is held in theory from the Crown. This means that possession by a squatter does not confer any rights of ownership under Scots law. Current property holding may be extended where there is an accumulation of silt carried downstream or a river or sea recedes.[2] As far as obtaining property ownership rights from others is concerned, this is done through the acquisition of an *ex facie* valid title. However, any defects in the title which the occupier may acquire can only be cured by the operation of the positive prescription which involves the existence of a valid title plus possession of the property for at least 10 years. Thus the impact of the positive prescription is to perfect an otherwise defective title. Moreover, as we have already noted, the recording of title to the land is crucial because it is this act which grants the possessor a real right effective against the whole world. The systems of registration of title operating in Scotland are discussed below.

Contracts to buy and sell heritable property are *obligationes litteris* and so require probative writing to be effectual. No special form of words is required.[3] Usually, the first step in the sale of heritage will be the exchange of missives which are holograph of the parties and encapsulate the terms and conditions of the sale. At this stage the parties owe personal obligations to each other based upon their agreement as specified in the missives. The right of the

---

[1] Erskine, II,i,11.

[2] Stair, II,i,35; Erskine, II,i,14; Bell, *Prin.*, § 935.

[3] A. J. MacDonald, *Conveyancing*; J. H. Sinclair, *Handbook of Conveyancing*.

purchaser will only become real once there has been delivery of the disposition. However, there are two major problems which should be noted. First, problems have arisen as to conditions in the missives and their impact in relation to any prior communings, since the missives supersede these earlier discussions. In turn missives are superseded by the terms of the disposition. However, the complexity of modern missives means that these rules can no longer be stated with confidence.

The issue was highlighted in *Winston* v. *Patrick*,[4] where there had been a sale of a bungalow with an extension. The missives indicated that the seller warranted that all local authority requirements in relation to the property had been fulfilled. This clause was not repeated in the disposition of sale. It transpired that a building warrant had not been obtained and the purchasers sued in damages for breach of contract on the basis that the sellers had not constructed the extension in accordance with their obligations under the missives. The Second Division considered that the clause did not incorporate any personal obligation on the seller to do anything in the future. At best the clause was merely a statement as to the condition of the property at the date of the missives. This meant that although the purchaser could found on the warranty prior to delivery of the disposition, once the disposition had been delivered no action of damages for breach of contract could be entertained. The result of this case has been the widespread use of clauses indicating that the missives are not to be superseded by the disposition of sale. Extensive litigation[5] now bedevils this once tranquil area where the major question in the past was whether or not certain items were included in the sale. This is the second problem to which we shall now turn.

The general rule is that if an item has become part of the heritage then it is carried in the sale. In order to avoid disputes such matters are normally dealt with expressly in the missives. However, where the missives are silent on a disputed item the rules relating to fixtures apply. The initial inquiry must be whether the item in question is a fixture, *i.e.* whether the moveable is so affixed to the heritage as to become a part of the heritable property. This is

[4] 1980 S.C. 246.

[5] For an excellent summary of the litigation and the academic literature on this subject see "Conveyancing," *Stair Memorial Encyclopaedia of the Laws of Scotland* (1988), Vol. 6, para. 566. For the question of passing of risk see *Sloan's Dairies Ltd.* v. *Glasgow Corporation*, 1977 S.C. 223 (risk of damage passes to purchaser on inclusion of missives which are not subject to any suspensive condition), and Scottish Law Commission, *Report on the Passing of Risk—Contracts for the Sale of Heritable Property* (Report No. 127, October 1990).

another application of the law of accession which was discussed earlier in this book. If an item is not a fixture it remains a moveable and so would not be covered by the missives so far as they specifically relate to heritage. The law of fixtures was explained by Lord Chelmsford in *Brand's Trs.* v. *Brand's Trs.*[6] He said that the meaning of the word fixture is:

> "anything annexed to the [heritage], that is, fastened to or connected with it, not in mere juxtaposition with the soil. Whatever is so annexed becomes part of the [heritage], and the person who was the owner of it when it was a [moveable] loses his property in it, which immediately vests in the owner of the soil."

An article which meets these requirements would be a fixture and would be regarded as being part of the heritage. In the *Brand's Trs.* case the Lord Chancellor stated that there were two general rules in relation to the law of fixtures. The first of these rules is that whatever is fixed to the heritage becomes part of the heritable property and belongs to the heritable owner. To this rule there are no exceptions. The second rule is that once something has become part of the heritage it cannot be removed by a limited owner, whether that person is a liferenter or a tenant. However, there are certain circumstances where the law would recognise exceptions to the second rule, particularly in relation to the right to remove trade fixtures which a tenant has erected in the course of trade. It is clear from the above two rules that in considering whether a moveable has become heritage the basic test was one based upon the degree of affixation.[7] The relationship of the parties would be an irrelevant consideration in deciding whether an item is a fixture, although their exact relationship could be important when considering whether or not there are any rights to sever.

It has been argued that this approach, which concentrates solely upon affixation as far as the Lord Chancellor's first question is concerned, runs contrary to the previous Scots law where account was also taken as to whether the article was intended for the

---

[6] (1876) 3 R.(H.L.) 16.

[7] In *Cliffplant Ltd.* v. *Kinnaird*, 1982 S.L.T. 2 the Inner House relied solely on the degree of affixation in deciding whether the article in that case was heritable. This part of the decision has been overruled by a Full Bench in *Scottish Discount Co.* v. *Blin*, 1985 S.C. 216.

permanent use of the land.[8] In this way it was possible to have some regard to the relationship of the parties when deciding whether or not the article was a fixture.[9] It has now been made clear by the decision of a Full Bench in *Scottish Discount Co.* v. *Blin*[10] that the question as to whether an item is a fixture should not be resolved solely on the basis of the degree of physical attachment but regard should also be paid to a number of other factors including the intention of the party who attached it.

(a) **Manner of Attachment**

In relation to the first question, it is now clear that the court must consider other factors beyond the simple issue of physical attachment. In the *Blin* case the Lord President declared that the correct test was that spelled out by Professor Gloag in the 1929 edition of the *Encyclopaedia of the Laws of Scotland.*[11] Thus as well as the degree and extent of attachment the following other elements should also be considered: whether the article can be removed *integre, salve et commode, i.e.* without the destruction of itself as a separate thing, or of the soil or building to which it is attached; whether its annexation was of permanent or *quasi*-permanent character; whether the building to which it is attached was specially adapted for its use; how far the use or enjoyment of the soil or building would be affected by its removal[12] and the intention of the party attaching it. This intention must be discovered from the nature of the article and the building and the manner in which it is affixed. It is not to be proved by extrinsic evidence or deducible from the fact that the relationship is one of landlord and tenant.

It is impossible to lay down any exact rules as to what constitutes a fixture. Each case will depend on its own facts and circumstances. However, the greater the attachment of an article (particularly if this involves dismantling it in order to remove it) the more likely it is

---

[8] Kenneth G. C. Reid, "The Lord Chancellor's Fixtures" (1983) 28 J.L.S. 49. See also the earlier decisions in *Fisher* v. *Dixon* (1843) 5 D. 775; *Dowall* v. *Miln* (1874) 1 R. 1180.

[9] In *Syme* v. *Harvey* (1861) 24 D. 202 greenhouses which had been erected by a market gardener were held to be moveable largely because they had been erected by a tenant in the course of trade.

[10] 1985 S.C. 216.

[11] See Vol. 7, paras. 362 and 363.

[12] In this regard see *Christie* v. *Smith's Exr.*, 1949 S.C. 572 where one reason why a summerhouse was held to be heritable was because of the gap that was left in a boundary wall when it was removed.

that the item will be a fixture irrespective of the intention of the party attaching it. On the other hand, it is possible for an article to be a fixture without there being any physical attachment. However, in such a case the burden of proof is on the person who asserts that the article is heritable to prove it is so.[13] For example, in *Howie's Trs.* v. *McLay*[14] it was held that five lace looms bolted to an iron soleplate attached by its own weight to the floor were heritable. Moreover, there are some types of fixture where there need be no physical attachment whatsoever. This applies in the case of constructive fixtures: a key would be a constructive fixture, because it is accessory to the heritage.

Another issue which is likely to be considered is the purpose of the affixation. In deciding the test as to purpose the question which the court generally asks itself is whether the aim of the attachment was to improve the heritage, or to permit the better enjoyment of the moveable itself? Even though a moveable is attached to the heritage to a considerable degree, it will not become heritable unless the purpose of the annexation is to improve the heritage. This means that carpets nailed to floors or pictures hung on walls do not become fixtures despite the fact that they are attached to heritage. In these cases the law holds that the purpose of the attachment is to enhance the moveable rather than the heritage.

(b) Right of Removal

Once it has been discovered that the article is a fixture, a second question arises as to whether the person wishing to take away the fixture has a right to remove it. This may well be a matter which the parties will consider expressly in their contract, and the terms of that contract would normally be accepted by the court in relation to any disputes over removal. However, the terms of such a contract would only bind the parties to it and may not affect third parties. In *Hobson* v. *Gorringe*[15] it was held that the terms of a hire-purchase agreement which permitted the owner to remove a fixture if the hirer defaulted in his payments did not affect the rights of the hirer's mortgagee to claim the article, since he had rights over the heritage. This general approach has found some favour in Scotland, although it may be that the hire-purchase agreement could be examined where the question whether the article is a fixture is in fine

---

[13] *Holland* v. *Hodgson* (1872) L.R. 7 C.P. 328.
[14] (1902) 5 F. 214.
[15] [1897] 1 Ch. 182.

balance.[16] If there is no express agreement over removal, the court is likely to take into account the relationship of the parties before deciding whether the fixture can be removed. This principle applies in a variety of relationships—seller and purchaser and landlord and tenant are the most important.

(i) Seller and purchaser

This is clearly a case where the terms of a contract are likely to determine any right of removal. Where there is no term in the contract of sale, the courts have generally considered that the fixture should remain with the heritage. The courts have concluded that the most important consideration is whether the fixture can be removed without injury to itself and to the heritage.[17] Some guide to the courts' approach can be gleaned from the rating cases under the Lands Valuation Acts. In *Cowans* v. *Assessor for Forfarshire*[18] one reason why the court considered that grates, gas fittings, chandeliers, blinds, curtain poles and picture rods could not be removed was that not only were they for the comfortable enjoyment of the house, but they were necessary in order to render it habitable.

(ii) Landlord and tenant

In this situation considerations of public policy have given the tenant a larger right to remove a fixture. This was accepted in the *Brand's Trs.* case, where the Lord Chancellor explained that a limited right of removal was given to tenants particularly in the case of trade fixtures. The reason why tenants are given greater rights of removal is in order to encourage them to improve the property which they are occupying. There is some incentive for tenants who know that they can take away the improvements made to the property during their occupation. The law divides fixtures removable by a tenant into three groups: trade fixtures; ornamental fixtures and agricultural fixtures.

Trade fixtures

It has long been established that a tenant may remove fixtures which he has attached to the heritage for the purposes of his trade. In *Syme* v. *Harvey*[19] it was held that since a number of greenhouses had been constructed by a market gardener for the purpose of his

---

[16] See esp. the judgment of Lord President Emslie in *Scottish Discount Co.* v. *Blin*, 1985 S.C. 216 at pp. 234–235.

[17] *Jamieson* v. *Welsh* (1900) 3 F. 176.

[18] 1910 S.C. 810.

[19] (1861) 24 D. 201.

trade, they could be removed on the expiry of the lease. However, this case was decided before the *Brand's Trs.* case and seems to be based on the view that the articles retained their moveable characteristics. Nonetheless, even *Brand's Trs.* recognises that tenants may at the end of the lease remove trade fixtures which they have erected.

Ornamental fixtures
   In this situation the tenant is also given limited rights of removal. In *Spyer* v. *Phillipson*[20] it was held that a tenant could remove an ornamental fixture so long as it was for the better enjoyment of the article itself.

Agricultural fixtures
   It seems that the common law was less favourable to the tenant in the case of agricultural fixtures.[21] To some extent, this is now regulated by statute. The Agricultural Holdings (Scotland) Act 1949 declares that any engine, machinery, fencing or other fixture affixed by the tenant, any building erected by him, remain the property of the tenant and are removable for up to six months from the expiry of the lease.[22]

2. IMPACT OF LAND TENURE REFORM (SCOTLAND) ACT 1974

(a) Introduction

The Land Tenure Reform (Scotland) Act 1974 has had a major impact upon the operation of the feudal system. However, like the Conveyancing and Feudal Reform (Scotland) Act 1970, which will be discussed in Chapter 8, the 1974 Act does not bring about the abolition of the feudal system, but merely creates a number of mechanisms for the disappearance of feuduty. The 1974 Act provided that there would be no payment of feuduty in new feus created after September 1, 1974, and also provided for the redemption of existing feuduties. These are dealt with in two ways. First, the Act allows a feuar to redeem the feuduty at any time: and second, it requires sellers of heritable property to redeem their feuduty prior to the sale of their properties.

---

[20] [1931] 2 Ch. 183.
[21] John Rankine, *The Law of Leases in Scotland* (3rd ed.), pp. 301–302.
[22] s. 14(1).

(b) **Prohibition of Feuduty on New Feus**

The Act provides that no deed executed after the commencement of the Act (September 1, 1974) shall impose a feuduty. The section also adds that any feudal grant made after September 1, 1974 shall have effect as if the grant were subject to feuduty.[23] In other words the 1974 Act only abolishes the payment of feuduty and does not otherwise affect the feudal relationship between superior and feuar.

(c) **Optional Redemption of Feuduty**

There is provision that any proprietor of a feu may, at any term of Whitsunday or Martinmas, redeem the feuduty which would otherwise fall due.[24] In order to redeem the feuduty the feuar must
(a) give to the superior or his agent a notice of redemption as prescribed in Schedule 1 to the Act, and
(b) pay to the superior such a sum of money as would, if invested in 2½ per cent Consolidated Stock at the middle market price at the close of business last preceding the date occurring one month before the appropriate term, produce an annual sum equal to the feuduty, and also any amount of feuduty unpaid in respect of the property.[25]
The effect of redemption is to terminate the obligation to pay the feuduty for the future, but the feu continues in all other respects.

(d) **Compulsory Redemption of Feuduty on Sale**

There is provision for the compulsory redemption of feuduty on sales of heritable property after September 1, 1974.[26] Where the property is transferred for "valuable consideration" the seller is obliged to redeem the feuduty before giving entry to the purchaser. The Act requires the person who was the proprietor of the feu (the seller) to pay to the superior the necessary redemption money computed once again in relation to the price of 2½ per cent Consolidated Stock one month before the redemption date (which is taken to be the date of entry under the conveyance of the property).

[23] s. 1.
[24] s. 4(1).
[25] s. 4(2).
[26] s. 5.

Once the redemption date has passed the purchaser is entitled to give to the superior a notice of redemption. Two months after the notice has been given the feuduty which was payable on the feu ceases to exist. This applies even where the seller has failed to make the necessary payment to redeem the feuduty. The superior, however, is still permitted to raise an action against the seller or his/her representatives for recovery of the redemption money and any interest which has accrued should the seller have failed to redeem the feuduty. It is only by order of the court that the superior can seek the redemption money from the purchaser when the seller has failed to make the necessary redemption, and the court will order this only when it is not reasonably practicable to recover the money from the seller or his/her representatives. It seems that this procedure only applies to allocated feuduties.[27] Redemption by law does not apply in the case of a *cumulo* feuduty which has not been allocated among the several feuars. This fact restricts the effect of the redemption procedure because it would not apply to tenement property, for example, where the property is under *cumulo* feuduty. Here no redemption can be made on the sale of one of the tenement flats unless the feuduty is first allocated under the procedure specified in the Conveyancing and Feudal Reform (Scotland) Act 1970.[28]

(e) Application to Ground Annuals

These rules in relation to feuduty also apply in the case of ground annuals. No deed executed after September 1, 1974 shall impose a ground annual and there are also provisions which authorise the voluntary and compulsory redemption of ground annuals.[29]

3. LAND REGISTRATION IN SCOTLAND

(a) The Movement for Reform

Demands for reform of the feudal land system in the past have also centred on the system of land registration. Since the start of the twentieth century there have been constant demands for reform

---

[27] s. 5.
[28] ss. 3–5.
[29] s. 2.

with the objective of creating a system of registration where only the title to the property need be registered.

In 1910 a Royal Commission under the chairmanship of Lord Dunedin examined "the expediency of instituting in Scotland a system of registration of title" and, although the report of the Commission did not recommend the immediate introduction of registration of title, it did make certain recommendations for reform.[30] In 1959 the Secretary of State for Scotland appointed a departmental committee under the chairmanship of Lord Reid to look at statutory conveyancing reforms. The report of this Committee[31] in 1963 recommended the creation of an expert committee to consider possible amendments to conveyancing statutes and also that another expert committee should be appointed to devise details of a scheme for registration of title. This recommendation led to the appointment of an expert committee, chaired by Professor G. L. F. Henry of Edinburgh University.[32] This was asked to work out details and provide the material for a Registration of Title Bill. To facilitate its work it carried out a pilot scheme in the Registers of Scotland.

The Report of the Henry Committee published in 1969 set out in detail a proposed scheme for registration of title, and this scheme eventually formed the basis of the Land Registration (Scotland) Act 1979. The provisions of this Act are being brought into effect in Scotland over a lengthy period, and it was hoped that land registration would cover the whole of Scotland by the early 1990s.[33] This turned out to be over-optimistic.[34] Consequently, before examining registration of title, it is necessary to look at the system of recording of writs in Scotland which it replaces.

(b) Writ Registration

(i) General Register of Sasines

Traditionally deeds affecting heritable property were recorded in the General Register of Sasines. This register has been since its inception the chief security in Scotland of the rights of land and other heritable property. The register dates back to the Act of the

---

[30] Cd. 5316.

[31] Cmnd. 2032.

[32] *Report on the Scheme for the Introduction and Operation of Registration of Title to Land in Scotland*, Cmnd. 4137 (1969).

[33] See Bulletin section, (1984) 29 J.L.S. 303.

[34] See below at p. 55.

Scots Parliament 1617 c. 16, but it is now regulated by the Land Registers (Scotland) Act 1868.

Where appropriate it is necessary to record any deed affecting heritable property in this register in order to create a real right over the property. This act transforms a personal right against the seller into a real right which is effective against the whole world. The Register of Sasines is one of 14 registers in Scotland. In 1978 more than 270,900 writs were presented for recording in the register. This number was increasing every year, but has started to drop off considerably as new areas of Scotland become affected by the 1979 Act.

(ii) **Recording of writs**

The Register of Sasines was divided into 33 divisions which correspond with the former local county areas. A presentment book for each county is kept in the public office. When a deed is presented for registration, the following details are entered in the book:

  (i) the daily running number;

  (ii) the date and hour of presentment;

  (iii) the name of the writ;

  (iv) the name of the person to or by whom the writ is granted;

  (v) the signature of the presenter;

  (vi) the name of the solicitor sending the writ to be recorded.

A minute of abridgment of the writ was thereafter made up, and details entered in the minute book. In addition each writ was photographed and bound together in order of presentation in a record volume and indexed. These volumes are open to public inspection.

Each writ was also entered on a search sheet: this is where the deed is ledgerised under the property or registration unit. All the entries in the minute book were posted under the separate headings of the property to which the deeds respectively referred, and the description of the property formed the heading of the related search sheet. The search sheet was necessary in order to find the deeds in the register.

(iii) **Why reform was needed**

This system had worked very satisfactorily since 1617: but the register was not geared to the volume of transactions which were taking place in Scotland every year. It was also a register of deeds, rather than one of title. Registration could also be rather cumbersome. The Land Registration system was introduced to overcome these difficulties.

(c) **Land Registration (Scotland) Act 1979**

There are three preliminary points that need to be made about this Act:

(a) It implements the recommendations of the Henry Committee with its introduction of a system of title registration in Scotland.[35]

(b) It abolishes the General Register of Sasines and replaces it with the "Land Register of Scotland" under the management and control of the Keeper of the Registers of Scotland.

(c) This reformed register is map-based (rather than deed-based as was the General Register).

Since the reformed system is based on area maps, the Act was not to be brought into effect for a couple of years to allow the Ordnance Survey time to draw up the necessary maps. In fact, the first area to move over to registration of title was Renfrew, when the land registration system became effective there on April 6, 1981. Thereafter the provisions of the Act were to be brought in over a nine-year period for various parts of Scotland. However, the process of change has actually taken place over a longer period than this. About 25 per cent of transactions are in the new form in four areas in 1990—Renfrew, Dumbarton, Lanark and Glasgow—with Stirling and West Lothian due to become operative in 1993. They will be followed by Edinburgh and Ayr, but it will not be until the next century that the process of changeover is completed.

The reformed system centres around the issuing and recording of a "land certificate" after application for registration has been made to the Keeper.[36] The certificate is the title sheet of the property, which is registered in the Land Register. It is drawn from a description based on the Ordnance Survey map. Once the title sheet is recorded a real right will be given to the person registered as entitled to that interest in land. Once an area starts to operate the new Register, the only method of creating interests in land is by registration of title in it.

---

[35] For criticisms of the scheme which was introduced by the 1979 Act, see Kenneth G. C. Reid, "New Titles for Old" (1984) 29 J.L.S. 171 and "Registration of Title: The Draftsman's Part" (1984) J.L.S. 212, and the replies by the Keeper, (1984) 29 J.L.S. 175 and 216.

[36] See generally, Land Registration (Scotland) Act 1979, Pt. I.

CHAPTER 7

IMPLIED RIGHTS OF LANDOWNERSHIP

OWNERSHIP of land carries with it the right to use and enjoy the property as well as the right to exclude others. Thus those who possess a title to land not only enjoy rights of occupation but obtain certain incidental rights which exist through their possession of the property. Proprietors are entitled to expect a level of support for their buildings and may also obtain mineral rights over their land. These incidental rights also entitle proprietors to prevent others entering their lands. However, the exercise of a person's rights of ownership is not absolute since it is also subject to the competing rights of others, both neighbours and others in the community.[1] It is the purpose of this chapter to consider the most important rights which exist through the ownership of land.

1. POSSESSION

It has already been noted in Chapter 6 that possession of heritage and no more creates no rights under Scots law. Clearly, a duly recorded or a registered title gives the possessor of that title certain rights. However, if there should be any defects in title these will only be corrected by the operation of the positive prescription. Thus possession which is referable to a title is vital if any flaws in that title are to be extinguished. Indeed, until the period of the positive prescription has run, it is possible that a person's land rights could be defeated by a claim from other people that they have better rights. Even where the period of the positive prescription has passed there is no guarantee that the defect in title will be extinguished, since for this to happen certain conditions must be satisfied. First, there must be a form of title which is recognised by the law, and, second, the prescriptive possession must be in accordance with legal requirements. However, prescriptive possession is not only important as regards titles to land generally, but also operates as a means of creating other rights such as rights over

[1] See Chap. 8 below.

Crown property or positive servitudes. It is important to discuss the question of prescription in more detail before returning to the question of possession.

(a) **Prescription**

There are two specified forms of prescription recognised by Scots law. These are the positive prescription and the negative prescription. Both prescriptions entail rights either being created or extinguished through lapse of time. While the passage of time in the positive prescription has the effect of establishing or defining a right to heritable property, lapse of time in the negative prescription extinguishes rights and obligations relating to both heritable and moveable property. The present law on prescription is contained in the Prescription and Limitation (Scotland) Act 1973.

(i) **Positive prescription**

Where a person seeks to acquire a title and interest to land, a person must possess that land for 10 years and such possession must be referable to a title. As the 1973 Act makes clear, the possession must be founded on and follow either the recording of a deed which is sufficient in respect of its terms to constitute an interest in the land, or the registration of that interest in the Land Register of Scotland subject to an exclusion of indemnity.[2] A title of either type permits the operation of the positive prescription. However, the positive prescription cannot run if the possession was founded on the recording of a deed which is invalid *ex facie* or was forged, or was registered in respect of an interest in land in the Land Register of Scotland proceeding on a forged deed and the person appearing from the Register to be entitled to the interest was aware of the forgery at the time of registration.[3] The period of the positive prescription will apply if there has been possession for a continuous period of 10 years exercised openly, peaceably and without any judicial interruption.[4] The possession can be natural or civil.[5] Clearly, possession by force, fear or stealth will not suffice. The possession must exist as a matter of right and be based upon a title as just described. Thus possession for 10 years based on no title at all will bestow no rights and will mean that the occupier's land rights

[2] 1973 Act, s. 1(1)(*b*) as amended by the Land Registration (Scotland) Act 1979, s. 10(*a*).
[3] *Ibid.*, s. 1(1A) inserted by the 1979 Act, s. 10(*b*).
[4] *Ibid.*, s. 1(1)(*a*).
[5] *Ibid.*, s. 15(1).

can be challenged even though the period of the positive prescription has elapsed.

In the case of the creation of a right of positive servitude or a right of way the positive prescription is 20 years' continuous, open and peaceable possession without any judicial interruption.[6] In the case of a positive servitude the possession must also be founded on, and follow the execution of, a deed which is sufficient in respect of its terms (whether expressly or by implication) to constitute the servitude.[7] The nature of the servitude or the right of way which is acquired in this way depends upon the extent of the possession which was exercised in order to create it. The period of the positive prescription is also 20 years in the case of the acquisition of an interest in the foreshore or in any salmon fishings from the Crown.[8] The effect of the running of the positive prescription is to exclude all inquiry into the previous title and rights to the lands.

(ii) Negative prescription

Prior to the 1973 Act there were a series of negative prescriptions which applied to different types of rights and obligations. The 1973 Act creates two specific negative prescriptions, the negative prescription of 20 years and the quinquennial prescription. In the case of the 20-year negative prescription, if an obligation has become enforceable and has subsisted for a continuous period of 20 years without any relevant claim having been made, and without an acknowledgment of the obligation, then as from the expiration of that period the obligation will be extinguished.[9] Equally, any right in heritable or moveable property will be extinguished if the right has subsisted for a continuous period of 20 years unexercised or unenforced, and without any relevant claim in relation to it having been made.[10] In land law the operation of the negative prescription will extinguish the right to object to the use of property in a way which creates a nuisance. The negative prescription also applies to extinguish a right to use of a servitude. However, as we shall see, the public's right of navigation in rivers cannot be extinguished in this way.

(iii) Rights which never prescribe

The 1973 Act does nothing to affect the rights which Scots law has

---

[6] *Ibid.*, s. 3(1) and (3). For further discussion on the law of servitudes see Chap. 8.
[7] *Ibid.*, s. 3(1)(*b*).
[8] *Ibid.*, s. 1(4).
[9] *Ibid.*, s. 7(1).
[10] *Ibid.*, s. 8(1).

accepted as being imprescriptible. These are rights which continue to apply no matter the length of time of the failure to take action. Such rights include any real right of ownership in land, the right of land given to a lessee under a recorded lease and the obligations of a trustee to produce accounts, make reparation in respect of fraud or make furthcoming of trust property. Any right exercisable as a *res merae facultatis* (a right which creditors may assert or not as they please) also cannot prescribe.[11]

(ii) **Other Incidents of Possession**

Possession is important in two other senses. First, a person who is in possession of heritage has the right to maintain and recover possession by the use of the possessory remedies. Second, even where a person has no valid title to the land that person may obtain certain advantages so long as the possession is *bona fide*. As far as the possessory remedies are concerned, these fall into two types. First, there are the specific or nominate remedies, of which the most important is an action of removing.[12] This is an action which entitles the pursuer to recover possession from a person who claims to have a title to possess, or who had a title to possess, and refuses to give up possession. The other and general possessory remedy is interdict, which is available to prohibit any act which amounts to an invasion or a threat of invasion of the pursuer's legal rights. It can be used as a means of preventing another from continuing to occupy or repeating any occupation in another person's lands.[13] Where a possessory judgment is sought the requisite possession must have lasted uninterrupted for at least seven years,[14] be open and peaceful and be based upon some sort of written title. This could be on the basis of a feu title, but a lease will suffice.[15]

A person who is a *bona fide* possessor of land is one who, although not truly the proprietor of the subject which he possesses, believes himself the proprietor on probable grounds and with a good conscience.[16] There must be some colourable title to found this possession, so that a person cannot have *bona fide* possession

---

[11] *Ibid.*, Sched. 3.

[12] For a discussion of the other specific remedies see W. M. Gordon, *Scottish Land Law* (1989), paras. 14–15 to 14–30.

[13] N. R. Whitty, "Positive and Negative Interdicts" (1990) 35 J.L.S. 510.

[14] *per* Lord Cowan for the 2nd Division in *Colquhoun* v. *Paton* (1859) 21 D. 996 at p. 1001.

[15] *McDonald* v. *Dempster* (1871) 10 M. 94.

[16] Erskine, II,i,25.

where there is no title and no reason to believe that a title exists. A person who is a *bona fide* possessor has the following rights:

(a) A right to the fruits of the thing possessed. Thus, where the true owner seeks the right to recover possession of the property, the *bona fide* possessor retains ownership of all the fruits (including rents and feuduties) which have been obtained during this possession.

(b) The right to recompense for meliorations. A *bona fide* possessor who has made improvements to the property is entitled to recompense for these, since they are likely to have improved the value of the property.

(c) No liability for violent profits. A *bona fide* possessor cannot be sued by the true owner for loss of profits over the subjects which would have been acquired had the property not been possessed by another.

2. RIGHTS OF SUPPORT

A person's right of support depends upon the state of the land. Land which is in its natural state must be maintained and must not be affected by operations on adjacent or subjacent properties which affect the level of support. This right is regarded as an incident of property, so that, by virtue of that ownership, owners can insist on having their land left in its natural state. If a person's right to support for land in its natural state is breached, the owner becomes entitled to damages for surface damage without the need to establish negligence.[17] It would seem that in such a case the owner's right is simply the right to sue for loss of support; owners do not enjoy a positive right to claim support.[18] On the other hand, the owner enjoys a fresh right of action for every occasion that further damage is caused to the land.[19] As well as damages to compensate for any appreciable damage to the land, the owner may also seek interdict to prevent the operations continuing. Although the right to support is a natural right and exists without express stipulation, the party who exercises it is at liberty to renounce it. Thus, where a superior does reserve the right to own and to work minerals and the feuar agrees that such working entails no liability for damage, interdict

---

[17] *per* Lord Justice-Clerk Thomson in *Angus* v. *National Coal Board*, 1955 S.C. 175 at p. 181.

[18] W. M. Gordon, *Scottish Land Law* (1989), para. 6–83; *Anderson* v. *Robertson*, 1958 S.C. 367.

[19] *Darley Main Colliery Co.* v. *Mitchell* (1886) 11 App.Cas. 127.

cannot be obtained to prevent the superior working the minerals even where this work is causing damage to the feuar's property.[20] There is no natural right of support for buildings which have been erected on the land. In this case an owner's rights do not depend upon any natural right of property but must be acquired in some way. It is conceivable that they might be acquired by express grant or express reservation when minerals are severed, although it is more likely that if they are to exist they will be obtained by implication. Thus where buildings have already been erected when the right to work the minerals under the land is severed, a right to sue for any damage caused may be implied. This would be on the basis that the grant or reservation of the minerals was presumed to have been concluded by reference to the current level of support which the buildings have received. However, if the buildings are erected after the rights over the minerals have been severed no rights of support for those buildings can be implied. As the Lord Chancellor stated in *Caledonian Railway Co.* v. *Sprot*,[21] where mineral rights have been severed and a person "thinks fit to build a house on the edge of the land he has acquired, he cannot complain of my workings or diggings, if by reason of the additional weight he has put on the land they cause his house to fall." The only exception to this rule would be where the land is conveyed for a specified purpose. In such a case the grant of land would imply a right of reasonable and necessary support for operations connected with that purpose.[22]

It is also possible that a proprietor may have a cause of action against the activities of neighbours which lead to a withdrawal of support by reference to the law of nuisance.[23] The Coal Mining (Subsidence) Act 1957 also grants rights to owners by placing a duty on the British Coal Corporation to conduct remedial works or pay for such works where subsidence damage is caused by the loss of support through coal-mining operations.

3. Rights as to Water

The question of rights as to water is clearly an area where the Crown exercises considerable rights, particularly as regards the sea and

---

[20] *Buchanan* v. *Andrew* (1873) 11 M.(H.L.) 13; see also *White* v. *Wm. Dixon Ltd.* (1883) 10 R.(H.L.) 45.

[21] (1856) 2 Macq. 449 at p. 451.

[22] *Caledonian Ry. Co.* v. *Sprot* (1856) 2 Macq. 449; *North British Ry.* v. *Turners Ltd.* (1904) 6 F. 900.

[23] *L.A.* v. *Reo Stakis Organisation Ltd.*, 1982 S.L.T. 140. This issue is discussed more fully in Chap. 8.

tidal rivers. These issues will be discussed later in this chapter when we consider the *regalia*. This section of the chapter will be concentrating upon the rights of landowners who have a quantity of water upon their properties. Rights as to water depend upon the category into which the water is classified—it may flow in a channel, be spread over the land, or percolate through the land.

(a) Rivers and Streams

A person's rights over running water depend upon whether or not the stream or river is navigable. Riparian proprietors[24] (*i.e.* those who own the land up to the banks of the river) undoubtedly have certain rights over water which flows through their land. However, their rights depend upon the critical distinction between navigable and non-navigable rivers.

(i) Navigable rivers

In the case of tidal navigable rivers the bed or *alveus* belongs to the Crown, and the public have rights of navigation and fishing and are also entitled to moor boats so long as this is not on a permanent basis.[25] Moreover, any activity (such as the mooring of fish-farm cages) which causes material interference with the public's right of navigation would breach this right and constitute grounds for the award of an interdict.[26] A river would be considered to be tidal to the extent of the high-water mark of ordinary spring tides.

In the case of navigable rivers which are non-tidal a right of navigation is given to the public, although the *alveus* and banks are the property of the riparian owners. Frequently, the courts are required to decide whether a right of navigation exists. In *Wills' Trs.* v. *Cairngorm Canoeing and Sailing School*[27] it was made clear that this right is not subject to the same requirements as to constitution as is the case with a public right of way over land. The correct approach is not only to consider the theoretical navigability of the river, but also to discover its regular, habitual use as a channel of communication or transportation since time immemorial (customarily for 40 years). Moreover, since the right of navigation is an example of an imprescriptible right it cannot be lost by non-use. In the *Wills' Trs.* case, the House of Lords concluded that as

---

[24] See *Marquess of Breadalbane* v. *West Highland Ry. Co.* (1895) 22 R. 307.
[25] *Crown Estate Commrs.* v. *Fairlie Yacht Slip Ltd.*, 1979 S.C. 156.
[26] *Walford* v. *David*, 1989 S.L.T. 876.
[27] 1976 S.C.(H.L.) 30.

since time immemorial the public had used the river for the purpose of floating logs down to the sea, a right of navigation had been established. However, given the nature of the use (the floating of logs to the sea), the right of navigation only operated in relation to traffic going downstream.

The next question is to discover the extent of the right of navigation. This will depend upon the physical capacity and quality of the river. The important issue is to establish whether and to what extent the river is capable of coping with the public's right of passage. In *Wills' Trs.* Lord Wilberforce declared that:

> "the fact that some stretch of water is navigable or passable by some acrobatic *tour de force* does not establish a public right of passage. Thus, again, the establishment of a public right of passage does not open the door to every kind of user which physical prowess or exorbitant technology may make possible. The right is one for the ordinary public to use conformably with the nature of the river as water flowing past other people's lands."[28]

As has been indicated, the public's right of navigation is essentially one of passage. Nonetheless the public may also acquire certain incidental rights,[29] such as the right to moor or anchor boats, so long as these are exercised on a wholly temporary basis consistent with the right of passage which is being exercised.[30] Equally, riparian proprietors retain the right to use the *alveus* so long as they do not do anything which interferes with or obstructs navigation.[31]

(ii) Non-navigable rivers

Rights here fall as incidents of ownership, so consequently the public has no rights. Where the stream or river flows over the property of one person, that person is the owner of the surface, bed and banks of the river or stream. Where the stream acts as a boundary between a number of owners, each owns the bed of the stream, so far as *ex adverso* (opposite to) his own lands, to the *medium filum* (middle line of river). Riparian proprietors also enjoy a common interest to ensure that the flow of the water is not

---

[28] 1976 S.C.(H.L.) 30 at p. 124. See also the speech of Lord Fraser of Tullybelton at p. 169.

[29] The issues are summarised by Lord McDonald in *Scammell* v. *Scottish Sports Council*, 1983 S.L.T. 463.

[30] *Campbell's Trs.* v. *Sweeney*, 1911 S.C. 1319; *Leith-Buchanan* v. *Hogg*, 1931 S.C. 204.

[31] *Orr Ewing & Co.* v. *Colquhoun's Trs.* (1877) 4 R.(H.L.) 116.

affected adversely by the activities of other riparian proprietors. Thus a person's ownership is subject to the obligation not to interfere with the character or quality of the water, nor may owners do anything which diminishes or increases the flow.[32]

Every proprietor is entitled to take water from the stream for primary purposes (drink for people or animals), and for domestic purposes (washing). The owner can do this even though the effect is to diminish or even exhaust the supply of water. Any surplus must be returned to the stream by proprietors within their own lands. Water cannot, however, be taken from the stream for secondary purposes, such as for manufacture, if the rights of the lower proprietor are infringed either as to quality or flow. On the other hand, there would be nothing intrinsically unlawful in a proprietor using the stream for secondary purposes so long as there is sufficient water left for other owners. The extent of a person's rights to draw water from a stream will also be affected by prescription. If a person has been drawing water for secondary purposes and there has been no objection by other riparian proprietors for the period of the negative prescription (20 years),[33] this would prevent the other proprietors complaining at a later date. Otherwise, an interdict is available to prevent a riparian proprietor affecting the flow of rivers or polluting them.[34]

(b) Water Not in a Definite Channel

This water is part of the land (*pars soli*) and belongs to the appropriating proprietor. Examples are water in a bog or water percolating through the ground. This water is often extracted by means of a well. Indeed it would seem that a proprietor is entitled to impound, and use for manufacturing purposes, water percolating through the ground, even though the water if not intercepted would go to feed a stream.[35] The water may be discharged on to lower proprietors' lands where it is naturally flowing that way and they must receive it although they cannot insist on its continuance. However, a proprietor has no right to discharge polluted water on to another's land.[36] Nor can an owner increase the flow to

---

[32] *Young & Co.* v. *Bankier Distillery Co.* (1893) 20 R.(H.L.) 76.

[33] Prescription and Limitation (Scotland) Act 1973, s. 8.

[34] For the statutory rules on pollution see the Rivers (Prevention of Pollution) (Scotland) Acts 1951 and 1964 and the Control of Pollution Act 1974.

[35] *Milton* v. *Glen-moray Glenlivet Distillery Co.* (1898) 1 F. 135.

[36] *Montgomerie* v. *Buchanan's Trs.* (1853) 15 D. 853.

neighbours through pumping operations or artificial alteration of the flow.[37]

Lochs

Four distinct situations exist:

(a) Sea loch which is treated as an extension of the sea, so that a landed proprietor acquires no rights to the *alveus* since this belongs to the Crown and the public enjoys rights of navigation.

(b) Loch surrounded completely by one owner's property gives that owner full rights of ownership and fishing over it.

(c) Loch with a stream running out of it. Here the proprietors by the loch must not prejudice the rights of the stream's riparian proprietors.

(d) Loch with several proprietors. There is a presumption that the loch is owned in common. Each proprietor has exclusive property in the *alveus ex adverso* (opposite) of their lands up to the centre, whilst the water is open to all the proprietors. They also have rights of navigation and fishing and can use the water for primary purposes.

4. RIGHTS IN MINERALS AND MINES

In Scots law a person is deemed to own property from the sky to the centre of the earth (*a caelo usque ad centrum*). This means that as well as owning the surface of the property the owner also has rights both to the air above it and to the ground underneath it. There are, however, certain rights to property which an owner cannot normally exercise. These exceptions include:

(a) The right of aeroplanes to pass over property without any legal action for trespass or nuisance under the Civil Aviation Act 1982, so long as their height is reasonable in all the circumstances.[38] Where material loss or damage is caused to any person or property or land by an aircraft, however, the owner of the plane is liable for such damage.[39]

(b) The right to gold and silver which belongs to the Crown as part of the *regalia minora*. As part of the *regalia minora* they are capable of being alienated to subjects. In any case, the Royal Mines Act 1424 c. 12 creates a procedure for the sale of the right to work precious metals in return for a royalty payable to the Crown.

---

[37] *Young & Co.* v. *Bankier Distillery Co.* (1893) 20 R.(H.L.) 76.
[38] s. 76; discussed in *Steel-Maitland* v. *B.A.B.*, 1981 S.L.T. 110.
[39] Civil Aviation Act 1982, s. 76(2).

(c) The right to coal and to mine for it is vested in the British Coal Corporation under the provisions of the Coal Industry Nationalisation Act 1946 (as amended).

(d) Petroleum and natural gas rights which vest in the Crown under the provisions of the Petroleum (Production) Act 1934.

Apart from the above exceptions, owners of property are entitled to the peaceful, open and uninterrupted enjoyment of their land. As we shall see, an owner can take action against those who commit trespass, nuisance or encroachment. As well as this, in terms of the *a caelo* maxim, owners also have rights to the minerals lying underneath their property. If a person should decide to sell the property, the rights to the minerals will pass in the sale unless the seller or superior specifically reserves the right to the minerals from the rest of the sale or grant. Equally, a person may grant a right to minerals to another as a separate transaction. It would also be possible for a right to minerals to be created on the basis of open and uninterrupted possession for the period of the positive prescription (10 years), so long as there is a title to the land.[40] In other words, although the maxim gives the present proprietor a *prima facie* right to minerals under the land, such right can be denied if there has been an earlier severance of the right to mine by grant, reservation or prescriptive use.

The law does not specifically define the meaning of the word mineral. The definition of a mineral depends upon the facts of each case. Clearly, much may depend upon the intention of the parties when the minerals were conveyed.[41] However, as a rule of thumb a mineral would be any substance which is known in the vernacular by mining engineers, commercial people and landowners in the locality as a mineral.[42] The substance should also be distinct from the ordinary subsoil of the area and be exceptional in its character, use and value.[43] A person who obtains the rights to minerals should also ensure that the necessary ancillary rights, such as a right of access and provision for storage and removing the minerals, are also provided, since without specific provision such rights will not necessarily be implied by the common law.

The above rules do not apply in the case of railways. Under the provisions of the Railway Clauses Consolidation (Scotland) Act 1845 (as amended) a railway is not entitled to the minerals under the

---

[40] Prescription and Limitation (Scotland) Act 1973, s. 1.

[41] *Borthwick-Norton* v. *Gavin Paul & Sons*, 1947 S.C. 659.

[42] *Borthwick-Norton, ibid.*; *Caledonian Ry. Co.* v. *Glenboig Union Fireclay Co. Ltd.*, 1911 S.C.(H.L.) 72.

[43] *Borthwick-Norton, ibid.*

land which has been purchased. It is only entitled to those minerals which must be dug out or taken away in the construction of the railway. If someone should be mining minerals close to a railway line the Act provides for an "area of protection." Works cannot be carried out within a distance of 40 yards (or some other prescribed distance) either side of the railway line.

5. NUISANCE

This is a relatively new concept in Scots law and is dealt with in more detail in Chapter 8. At present we simply wish to make it clear that proprietors of land have the right to prevent any offensive or intolerable behaviour by others which affects their enjoyment of their property. The classic definition was given by Professor Bell in *The Principles of the Law of Scotland*. He declared that:

> "whatever obstructs the public means of commerce and inter-course, whether in highways or navigable rivers, whatever is noxious or unsafe, or renders life uncomfortable to the public generally, or to the neighbourhood: whatever is intolerably offensive to individuals in their dwelling-houses, or inconsis-tent with the comfort of life, whether by stench (as the boiling of whale blubber), by noise (as in a smithy on an upper floor), or by indecency (as a brothel next door), is a nuisance."[44]

The essence of a nuisance is that it abuses a person's natural rights of property. As well as covering the situation where a neighbour infringes one's natural rights of enjoyment and use of land, it is also broad enough to cover what is, in effect, a public nuisance. In other words, it is broad enough to cover matters which refer not to the neighbourhood but which affect the public generally. Thus in *Slater v. McLellan*[45] the owner of a traction engine travelling on the highway was held to have committed a nuisance when he allowed sparks to be emitted by the engine, causing surrounding trees and houses to be damaged. The most common forms of nuisance in Scotland involve breaches of the law of neighbourhood. Thus the commoner types of nuisance involve pollution, the emission of noise or heat or the causing of vibrations. In addition a person whose building has suffered loss of support as a result of activities carried out by a neighbour may have an action in nuisance for a

[44] § 974.
[45] 1924 S.C. 854.

remedy, without the need to show interest required for a normal loss of support action.[46]

6. ENCROACHMENT

As we have seen, in terms of the *a caelo usque ad centrum* maxim it is clear that proprietors enjoy ownership of their land both above and below ground. A proprietor would have a cause of action where there is any temporary or permanent encroachment upon or below the surface of his land or in the airspace above it.[47] A proprietor can take action, for example, if a neighbour's trees should overhang the property,[48] or a jib of a crane should pass overhead.[49] But a person's property rights would also be infringed when roots from a neighbour's tree penetrate through onto one's land. The concept of encroachment would also be breached where the owner of minerals attempts to extract them from under a person's property without having the necessary title to work them. The usual action for encroachment would be interdict to prevent the encroachment continuing.

7. TRESPASS

Trespass involves any temporary intrusion or entering upon the lands or heritage of another without that person's permission. Trespass can be committed in a number of ways. It can be committed by foot, by an animal or by use of a bicycle etc. The proprietor of land is quite at liberty to warn any person who is trespassing thereon. A person with title to the land cannot eject a trespasser forcibly unless the trespasser occasions or threatens violence on the proprietor or does damage to the property.[50] If proprietors require to use force they can only use such force as is reasonably necessary in the circumstances. Although damages can be claimed against a trespasser for damage done to the property, the principal remedy available to a proprietor under Scots law is interdict.

[46] *L.A.* v. *Reo Stakis Organisation Ltd.*, 1982 S.L.T. 140. But see now *R.H.M. Bakeries (Scotland) Ltd.* v. *Strathclyde R.C.*, 1985 S.L.T. 214 (H.L.).

[47] But see the Civil Aviation Act 1982, s. 76, as far as flights by civil aircraft are concerned.

[48] *Halkerston* v. *Wedderburn* (1781) Mor. 10495.

[49] *Brown* v. *Lee Constructions Ltd.*, 1977 S.L.T. (Notes) 61 (interdict granted on the basis of a trespass).

[50] *Wood* v. *N.B. Ry. Co.* (1899) 2 F. 1.

The court, however, will only award interdict if there is a threat or probability of continuance or repetition of the trespass. Award is therefore discretionary.[51] In *Hay's Trs.* v. *Young*[52] the principal reason why the court refused the interdict was because repetition of the entry on the pursuer's lands was not to be expected. Neither will an interdict be granted where the trespass is having a minimal impact on the property (the application of the *de minimis* rule). In *Winans* v. *Macrae*[53] a landholder was refused interdict when he attempted to stop a pet lamb belonging to a cottar straying on to his lands. The court considered that this was a *de minimis* situation and that other remedies existed beyond interdict.

A proprietor's right to prevent trespass on land is subject to one major limitation. As Professor Bell has put it:

> "the exclusive right of a landowner to use his property as he pleases yields wherever public interest or necessity requires that it should yield."[54]

This means that at common law it is permissible to trespass during an emergency such as in the case of fire, or in pursuit of a criminal, or to obtain evidence in connection with a crime,[55] or to avoid danger. The English courts, however, took the view that this exception did not extend to a permission to homeless people to enter property, since otherwise no one's house would be safe from intrusion.[56] There are also a number of statutes which grant rights of entry to public officials.[57]

Although under Scots law the action of trespass does not normally give rise to criminal proceedings, there are particular Acts which allow certain organisations, such as British Rail, to prosecute trespassers. Further, the Trespass (Scotland) Act 1865 makes it criminal for a person to lodge in any premises, or occupy any land without the consent and permission of the owner.

---

[51] See, *e.g. Plessey Co. plc* v. *Wilson*, 1983 S.L.T. 319.

[52] (1877) 4 R. 398.

[53] (1885) 12 R. 1051.

[54] *Prin.*, § 956.

[55] *Shepherd* v. *Menzies* (1900) 2 F. 443; *Southern Bowling Club* v. *Ross* (1902) 4 F. 405.

[56] *London Borough of Southwark* v. *Williams* [1971] Ch. 734.

[57] See, *e.g.* Rights of Entry (Gas and Electricity Boards) Act 1954, s. 2 (grant of warrant by sheriff to enter premises by force); Health and Safety at Work etc. Act 1974, s. 20 (right of inspectors to enter premises without permission).

8. PROPERTY RIGHTS OF THE CROWN

There are certain rights in heritable property which are presumed to be owned by the Crown. Two specific forms of Crown ownership are recognised by Scots law.

(a) **Regalia majora**

Rights to the *regalia majora* are held by the Crown in trust for public purposes. It is impossible for these rights to be alienated to anyone else by the Crown. They are more in the way of a right of sovereignty than one of property.

(b) **Regalia minora**

These rights are in Crown ownership also. In this case the Crown does possess a property right which can be alienated to others.

Examples of these two groups of rights are given below.

The sea

The sea below the foreshore and within the territorial limit,[58] as part of the *regalia majora*, belongs to the Crown in trust for the public rights of navigation and fishing.

The foreshore

This area encompasses the shore between the high- and low-water marks of ordinary spring tides. The foreshore is an example of Crown property where both the *regalia majora* and the *regalia minora* apply. Thus the Crown possesses two specific rights. First, it has a right of sovereignty which means that the foreshore is vested in the Crown in trust for public purposes. This right cannot be alienated. The public purposes recognised by this right include a right of navigation and of fishing. The right to navigation also covers certain ancillary rights such as the right to anchor or moor, so long as this is done in the course of passage. The right of navigation does not extend to the laying of fixed moorings, because this is not incidental to the public's right of passage but involves the provision of a facility which a vessel may use from time to time.[59] It is probable that the public also has a right to use the foreshore for recreation purposes. The other right to the foreshore vested in the Crown is a right of property. Although the Crown is taken to own the foreshore, it can be alienated to another by the Crown. It can be alienated to an adjacent proprietor, for example, if he has been

---

[58] Now 12 international nautical miles—Territorial Sea Act 1987, s. 1(1)(*a*).

[59] *Crown Estates Commrs.* v. *Fairlie Yacht Slip Ltd.*, 1979 S.C. 156.

given a specific grant of ownership from the Crown. Such a grant need not refer to the foreshore in specific words.[60] Equally, the foreshore can be acquired by prescriptive possession based on a *habile* title.[61] If the foreshore is owned by someone other than the Crown, that person must recognise the rights of the public to use the foreshore for navigation, fishing, etc.

Navigable rivers

Rivers which are navigable and tidal are part of the *regalia majora* and are the property of the Crown in trust for the public's right of passage. The law applying to rivers and lochs was discussed above.

Ferries, ports and harbours

These rights are part of the *regalia minora* and belong to the Crown, but can be alienated to others by express grant or by operation of prescription. Thus they can be items of private property so long as the owner allows the public access to them on making the relevant payment.

Salmon fishing

Salmon fishing is a separate feudal right which is vested in the Crown. As part of the *regalia minora* it can be granted by the Crown to a subject either by express grant or through a general grant with exercise of the right for the prescriptive period. As we have seen, this is 20 years.[62]

---

[60] *L.A.* v. *Wemyss* (1899) 2 F.(H.L.) 1.

[61] Prescription and Limitation (Scotland) Act 1973, s. 1(1) and (4). The prescriptive period is 20 years when the positive prescription is pleaded against the Crown.

[62] For a more detailed discussion of this topic, see W. M. Gordon, *Scottish Land Law* (1989), paras. 8–49 to 8–75.

CHAPTER 8

RESTRICTIONS ON LANDOWNERSHIP

OWNERSHIP of land in society involves certain limitations flowing from the potential conflict between the rights of different landowners as well as of other members of the public. These restrictions stem from individual agreements, from the law protecting amenity as well as from statutory schemes on the use of land and the protection of certain disadvantaged groups like tenants, the homeless or women (see Chapter 12).

1. RESTRICTIONS BY AGREEMENT

(a) Personal Burdens on Land

It is open to any landowner to enter into any agreement with any other person to provide lawful rights to that other person over the landowner's property. Such an agreement would give rise to personal rights—only the parties to the agreement are bound by such arrangements. An agreement to allow a person to fish on one's property would be personal to the angler and would not bind any subsequent purchaser of the land. It is possible by agreement to create rights which bind later owners of land provided that these meet certain requirements. These are known as "real burdens."

(b) Real Burdens on Land

Under the feudal system the superior was permitted to lay down restrictions on the use of the property by the feuar. These restrictions are generally referred to as real burdens or, more properly, real conditions.[1] Real burdens are conditions which permanently run with the land irrespective of the fact that the original grantor and grantee have long ceased to have an interest in the property.

---

[1] Kenneth G. C. Reid, "What is a Real Burden?" (1984) 29 J.L.S. 9.

Typically a real burden is imposed by the superior on the feuar's use of the land. Real burdens could, for example, prohibit the feuar from using the property as "a factory, warehouse, office or piggery." They could even restrict the use of the property to a dwelling-house for one family only. Indeed, the real burden could cover almost anything, even down to a requirement that the subjects be insured at a certain minimum value.

In *Tailors of Aberdeen* v. *Coutts*[2] the Court of Session laid down seven requirements which a restriction must satisfy before it is given the status of a real burden. Any condition which does not meet the requirements of these seven rules may apply to the original superior and feuar who created it, but it will not affect singular successors of either of them. Since the principal feature of a real burden is that it runs with the land and does not only affect the parties who created it, a restriction will not apply to all successors of the original grantor and grantee unless it satisfies the rules as laid down in the *Tailors of Aberdeen* case.

(i) Clear intention
To constitute a real burden or condition effectual against singular successors no technical words are required, but the words that are used must clearly show an intention to affect the property itself and not merely the grantee.

In *Tailors of Aberdeen* the Court of Session declared that it was not necessary that any technical forms of words should be employed in order to create the real burden. The grant need not even declare that the burden is real, or that it should be inserted in all future grants or that it attaches to singular successors. It is sufficient if the intention of the parties is clear.

(ii) Acceptable purpose
The burden or condition must not be contrary to law or public policy; useless or vexatious; too vague; nor inconsistent with the nature of the property.

(a) *Contrary to law or public policy*
Where the real burden is so created that its performance would require the commission of an unlawful act, or if it is of such a nature that its performance would give the superior a monopoly, the real burden will be struck down as being illegal or contrary to public policy. So a condition which required the superior to maintain a brothel on his property, or which required the feuar to grind all his

---

[2] (1840) 1 Rob.App. 296.

grain at the superior's mill, would not be enforceable. In *Yeaman* v. *Crawford*,[3] where there was a stipulation that the feuars were to have all their blacksmith work done at the barony blacksmith, the real burden was struck down as being contrary to public policy. In a more recent case, *Aberdeen Varieties* v. *James F. Donald*,[4] a company had sold one of its theatres to another company with a restriction which was declared to be a real burden, that the theatre could not be used in all time coming for any stage play. Singular successors of the seller sought to enforce this restriction. One reason why the condition was struck down in the Inner House was that it was unlawful because, if enforced, it would mean the imposition of a perpetual commercial monopoly. This case would suggest that it will be difficult for a seller to create a real burden for the sale of business, since any restriction as to use may be construed as bestowing monopoly powers in the seller.[5]

(b) *Useless or vexatious*

In *Tailors of Aberdeen* a condition which required every singular successor of the feuars to grant personal obligations to the superior for payment of feuduty was held to be both unnecessary and vexatious. This was because the payment of feuduty was implied by feudal law.

(c) *Inconsistent with the nature of the property*

This point is illustrated in *Beckett* v. *Bisset*,[6] where Beckett claimed that the exclusive rights of shooting she alleged she possessed over Bisset's property constituted a real burden. Her action failed, however, because Lord Blackburn had the greatest difficulty in seeing how this exclusive right could be a real burden. As far as he was concerned, the right alleged to be created was "inconsistent with the nature of the species of property and so was not enforceable."

(iii) Specific wording

The burden or condition must be specific, and will be construed strictly *contra proferentem* (*i.e.* against the party seeking to apply it). The real burden must be specific in all the material requirements necessary to enforce it as a legal obligation. Thus in a number of cases the real burden has been struck down because the words

---

[3] (1770) Mor. 14537.
[4] 1940 S.C.(H.L.) 45. But for present purposes see 1939 S.C. 788.
[5] *Phillips* v. *Lavery*, 1962 S.L.T.(Sh.Ct.) 57.
[6] 1921 2 S.L.T. 33.

which created it were susceptible of a doubt as to the superior's intention. So in *Murray's Trs.* v. *St Margaret's Convent Trs.*[7] the proprietors of a piece of property in a villa area granted a condition over it in favour of the proprietor of an adjoining house. This condition bound the proprietors of the property and their successors not to erect on the property any building "of an unseemly description." A singular successor of the grantor proposed to build a four-flatted tenement. The other proprietor sought interdict to prevent the building going ahead. The House of Lords held that the restriction against the erection of an unseemly building was too vague and indefinite to be valid as a restraint against the use of property. This decision was followed in *Kirkintilloch Kirk Session* v. *Kirkintilloch School Board*,[8] where "a perpetual right of occasional occupation" was held to be too vague.

It is also the case that the court will if possible so construe the burden as to take the least possible constraint from the restriction. In *Kemp* v. *Magistrates of Largs*,[9] a proprietor of a piece of land in Largs adjoining the harbour wished to build an amusement arcade. His superior, the Burgh of Largs, objected on the basis that this would be in contravention of their feu right whereby the use to which the property could be put was restricted to works necessarily connected with the harbour. The House of Lords held that the terms of the original feu disposition had not been constituted as a real restriction. It was concluded, therefore, that the grantor had not clearly signified his intention that the land should be subject to a real burden against the use of the property for any other purpose than the maintenance of a harbour.

(iv) Clear financial obligation

If the burden refers to the payment of money, the amount must be definite and the creditor identifiable.[10] In *Tailors of Aberdeen* the feuars were required to pay a proportion of two third parts of the expense of forming and enclosing the area in the middle of the town square and of upholding it in good repair. This was held not to be a real burden because it was made up of an obligation to pay an indefinite sum of money. While the creditors must be stated and clearly identified, there is no requirement that they need actually be named. In *Erskine* v. *Wright*[11] a real burden was accepted by the

---

[7] 1907 S.C.(H.L.) 8.

[8] 1911 S.C. 1127.

[9] 1939 S.C.(H.L.) 6.

[10] This rule is obviously subject to the provisions of the Land Tenure Reform (Scotland) Act as regards the redemption of feuduty.

[11] (1846) 8 D. 863.

court in favour of children who were not named but whose parents were.

(v) Record in Register of Sasines or Land Register

The real burden or condition must be recorded in the General Register of Sasines or the Land Register of Scotland. Failure to record a real burden in the General Register or Land Register means that the condition will attach only to those persons who were parties to the original contract. The harsh result of a failure to record is illustrated in *Wallace* v. *Simmers*.[12] The owner of a farm entered into a minute of agreement with his son whereby the farm was sold to the son under the stipulation that a right of occupancy of one of the farm cottages would be made in favour of himself, his wife and his daughter for as long as they desired. This minute was not recorded in the General Register. The farmer occupied the cottage until his death when his daughter continued to live there. The farm was later sold by the son at an auction. The purchasers of the cottage were informed that the sale was subject to the daughter's occupancy of the cottage. After the sale the purchasers sought to eject the daughter. The Court of Session held that, as the daughter's right of occupancy was a personal right exercisable only against the grantor and was not capable of being made a real right, it was not valid against singular successors even if they knew of its existence.[13]

(vi) Supporting clauses not necessary

There is no need in the feudal grant to fence the burden or condition with irritant or resolutive clauses which grant rights to the superior to recover possession of the land if the real burden is breached. Although these clauses are generally inserted in feudal grants they are not strictly necessary because they are implied by feudal law.

(vii) Interest needed for enforcement

The party seeking to enforce a real burden must not merely have a title to do so but in interest as well. This question must be examined in relation both to the superior and to co-feuars.

---

[12] 1960 S.C. 255.

[13] Even if the minute of agreement had been recorded in the General Register it would not have been enforceable against singular successors. See *Campbell's Trs.* v. *Glasgow Corpn.* (1902) 4 F. 752.

(a) *The superior*

The superior's title to enforce a real burden will generally be based on the contract contained in the feudal grant. This is really a question of fact rather than law, and it is here assumed that the superior has the necessary title. The question of interest is rather more complicated. The rule is that, in any court action that the superior wishes to take to prevent the contravention, an interest to take the action is assumed to exist. It has been stated in a number of cases that the existence of the feudal relationship is *prima facie* evidence of the superior's interest. In *Macdonald* v. *Douglas*,[14] for example, Lord Justice-Clerk Grant declared that:

> "So far as the superior's interest is concerned, it was not disputed that, *prima facie*, a vassal, in consenting to be bound, concedes the superior's interest and that the *onus* is on the vassal to prove that, owing to some change of circumstances, any legitimate interest that the superior may originally have had has ceased to exist."

It is clear, therefore, that the onus is upon the feuar to rebut the presumption in favour of the superior's interest to enforce the real burden. This would be achieved by showing that there has been a change of circumstances. As Lord Watson declared in *Earl of Zetland* v. *Hislop*[15]:

> "*Prima facie*, the vassal in consenting to be bound by the restriction concedes the interest of the superior; and, therefore, it appears to me, that the *onus* is upon the vassal who is pleading a release from his contract to allege and prove that, owing to some change in circumstances, any legitimate interest which the superior may originally have had in maintaining the restriction has ceased to exist."

There can be no doubt that there is a heavy onus on a feuar seeking to prove a change in circumstances. In *Earl of Zetland* the superior sought to enforce a condition which prevented feuars using their premises for retailing spirits or as eating-houses without the superior's consent. Here a feuar argued that a substantial increase in the population of the town covered by the restriction amounted to a change in circumstances. Lord Watson accepted that an

---

[14] 1963 S.C. 374 at p. 389.
[15] (1882) 9 R.(H.L.) 40 at p. 47.

increase in population could be an element in estimating the change. He went on to state as follows:

> "If all the dwelling-houses, save one, in a particular street were by license of the superior used for the sale of liquor, I can conceive that the superior might have difficulty in showing a legitimate interest to prohibit the sale of liquor in that one house. But I am at a loss to understand why the existence of a whole street of public-houses in one part of the burgh should disable him from enforcing the prohibition in a street of villa dwellings in another quarter of the town."[16]

Equally, in *Howard De Walden Estates Ltd.* v. *Bowmaker Ltd.*[17] the First Division held that the test as to whether the feuar had proved that the superior had lost his interest to enforce the conditions of the feu was whether the original residential character of the neighbourhood and every part of it had been wholly lost by a change in circumstances. In this case the feuars were unable to prove that the superior had lost his interest despite the fact that over one-third of the houses in the street were no longer used as dwelling-houses (which their feudal grant required them to be).

There is clearly a very high burden on the feuar to prove the necessary loss of interest. This is illustrated in *Waddell* v. *Campbell*,[18] where it was held that the superior had an interest to enforce a condition in the feu grant for the use of "blue Scotch slates." This was in the face of evidence that the type of slate the feuar wanted to use was of better quality and less unsightly. Moreover it would seem that the interest of the superior need not be patrimonial or even beneficial.[19] In *Menzies* v. *Caledonian Canal Commissioners*[20] it was held that the commissioners could prevent a hotel being built which would have been in contravention of the conditions of the feu. This condition had been inserted in the feudal grant in order to prevent the workers on the canal getting drunk during working hours. The court concluded that the superior had an interest in ensuring that the canal was used safely by securing the sobriety of those who worked on the canal.

It is also possible to prevent the superior taking action to enforce feuing conditions by showing that the superior has acquiesced in

---

16 *Ibid.* at p. 51.
17 1965 S.C. 163.
18 (1898) 25 R. 456.
19 *Cf. Earl of Zetland* v. *Hislop* (1882) 9 R.(H.L.) 40.
20 (1900) 2 F. 953.

earlier contraventions by the feuar. Thus the superior may be personally barred from enforcing a real burden if a material breach of the conditions has been knowingly allowed to take place and to subsist for some substantial time. As Lord Adam said in *Johnston* v. *Walker Trs.*[21]:

"A superior who stands by and knows of and allows the vassal to incur considerable expense in doing that to which objection may be taken as a contravention of a restrictive feuing condition is barred from objecting at a later stage to that particular contravention."

The law on acquiescence was explained in *Ben Challum Ltd.* v. *Buchanan.*[22] The feuar in this case was obliged by his feu charter to erect a dwelling-house and shop with suitable offices. It was also stated that he should not alter nor add to these buildings without the superior's written consent. Over a period of 12 years the feuar erected five petrol pumps and a wooden bungalow for fodder storage without the consent of the superior. After the 12 years the superior decided to raise an action against the erection of the petrol pumps and the bungalow. The feuar argued that the superior had acquiesced in the breach of the feuing conditions. In the course of their decision the First Division outlined the necessary factors for acquiescence as follows

(i) It must be shown that the party seeking to enforce the restriction knew that it was being disregarded.

(ii) There must be more than mere silence on the part of the superior. It must be shown that the superior actually permitted the feuar to proceed and to incur the expense of structural alterations.

(b) *Co-feuars*

Normally it is only the superior who has the interest and right to enforce the conditions of the feu, but a neighbouring feuar may have a right to sue provided there is a *jus quaesitum tertio* (*i.e.* the right of a third party to sue). The right to sue rests on some element of mutuality of rights and obligations between the feuars. The issue was discussed by the House of Lords in *Hislop* v. *MacRitchie's Trs.*[23] where it was stressed that a *jus quaesitum tertio* will not be estab-

---

[21] (1897) 24 R. 1061.
[22] 1955 S.C. 348.
[23] (1881) 8 R.(H.L.) 95.

lished easily. In this case Lord Watson examined the existing law and made the following points:

(i) The fact that the same condition appears in feu charters derived from the same superior coupled with a substantial interest in its observance does not create a right to sue. Thus a right to sue cannot be created simply because co-feuars share common conditions.

(ii) The right can be created either expressly or by implication from the feudal grant. An express right will be created where the superior stipulates expressly in the several feudal grants that each vassal will have a right to sue. A right to sue can also be created by reasonable implication from a reference in each feudal grant to a uniform plan of building or a common feuing plan.

It is also possible for a *jus quaesitum tertio* to be created where the feuars mutually agree amongst themselves that each may enforce the conditions against the others.

Thus it is clear that the mere fact that there are several feus adjoining or in close proximity to one another and possessing a common superior does not of itself permit any one of them to enforce compliance with the conditions of the feu. Co-feuars must show that they have a *jus quaesitum tertio* by express grant from the superior, by implication in the feudal deeds or by agreement among the co-feuars. It is not enough that a co-feuar will be prejudiced by the contravention of the feuing conditions or that the superior concurs in the action. In *Hislop* v. *MacRitchie's Trs.*[24] it was held that the consent and concurrence of the superior did not give a co-feuar a right to object where a right to sue could not be set up either expressly from the feu grant or by implication. The fact that the grants given to the co-feuars contained the same restrictions did not give them a right to sue.

The right of the superior to sue and those of co-feuars are independent and separate rights. The right of the superior rests upon a contract created by the feudal grant, whereas the right of a co-feuar is more in the nature of a proper servitude.[25] This means that a loss of an interest to sue by the superior will have no effect upon co-feuars. In *Lawrence* v. *Scott*[26] it was held that the fact that the superior was barred from complaining about a breach of feuing conditions did not prevent a co-feuar from suing on the basis that a *jus quaesitum tertio* had been expressly conferred upon him in the

---

[24] (1881) 8 R.(H.L.) 95.
[25] *per* Lord Watson in *Hislop* v. *MacRitchie's Trs.* (1881) 8 R. 95 at p. 102.
[26] 1965 S.L.T. 390.

feudal grant. Co-feuars who enjoy a right to sue may become personally barred from suing through acquiescence. However, this will depend upon the extent of the harm and its seriousness for the relevant objector. Thus the fact that there have been breaches of feuing conditions in other parts of the area feued to which the co-feuar has not objected will not necessarily bar that person from complaining in the case of breaches closer to home.[27] Co-disponees might also have a right to sue where other disponees have breached conditions of their sale and similar rules to those which affect co-feuars will be applied.[28]

Discharge and Variation by Lands Tribunal

It is clear from the above discussion that feudal law made it difficult for feuars to avoid their feudal conditions. At common law a feuar may obtain a waiver of a particular feuing condition from the superior or, more radically, a charter of novodamus may be arranged which involves a regrant of the feu minus the offending conditions. Alternatively, the feuar may seek a declarator that the superior no longer has an interest to enforce the condition.[29] As we saw in earlier chapters, various aspects of the feudal system (such as feuduty and land registration) have been the subjects of public concern and ultimately legislative amendment. The operation of feuing conditions has been the subject of particular scrutiny in the twentieth century.

The White Paper, *Land Tenure in Scotland: A Plan for Reform*, published in July 1969,[30] examined the feudal system in some detail. It criticised the system as being both autocratic and obsolete and considered that in cases where the superior had no real concern for the amenity of the area the only basis upon which a superior was likely to enforce feuing conditions was financial. Moreover, since in the great majority of cases superiors no longer lived in the area there was no real pressure on them to ensure that the conditions of the feudal grant were being complied with. The White Paper argued that the answer did not lie in minor patchwork reforms. It was convinced that the feudal system should be replaced by a new

[27] *Mactaggart & Co.* v. *Roemmele*, 1907 S.C. 1318.

[28] *Nicholson* v. *Glasgow Blind Asylum*, 1911 S.C. 391; *SCWS* v. *Finnie*, 1937 S.C. 835.

[29] See, *e.g. Menzies* v. *Caledonian Canal Commrs.* (1900) 2 F. 953. This right cannot be delegated to the tenant of a feuar—*Eagle Lodge Ltd* v. *Keir and Cawder Estates Ltd.*, 1964 S.C. 30.

[30] Cmnd. 4099.

system altogether. The suggested solution was that on an appointed day existing feuars who were owners of the *dominium utile* should be declared to own their lands in terms of some new form of absolute ownership.[31]

As a direct result of the White Paper's criticisms the Conveyancing and Feudal Reform (Scotland) Act was enacted in 1970. This Act implemented many of the proposals contained in the Halliday Report,[32] but did not bring about the abolition of the feudal system as the White Paper of 1969 had demanded. Instead, it provided a completely new way of discharging the land conditions which were an integral part of the feudal system. Sections 1 and 2 of this Act provided an opportunity for disputed land conditions to be referred to the Lands Tribunal for Scotland for possible discharge or variation.

The Lands Tribunal for Scotland

(a) **Constitution**

The Lands Tribunal was created by sections 1 to 4 of the Lands Tribunal Act 1949. In Scotland, however, the Lands Tribunal did not actually come into being until March 1, 1971, when an Order in Council brought into force the relevant provisions of the 1949 Act for Scotland. The Lands Tribunal is made up of professional people of two types—lawyers who deal with the purely legal points and surveyors who can value the property and consider claims for compensation. It is usual for the Tribunal to sit in pairs consisting of one lawyer and one surveyor, although larger tribunals have been convened. If necessary cases are decided by vote, with the chairman having a casting vote in the case of a tie. The procedure which the Tribunal is to follow is laid down in the Lands Tribunal for Scotland Rules 1971.[33]

(b) **Jurisdiction**

The Tribunal has jurisdiction over the discharge and variation of "land obligations." A land obligation is defined in section 1(2) as an obligation relating to land which is enforceable by a proprietor of an interest in land, by virtue of his being such proprietor, and which is binding upon a proprietor of another interest in that land, or of an

---

[31] See also the Green Paper, *Land Tenure Reform in Scotland*, published by the Conservative government in 1972.

[32] *Conveyancing Legislation and Practice*, Cmnd. 3118 (1966).

[33] S.I. 1971 No. 218.

interest in other land, by virtue of his being such proprietor. The definition covers not only land conditions as set up under the rules as laid down in *Tailors of Aberdeen*, but also other obligations in feu grants which, although not created real, or lacking the precision of a real burden, are nevertheless binding upon successive feuars as inherent conditions of the grant. Private servitudes both positive and negative are also included, as are obligations created in deeds of declaration of conditions and registered long leases. However, excluded from the definition are feuduties and other periodic payments of money, rights to work minerals, obligations imposed by the Crown for the protection of royal parks, gardens or palaces, obligations created for military purposes and obligations under statutes relating to agriculture.[34] The Act also excludes all land obligations which are less than two years old.[35]

(c) Right of hearing

The Lands Tribunal can only hear cases from those people who are "burdened proprietors" as defined in the Act. A burdened proprietor petitions the Tribunal requesting it to vary or discharge the land obligation where the obligation is enforced upon that property by a "benefited proprietor." The phrases "benefited proprietor" and "burdened proprietor" are defined as follows:

   (i) A benefited proprietor is a proprietor of an interest in land who is entitled by virtue of his being such a proprietor to enforce the obligation (*e.g.* the superior or proprietor of a dominant tenement)[36];
   (ii) A burdened proprietor is a proprietor of an interest in the land upon whom, by virtue of his being such a proprietor, the obligation is binding (*e.g.* the feuar or proprietor of the servient tenement).[37]

If the Tribunal should vary or discharge the obligation, the benefited proprietor may be entitled to compensation.

(d) When obligations may be varied or discharged

The Act gives the Tribunal directions as to when it has authority to vary or discharge a land obligation. It can only do so when it is satisfied that one or other of the following conditions have been met[38]:

[34] 1970 Act, s. 1 and Sched. 1.
[35] 1970 Act, s. 2(5).
[36] A co-feuar with a *jus quaesitum tertio* is also a benefited proprietor.
[37] 1970 Act, s. 2(6).
[38] s. 1(3).

    (i) by reason of changes in the character of the land affected by the land obligation or of the neighbourhood or other circumstances which the tribunal deems material, the obligation is or has become unreasonable or inappropriate[39]; or

    (ii) the obligation is unduly burdensome compared with any benefit resulting or which would result from its performance[40]; or

    (iii) the existence of the obligation impedes some reasonable use of the land.[41]

A burdened proprietor can petition the Lands Tribunal on each one of these three grounds—they are not mutually exclusive.

(e) Conditions of jurisdiction

Since the jurisdiction of the Lands Tribunal is defined and limited by the Act which created it, the Tribunal must ensure that it acts in conformity with the statutory directions. Before the Tribunal can hear a case it must be satisfied that the conditions of jurisdiction have been met. The conditions are as follows:

    (i) the application must relate to a land obligation;

    (ii) the applicant must be a burdened proprietor; and

    (iii) the facts of the case must fall within one or more of the sets of circumstances listed in section 1(3)(*a*)–(*c*).

(f) Right to award compensation

As noted the Tribunal if it discharges the land obligation can award compensation to the benefited proprietor. The Tribunal can award compensation in one of two cases[42]:

    (i) as a sum to compensate for any substantial loss or disadvantage suffered by the benefited proprietor in consequence of the variation or discharge[43]; or

    (ii) as a sum to make up for any effect which the obligation produced at the time when it was imposed, in reducing the consideration then paid or made payable for the interest in land affected by it.[44]

---

[39] s. 1(3)(*a*).
[40] s. 1(3)(*b*).
[41] s. 1(3)(*c*). It is clear that s. 1(3)(*c*) concentrates on the proposed new use of the burdened land whereas s. 1(3)(*a*) looks to the past and the continuing unreasonableness of the restriction. See *North East Fife D.C.* v.*Lees*, 1989 S.L.T. (Lands Tr.) 30.
[42] s. 1(4).
[43] s. 1(4)(*a*).
[44] s. 1(4)(*b*).

Variation or Discharge through Change of Character[45]

(a) **Introduction**

Section 1(3)(*a*) deals with cases where a change in character in the neighbourhood has taken place subsequent to the imposition of the land obligation and which has affected the amenity of the property rendering the obligation unreasonable or inappropriate. There are three issues here—changes in the character of the land; changes in the neighbourhood and other circumstances deemed material by the Tribunal.

(b) **Change of character of land**

Generally, an obligation will be discharged under this provision where it can be established that the land has become useless in terms of the purpose for which the obligation was originally created.[46] A change in the profitability of the use of the land will not necessarily lead to a discharge. In *Bolton* v. *Aberdeen Corporation*[47] the applicant owned a grocery shop in Aberdeen and sought discharge of a condition which prevented him opening it as a betting shop. He claimed that because of increased competition his profits as a grocer had slumped. However, the Tribunal denied discharge because the land continued to have an economic use as a grocery shop.

(c) **Changes in the neighbourhood**

This question was considered in *Main* v. *Lord Doune*,[48] where there was a restriction against the use of the property for anything other than residential purposes. The feuar wished to open up a nursery on the property. This clearly was prohibited under the terms of his feudal grant. It was shown that one side of the crescent where the feuar lived was no longer residential but that the other side retained its residential character. The Tribunal could see no reason why, when a particular small section of a large feu has lost its residential character, it should be said that any of the adjoining parts which had not done so should be deemed to have acquired a non-residential character. Thus the Tribunal concluded that the burdened proprietor had not shown a change in the residential character of the neighbourhood and so discharge was refused. This

---

[45] s. 1(3)(*a*).
[46] *Solway Cedar Ltd.* v. *Hendry*, 1972 S.L.T. (Lands Tr.) 42; *Ross and Cromarty D.C.* v. *Ullapool Property Co. Ltd.*, 1983 S.L.T. (Lands Tr.) 9.
[47] 1972 S.L.T. (Lands Tr.) 26.
[48] 1972 S.L.T. (Lands Tr.) 14.

case sets a very high standard for change of character, but the same approach seems to have been favoured in later cases.[49] The other issue under this head is for the Tribunal to identify the "neighbourhood." In this regard the Tribunal will look at all the circumstances so that it may come to a decision as to the area of protection of the obligation.[50]

(d) Changes in social habits

Although section 1(3)(*a*) relates to changes in the character of the land, the Tribunal may also grant discharge where there are other circumstances which the Tribunal thinks material. This was discussed in *Murrayfield Ice Rink* v. *Scottish Rugby Union,*[51] where the proprietors of an ice rink applied for discharge of a land obligation which prevented them from using the premises as a supermarket. The application was opposed by the superior, the SRU. The ice rink argued on the basis of section 1(3)(*a*) that there were other circumstances which rendered the obligation unreasonable or inappropriate. It was claimed that there was a change of social habits over the years and that there was a decline in demand for ice sports. The Tribunal, however, could find no evidence of this. According to the Tribunal, if there was such a decline it was prior to 1960 when the land obligation was imposed in the feu grant. Consequently they refused discharge on this ground. The Tribunal did admit, however, that in relation to social habits and public taste these might constitute other circumstances.

Discharge was successful under section 1(3)(*a*) in *Manz* v. *Butter's Trs.*[52] In this case a hotel in the High Street in Pitlochry had been limited to temperance purposes since 1924. Discharge was sought under section 1(3)(*a*) since Pitlochry had now become a major tourist area. The Tribunal accepted that changes in the type of visitor going to the area and changes in social habits regarding drink meant that the obligation could be discharged.[53] It was pointed out by the Tribunal, however, that a prohibition against liquor might still be reasonable in a particular area. Nonetheless, the case does illustrate that a change in social habits can be deemed material circumstances and bring about a discharge under section 1(3)(*a*).

---

[49] *Pickford* v. *Young*, 1975 S.L.T. (Lands Tr.) 17; *Cameron* v. *Stirling*, 1988 S.L.T. (Lands Tr.) 18; *Tully* v. *Armstrong*, 1990 S.L.T. (Lands Tr.) 42.

[50] *Bolton* v. *Aberdeen Corpn.*, 1972 S.L.T. (Lands Tr.) 26.

[51] 1972 S.L.T. (Lands Tr.) 20, app. by Inner House, 1973 S.L.T. 99.

[52] 1973 S.L.T. (Lands Tr.) 3.

[53] See also *Owen* v. *Mackenzie*, 1974 S.L.T. (Lands Tr.) 11.

Variation or Discharge through Undue Burden[54]

The Act also provides a test based on whether any benefit would be provided by the discharge of the obligation. This test does not depend upon the personal circumstances of the burdened proprietor. The test is objective in terms of the locality. This point was made clear in *Murrayfield Ice Rink*, where the Tribunal was at pains to point out that the fact that a discharge would benefit the burdened proprietor did not automatically mean that it would bring benefit to the locality. The Tribunal's approach to this test is best illustrated in *Bolton*. Under this head Bolton claimed that his land obligation was unduly burdensome on him because as a grocer he was making far smaller profits than he would make as a bookmaker. The Tribunal did not accept this contention, however, and were not satisfied that Bolton's decline in profits was due to the restrictive land obligation. It could also have been due to Bolton's personal skills as a grocer. Thus the mere fact that the land would become more profitable if the obligation were discharged is not of itself sufficient grounds under section 1(3)(*b*).[55]

Variation or Discharge because Reasonable Use Impeded[56]

This has proved to be the most fruitful ground on which an applicant can obtain discharge or variation of a land obligation. The Tribunal has considered four separate issues under this test.

(a) **Is there a need for the proposed change of use?**

Murrayfield Ice Rink has made it clear that this question must be looked at in all the circumstances. In it the Tribunal asked itself whether wholesale and retail trade at the ice rink was a reasonable use of the land in all the circumstances. The Tribunal discovered that adequate access to the ice rink as an "island site" could not be arranged. There was also no proof that adequate parking space would be available to meet the increased traffic generated by a supermarket. Consequently the Lands Tribunal held that the relevant land obligation was not presently impeding some reasonable use of the land and that the proposed supermarket was not reasonable in all the circumstances.

---

[54] s. 1(3)(*b*).
[55] *Sinclair* v. *Gillon*, 1974 S.L.T. (Lands Tr.) 18.
[56] s. 1(3)(*c*).

On the other hand, in *Main*[57] the restriction was found to impede a reasonable use of the land. This was because it was proved to the satisfaction of the Tribunal that the provisions of a nursery in the locality would fulfil a social need.

(b) Would the discharge provide a beneficial utilisation of land?

This was a question which the Tribunal considered in *West Lothian Co-operative Society Ltd.* v. *Ashdale Land and Property Co Ltd.*[58] The case concerned certain disused property in Broxburn which had been sold with the intention of building a factory. The feuing conditions in question, however, required that certain derelict buildings be maintained on the feu and also prevented the premises being used as a factory. The Tribunal granted discharge under section 1(3)(*c*) because the requirement that the buildings be maintained impeded the redevelopment of the feu.

(c) Has planning permission been obtained?

It is relevant to the applicant's case if planning permission has been obtained for the proposed change in use. In *Main*[59] planning permission had already been obtained for the proposed nursery. The Tribunal took this into account when considering whether the land obligation impeded a reasonable use of the land.

(d) How will the amenity of the area be affected by the discharge?

This is the most common ground of objection to applications under section 1(3)(*c*). The superior or local residents may object on the basis of a consequent loss of amenity if the obligation is discharged. In *Bolton*[60] the application was also rejected under this ground. The Tribunal agreed with the position that Aberdeen Corporation had adopted, that the restriction was necessary to uphold the amenity of the area. This question was also considered in *Smith* v. *Taylor.*[61] In this case there was an application for discharge of an obligation which forbade the sale of liquor in a private hotel. The feuar sought discharge in order to obtain a liquor licence for the hotel. There were objections to the discharge from a number of neighbouring proprietors because of the noise and smell and increase in traffic and the parking of cars which licensed pre-

---

[57] 1972 S.L.T. (Lands Tr.) 14.
[58] 1972 S.L.T. (Lands Tr.) 30.
[59] *Loc. cit.* Issue is also discussed in *British Bakeries (Scotland) Ltd.* v. *City of Edinburgh D.C.*, 1990 S.L.T. (Lands Tr.) 33.
[60] 1972 S.L.T. (Lands Tr.) 26.
[61] 1972 S.L.T. (Lands Tr.) 34.

mises would create. The Tribunal considered that it was helpful to the applicant's case that his property had already been used without objection as a private hotel and boarding house.

Power of Addition

Under section 1(5) the Tribunal has the power when varying or discharging a land obligation to add or substitute any such provision as appears to it to be reasonable as a result of the variation or discharge and as may be accepted by the applicant. The tribunal has been able to use this procedure as a way of protecting the amenity of the area or preserving privacy.[62]

Compensation[63]

For compensation to be awarded under section 1(4)(i) the loss or disadvantage must be substantial. Compensation is often awarded for loss of amenity. In *Smith* v. *Taylor*,[64] for example, the surrounding householders claimed compensation for the increased noise and smells that would be created by a licensed hotel. Their claims were successful and they were awarded compensation of between £100 and £800 depending on their proximity to the boarding-house. Equally, compensation may be awarded under this head where the discharge is likely to lead to a depreciation in the value of premises.[65] However, compensation will not be awarded simply because the discharge of the obligation means that the superior will not receive the amount of money that a waiver of the obligation would provide.[66]

The second ground upon which compensation can be awarded is as a sum to make up for any effect which the obligation produced, at the time of its imposition, in reducing the consideration paid. The basic issue here is whether the superior charged a lower feuduty on the basis of the obligation which has now been discharged. In *Manz* v. *Butter's Trs.*[67] the Tribunal held that the superiors were not

---

[62] *Crombie* v. *George Heriot's Trust*, 1972 S.L.T. (Lands Tr.) 40; *Bruce* v. *Modern Homes Investment Co. Ltd.*, 1978 S.L.T. (Lands Tr.) 34.

[63] s. 1(4).

[64] *Loc. cit.*

[65] *Co-operative Wholesale Society* v. *Ushers Brewery*, 1975 S.L.T. (Lands Tr.) 9.

[66] *West Lothian Co-op. Soc.* v. *Ashdale Land and Property Co. Ltd.*, 1972 S.L.T. (Lands Tr.) 30.

[67] 1973 S.L.T. (Lands Tr.) 2; *West Lothian Co-op. Soc.*, above.

entitled to compensation under section 1(4)(ii) because they had failed to prove that a lower feuing rate was charged in 1924 when the land was first feued than would have been charged if the relevant feuing conditions had not been imposed. It is very rare for compensation to be awarded under this head.

(c) Servitudes over Land

As in other areas of Scots law, much of the law on servitudes is derived from Roman law.[68] A servitude has been defined by Bell as:

> "a burden on land or houses, imposed by agreement—express or implied—in favour of the owners of other tenements: whereby the owner of the burdened or 'servient' tenement, and his heirs and singular successors in the subject, must submit to certain uses to be exercised by the owner of the other or 'dominant' tenement or must restrain in his own use and occupation of their property."[69]

A servitude is, therefore, nothing more than a burden on heritable property in favour of the "dominant" tenement by the property itself. The benefit granted to the owner of the dominant tenement is not personal, but is derived from the ownership of the dominant tenement. Thus a servitude is always praedial, that is, it is real and binds singular successors. Personal rights of skating, shooting, fishing, etc., are not servitudes but privileges, which subsist only as personal licences.

Servitudes are divided into two groups, positive and negative:
- (a) A positive servitude permits the owner of the dominant tenement to do a positive act, such as walk over the servient tenement or pasture cattle there.
- (b) A negative servitude allows the dominant tenement to prevent or restrain the servient tenement from doing some action.

(i) Essentials of a servitude
(i) There must be two tenements owned by different persons,[70] both comprising subjects which are corporeal heritable

---

[68] Justinian's *Institutes*, II. 2, 3.

[69] *Prin.*, § 979.

[70] As to whether a servitude can be created in favour of a tenement held by a tenant, see W. M. Gordon, *Scottish Land Law* (1989), para. 24–09.

property, and which are neighbouring or reasonably adjacent to one another.

(ii) There must be benefit to the dominant owner, for this is the reason for the existence of the servitude. Thus the servitude must benefit the land and not merely be for the personal advantage of the holder of the dominant tenement.[71]

(iii) When a servitude is created by express grant, the words creating it must be unambiguous, definite and precise. Since a servitude is a restraint on the freedom of property, strict proof is required in order to set it up.[72]

(ii) **Creation of a servitude**
There are four ways of creating a servitude:

(a) *By express grant*
This is the only way that a negative servitude can be created, since prescriptive possession is out of the question and other methods would be almost impossible to establish. The document creating the servitude must be probative or holograph. It would also be possible to create the servitude by an improbative grant which has been set up by homologation or *rei interventus*. This means that there must be subsequent actings which are referable to the grant and which have been carried out on the faith of it.[73] There is no need for the agreement to be registered in the General Register of Sasines or Land Register. Nonetheless, if it is a positive servitude it may be difficult to show that it was intended to apply to singular successors of the grantor. However, in theory at least, a person who acquires the dominant tenement can exercise the rights created by the servitude so long as there has been inspection of the property and inquiry followed by possession. Since in the case of a negative servitude there is no question of possession if the agreement is not recorded, it would not otherwise come to the notice of singular successors.

(b) *Implied grant*
This is an exceptional method by which a servitude can be created, since it means placing a burden on another property as well as a benefit to the dominant tenement, and this would impinge upon the concept of freedom of property. Typically, a positive servitude

---

[71] *Patrick* v. *Napier* (1867) 5 M. 683.

[72] See the speech of Lord Reid in *Hunter* v. *Fox*, 1964 S.C.(H.L.) 95.

[73] See, *e.g. Safeway Foodstores Ltd* v. *Wellington Motor Co. (Ayr) Ltd.*, 1976 S.L.T. 53. For the extent of a servitude of access provided by express grant, see the decision of the House of Lords in *Alvis* v. *Harrison*, 1991 S.L.T. 64.

may be created in this way if the property was originally owned by one person and the parts were later sold separately so that a servitude of access out of necessity would have to be implied. Such an implied servitude would have to be necessary, or, at least, reasonably necessary for the comfortable enjoyment of the dominant tenement.[74]

(c) *Express or implied reservation*

In this case both tenements must have been in ownership of the one person and later separated. This would occur when a seller sells off part of the land and reserves certain servitude rights which appear on the deed of conveyance. It is also possible to reserve a servitude right impliedly, but this is seldom upheld. An implied reservation cannot be set up where the right sought is merely for the more comfortable or convenient enjoyment of the retained subjects, because this would be a derogation from the disponer's own grant.[75]

(d) *Prescription*

Where there has been an actual use of a servitude and possession for 20 years, continuously, openly, peaceably and without judicial interruption, a positive servitude will be created.[76] It may be possible to establish the servitude without proof of actual possession for 20 years. So long as for most of this period the relevant possession can be proved, the court will be prepared to infer user for the entire period of the positive prescription.[77] If acquired in this way, the kind of servitude created is determined by the prescriptive possession which has been established.

(iii) Positive servitudes

These may be either *urban* (affecting buildings in town or country), or *rural* (affecting lands).

(a) *Urban servitudes*

These can be further classified into various types:

(i) **Support**. Two servitudes of support are recognised, stemming from the civil law:

---

[74] *Cochranes* v. *Ewart* (1860) 22 D. 358; *Fraser* v. *Cox*, 1938 S.C. 506.

[75] Rankine, *Landownership*, p. 438. See also *Ferguson* v. *Campbell*, 1913 1 S.L.T. 241.

[76] Prescription and Limitation (Scotland) Act 1973, s. 3.

[77] *McGregor* v. *Crieff Co-op. Soc.*, 1915 S.C.(H.L.) 93.

Tigni immitendi—the right to insert, into the wall of the servient tenement, a beam or other structural member forming part of the dominant tenement and to maintain it there and renew it when necessary.

Oneris ferendi—the right of the dominant tenement to rest beams on the wall of the servient and to have whole rooms resting on the other's tenement. There is an implied duty on servient owners to maintain their individual tenement.

(ii) **Stillicide**. This is a right of eavesdrop which allows the dominant tenement to discharge rainwater from the roof on to the tenement which is servient.

(b) *Rural servitudes*
Again these can be classified:

(i) **Fuel, feal and divot**. This is a right to dig peat for fuel and to take clods for fencing and roofing. Under this servitude there is implied a right of access to the locality. The right may be restricted to such parts of the servient tenement as is sufficient for the needs of the dominant tenement.

(ii) **Pasturage**. This servitude confers on the dominant tenement the right to pasture stock on the servient tenement, or, more frequently, on common ground.[78] If it is created by express grant, but if no numbers are specified, the extent of the right is measured by the benefit to the dominant tenement. In practice, since there are likely to be several dominant tenements, their rights are determined either by rentals or the stock each can winter.

(iii) **Water**. *Aquaehaustus*. This servitude allows the owner of the dominant tenement to take water proper to one tenement for his use. It often exists so that the dominant owner can take water for cattle, but it may apply for other purposes. The owner of the servient tenement may use the water, at least for primary purposes, provided the dominant tenement is left with the appropriate entitlement.

Aqueduct. This is the right to lead water over the servient tenement. There is implied a right of access for the dominant tenement in order that the works can be maintained. This form of servitude is generally linked with the right to rest a weir on the servient tene-

[78] *Fraser* v. *S. of S. for Scotland*, 1959 S.L.T. (Notes) 36.

ment. It was held in *Central Regional Council* v. *Ferns*[79] that a servitude of aqueduct could be created by implication through the existence of legislation. In such case the owner of the servient tenement was not entitled to do any act which materially interfered with the right of access to the works.

(iv) **Passage**. This form of servitude exists in four degrees—footways; horse roads; drove roads and carriageways. A grant of wider use covers the narrower uses also, so that for example a right of carriageway implies a right of footway. The type of passage the dominant servitude possesses will depend on the grant[79a] or the type of possession which has been exercised. The right may be restricted to use for a particular purpose, *e.g.* to go to a church or a mill, etc. A right of carriage road permits the dominant owner to use cars over it. The servient tenement can erect gates over the road but may not lock them. In some circumstances the course of a servitude road may be altered if provision is made of a substitute equally convenient to the dominant owner.[80]

(v) **Other rural servitudes**. Other rights have also been recognised as rural servitudes, for example bleaching, quarrying stone and taking sand and gravel. The modern development rights to run a pipeline through land, or an electricity or telephone line over it are dealt with under the Pipelines Act 1962. This grants bodies wishing to construct such pipelines the authority compulsorily to acquire the necessary rights.

(iv) **Negative servitudes**

These are rights which do not require the dominant owner to perform any acts but exist to prevent or restrain some action by the servient owner (*in non faciendo*). They are of three types—light, air and prospect. As a general rule they restrict the otherwise natural right of servient owners to build where and as high as they choose on their own property and thus block their neighbours' windows.

A servitude *non aedificandi* prevents the construction of any building however harmless, while one which is *altius non tollendi* permits the servient owner building to a certain height. These servitudes are always construed in favour of the servient tenement.

---

[79] 1979 S.C. 136.
[79a] See generally *Irvine Knitters Ltd.* v. *North Ayrshire Co-operative Society Ltd.*, 1978 S.C. 109.
[80] See, *e.g. Mags. of Rutherglen* v. *Bainbridge* (1886) 13 R. 745.

In *Craig* v. *Gould*[81] there was a prohibition against building higher than 10 feet, "because of the light" of the dominant owner. It was held that the servient owner could build up to 10 feet even although by so doing he blocked some windows of the dominant tenement. A servitude *non officiendi* is less specific. It restrains the servient tenement from constructing a building which interferes with the dominant owner's view.

(v) Transmission of servitudes

Servitudes have nothing to do with the superior/vassal relationship. They run with the land, and a singular successor of the dominant tenement automatically has a right to them if followed by infeftment (the recording of title in the Register of Sasines or Land Register) or by possession and enjoyment by the owner of the dominant tenement.

(vi) Extinction of servitudes

Servitudes can be extinguished in the following ways:

(a) *Express discharge or renunciation*. Such renunciation must be by the dominant owner in probative writing. This will bind singular successors to the dominant tenement. As with the rules for creation of a servitude, there is no need that the deed of renunciation be recorded in the Register of Sasines or Land Register. However, it is preferable to register such a deed, particularly when the original grant creating the servitude has been recorded.

(b) *Confusio*. This arises where both tenements come into the ownership of the one person. In such a case the servitude disappears and does not later revive if the tenements are later separated. However, this presumption may be rebutted if it can be established that the properties were held on separate titles.[82]

(c) *Negative prescription*. If a positive servitude has not been exercised or a relevant claim made by the owner of the dominant tenement for a continuous period of 20 years the servitude will be extinguished.[83] The time will run from the last date when the owner of the dominant tenement exercised the right. Equally, a negative servitude will cease to exist where the dominant tenement has failed to enforce it for 20 years. In this case, the time is calculated from the date of the first contravention by the servient tenement which went unchallenged.

---

[81] (1861) 24 D. 20.

[82] Bell, *Prin.*, § 977. See *Donaldson's Trs.* v. *Forbes* (1839) 1 D. 449. *Cf. Walton Bros.* v. *Mags. of Glasgow* (1876) 3 R. 1130.

[83] Prescription and Limitation (Scotland) Act 1973, s. 8.

(d) *Acquiescence*. This occurs where the owner of the dominant tenement evidences by conduct an intention to give up the right so as to be subsequently personally barred from enforcing it.

(e) *Change of circumstances*. The servitude will be extinguished if either the dominant or the servient tenement is destroyed. In such a case there must be total destruction for the servitude to disappear. If there is merely a temporary unfitness of either tenement, the servitude will simply be suspended until the necessary remedial action is taken. Servitudes may also be affected by the compulsory requisition of the servient tenement. In such a case the servitude will be suspended until the property is returned to private hands.

(f) *Statute*. It is possible that a statute which provides for the compulsory acquisition of the servient tenement will declare that the land is to be free from any servitudes. In any case any servitude which is incompatible with the compulsory purchase is likely to expire.

Public Rights of Way

A public right of way is not a servitude, but a right whereby the public can pass from one public place to another along a definite route. It is usually acquired by use for the prescriptive period of 20 years. The Prescription and Limitation (Scotland) Act 1973, s. 3(3) makes it clear that the use possessed by the public must be open, peaceable and without judicial interruption, and declares that once the 20-year period has expired a right of way will exist and be exempt from legal challenge. The difference between a servitude and a public right of way was discussed in *Ayr Burgh Council* v. *British Transport Commission*,[84] where the council, as proprietors of the local cattle market, raised an action of interdict against British Rail from levying a charge against cars, etc., making use of the British Transport Commission's livestock bank beside the cattle market. The council based their case on the fact they had acquired a public right of way for the purpose of getting to the cattle market. They also claimed that if no public right of way could be set up they had acquired a private servitude of access either by prescription or agreement. The court held that as the market was open only four days a week and was closed at nights, no public right of way could be set up since the essence of a public right of way is that the public place should be kept open for passage by the public at all times. The court also held that no servitude right of way in favour of the public

[84] 1955 S.L.T. 219.

was known to Scots law, since the essence of a servitude is to benefit one particular property, *viz.* the dominant tenement. Rights of way are basically extinguished in the same ways as servitudes.[85]

2. LAW OF NEIGHBOURHOOD

The social nature of property ownership was recognised by the common law in two major forms prior to the emergence of statutory limitations on what property owners could do with their heritage. Initially the option of freedom of property dominated and for any limitation an element of malice was required. However this was modified in the doctrine of nuisance which merely limited property owners to using their property in such a way as not to harm the property rights of others. This is in accordance with the maxim *sic utere tuo ut alienum non laedas* (so use your property as not to injure that of another). Whilst this provided the basis for complaint, it relied for its effectiveness on active complaints and litigation. It was greatly supplemented by regulation by public officials on behalf of the community in the form of statutory nuisance on a national basis in Scotland from 1867 onwards.

(a) The Use of One's Property with Malice against Neighbouring Property (in aemulationem vicini)

The common law prohibits any use of property whose sole benefit is to harm neighbouring property without there being any benefit to the property owner.[86] The spite or malice involved must be proved rather than merely assumed. Fishing beyond the mid-point of a river was taken to amount to malicious use against the rights of the owner of the opposite bank in *Campbell* v. *Muir*[87]; whilst more recently, in *More* v. *Boyle*,[88] the act of closing a water-pipe running through a garden was accepted as amounting to an act of spite or malice. Here there was a dispute about a repair to the water supply, and the response of the defender thereafter was to excavate in his

---

[85] See W. M. Gordon, *Scottish Land Law* (1989), paras. 24–147 to 24–154.

[86] Lord Watson questioned the existence of such a concept in *Mayor of Bradford* v. *Pickles* [1895] A.C. 587 at p. 598. His statement must be considered *obiter* and cannot be reconciled with later Scottish decisions. See also "Reparation," in *Encyclopaedia of the Laws of Scotland* (1931), Vol. 12, paras. 1076–1078.

[87] 1908 S.C. 387.

[88] 1967 S.L.T.(Sh.Ct.) 38.

garden and close up the pipe supplying his neighbours including the
pursuer.

(b) Nuisance Under the Common Law

Owners are restricted by the common law of Scotland to using their
property in such a way as not to harm others' enjoyment of their
property. Property owners are entitled to an environment free from
pollution. This covers physical discomfort—smoke, smells, noise or
vibration as well as things offensive to decency.[89]
    The broad approach is whether or not the acts complained of
interfere with the enjoyment of life of another property owner. The
proper angle of approach is from the standpoint of the victim of the
loss or inconvenience rather than from that of the alleged
offender.[90] What is acceptable conduct has varied between different
times and different geographical locations. Whether a particular act
or omission amounts to a nuisance is largely a question of
neighbourhood, circumstance and degree. Typically the important
element of the locality will mean that what is a nuisance in a
residential area need not be one in an industrial estate. Some
activities might be dealt with by either the criminal law or by the
relevant Public Health or Control of Pollution legislation. Nevertheless there is no limitation on the use of the common law merely
because the activities complained of are illegal or subject to regulation by statutory agencies. Indeed, given the limitations on the rôle
of the courts in controlling the discretion of the police and local
authorities, the common law of nuisance may prove a crucial
mechanism of control, as witness the successful interdict secured
against the erection of the stands for the Edinburgh Military Tattoo
in *Webster* v. *Lord Advocate.*[91]
    The complainer at common law may seek interdict as well as
damages and, where appropriate, restitution. It is now clear that
where the pursuer's chosen remedy is damages some reference to
culpa must be made.[92] The right to complain about a nuisance can

---

[89] See the classic definition of nuisance provided by Professor Bell (*Prin.*, § 974)
and quoted in full in Chap. 7.
[90] *per* Lord President Cooper in *Watt* v. *Jamieson*, 1954 S.C. 56 at p. 57, who also
made clear that the activity must be *plus quam tolerabile.*
[91] 1984 S.L.T. 13.
[92] See the decision of the House of Lords in *RHM Bakeries (Scotland) Ltd.* v.
Strathclyde R.C., 1985 S.L.T. 214, and see generally W. J. Stewart *An Introduction
to the Scots Law of Delict* (1989), paras. 2.11–2.15.

be lost through consent or acquiescence.[93] In addition, the right of a property owner to object may be lost through the operation of the period of the negative prescription which is 20 years[94] unless there is an increase in the nuisance. It is also possible that statute may specifically authorise the activity in question.

(c) **Statutory Nuisance**

Whilst there is no distinction in Scots law between public and private nuisance, which is a feature of the law south of the border, there is a more formal system of nuisance-regulation set up under various statutes dating for the most part from the nineteenth century. The statutory control system for general neighbourhood nuisances is to be found in the Public Health (Scotland) Act 1897. Specific forms of pollution have their own detailed statutory codes—air pollution is dealt with in the Clean Air Acts 1956 and 1968 and in the Alkali etc. Works Regulation Act 1906, whilst noise nuisance and water pollution are covered by the Control of Pollution Act 1974 and radioactive waste by the Radioactive Substances Acts 1948 and 1960.[95]

Statutory Nuisance in Outline

The Public Health (Scotland) Act 1897 states that a wide range of operations and activities shall be deemed to be statutory nuisances. The Act lists those items which are either injurious or dangerous to health and hence are liable to be dealt with summarily as provided under the Act.[96] These cover premises which are of such a construction or in such a state as to be a nuisance or injurious or dangerous to health. They also cover a host of matters whose condition is tested against this general standard of injurious or dangerous to health. It includes streets, gutters, drains, stables, byres or other buildings in which animals are kept, rubbish tips within 50 yards of any public road, any work, manufactory, trade or business, injurious to the health of the neighbourhood or so conducted as to be injurious or dangerous to health, any house or part of a house so

[93] *Bargaddie Coal Co.* v. *Wark* (1859) 21 D.(H.L.) 1.
[94] Prescription and Limitation (Scotland) Act 1973, s. 8.
[95] See F. Lyall, *Air, Noise, Water and Waste: A Summary of the Law in Scotland*, (1984).
[96] s. 16.

overcrowded as to be injurious or dangerous to the health of the inmates, any schoolhouse, or any factory which is not a factory subject to the provisions of the Factories Act 1961 with respect to cleanliness, ventilation, or overcrowding and is not kept in a cleanly state and free from waste products or is not properly ventilated or is so overcrowded while work is carried on as to be injurious or dangerous to the health of those therein employed, any churchyard or cemetery so situated or so crowded or otherwise so conducted as to be offensive or injurious or dangerous to health.

In *Connell* v *Duncan*[97] a broken lavatory basin was held to constitute nuisance and in *Corporation of Glasgow* v. *Purdon*[98] the nuisance consisted of dampness resulting from the defective condition of the property roof. The defender accepted that the condition of the property was such as to constitute a nuisance under section 16(i) of the Act.

It is, of course, the case that the wording of the Act is archaic but it still provides valuable rights. Typically action may be taken in respect of dwelling-houses affected by damp or condensation, or in respect of a house not served by an efficient drainage system.[99] It seems clear that the question whether or not a house meets the tolerable standard under the housing legislation is quite a different matter from whether or not the premises constitute a nuisance or a danger to health under the 1897 Act.

It would seem that unless there is some danger to health, or unless there is a nuisance of the common law type (*i.e.* there is some interference with the enjoyment or use of neighbouring property), there cannot be a statutory nuisance for the purposes of section 16 of the 1897 Act. In *National Coal Board* v. *Thorne*[100] the court held that the fact that a house had defective windows and gutters did not mean that there was a statutory nuisance. There was no evidence of prejudice to the health of the occupants and the court took the view that the word "nuisance" as used in the legislation had to be given the same meaning as it has in common law. There was, therefore, no nuisance in this case, as the only people affected by the defects were the occupiers of the house—neighbours were not affected.

---

[97] (1949) 65 Sh.Ct.Rep. 95.
[98] 1949 S.L.T. 44.
[99] s. 16(8)(i).
[100] [1976] 1 W.L.R. 543. See also *Salford City Council* v. *McNally* [1976] 1 W.L.R. 543.

(i) **The abatement of nuisances**

(a) *Inspection*
Under the 1897 Act, the local authority have a duty to have their district inspected from time to time in order to ascertain what nuisances exist and to enforce the provisions of the Act so as to secure the proper sanitary condition of all premises in their district.[101]

(b) *Entry*
If the local authority or a proper officer of the authority have reasonable grounds for believing that a nuisance exists on any premises, they may demand entry, and if refused may obtain a warrant to do so. They are also entitled to make such tests as are necessary on condition that, if no nuisance is found, they must restore the premises to their former condition.[102]

(c) *Notice*
If satisfied that a nuisance exists the authority must serve a notice on the author of the nuisance or, if the author cannot be found, on the occupier or owner of the premises, requiring the removal of the nuisance within the time stated in the notice.[103] The authority may also serve notice on the occupier, owner or any other person requiring them to do what is necessary to prevent a recurrence of the nuisance, even though the nuisance has ceased for the time being, if the authority consider it likely to recur. If a nuisance arises from a structural defect, notice must be served on the owner.[104]

(d) *Non-compliance with notice*
If the notice is not complied with and the authority consider the nuisance is likely to recur, then they may apply to the sheriff for an order for the removal or remedy or discontinuance of the nuisance. If the sheriff considers that the nuisance arose from wilful fault or culpable negligence, a fine may also be imposed. The sheriff may order whatever is necessary to remove the nuisance within a specified time, and, if it is likely to recur, may grant interdict against its recurrence.[105] The occupation of a house or building until it is

---

[101] s. 17.
[102] s. 18.
[103] *Clydebank D.C.* v *Monaville Estates Ltd.*, 1982 S.L.T.(Sh.Ct.) 2.
[104] s. 20.
[105] *McGourlick* v. *Renfrew D.C.*, 1982 SCOLAG 185 (Sh. Ct.); 1987 S.L.T. 538 (O. H.); 1988 S.L.T. 127 (I. H.). The case deals with the powers of a sheriff to help secure damp-free houses under the 1897 Act.

rendered fit for human habitation or use may also be prohibited. Contravention of such decree or interdict is punishable by a fine. On default by the owner or occupier, or if the author of a nuisance cannot be found, the sheriff may grant warrant to any person (including the local authority) to enter the premises and remedy the nuisance. Any expense may be recovered from the author of the nuisance, whom failing, the owner of the premises.[106]

(e) *Failure to act by the local authority*

If the local authority fail in their duty in regard to nuisances, it is within the rights of any 10[107] community charge payers[108] residing in the district, or of the procurator fiscal or of the Secretary of State, to give written notice to the authority of the alleged neglect, and if the authority do not take action within 14 days to remedy the nuisance, a petition may be presented to the sheriff who may enforce the removal or remedy of the nuisance at the expense of the local authority.[109]

Alternatively the procurator fiscal may,[110] with the approval of the Lord Advocate, institute proceedings to compel the authority to carry out their duty or may himself have steps taken to remove the nuisance at the expense of the authority.[111] There is effectively no appeal from the decree of the sheriff.[112]

Noise Nuisance

The Control of Pollution Act 1974 takes noise out of the general provisions of the Public Health (Scotland) Act 1897 relating to statutory nuisances, and sets up a new independent nuisance code.[113] Where a local authority is satisfied that noise amounting to a nuisance exists, or is likely to recur, it shall serve a notice on the person responsible, requiring the nuisance to be abated or prohibit-

---

[106] ss. 21–26

[107] *Cameron* v. *Glasgow D.C.* (No. 3) Oct. 5, 1984 (*Scottish Housing Law Reports*, Vol. 1, (1991)), 112.

[108] Formerly 10 ratepayers—now amended in the Law Reform (Miscellaneous Provisions)(Scotland) Act 1990—this was apparently overlooked in the Abolition of Domestic Rates legislation in 1987.

[109] s. 146.

[110] s. 148.

[111] See Scottish Affairs Committee, *Report on Dampness in Housing* (1984), where the Lord Advocate indicated that this power was not going to be used by fiscals on his instructions, due to their lack of expertise.

[112] s. 157, as interpreted in *McGourlick, supra.*

[113] s. 58.

ing, restricting its occurrence or recurrence. If the person responsible cannot be found, the notice is served on the owner or occupier of the premises from which the noise is emitted. The notice *may* specify work to be executed or steps to be taken, but the notice *must* specify the time period for compliance. It is an offence not to comply with the requirements of the notice, but it is a defence to prove that there was a reasonable excuse, or that the best practicable means have been used to prevent or counteract the noise.[114]

(ii) Noise abatement zones

A local authority is empowered to designate by order all or part of its area as a noise abatement zone and to specify the premises to which the order applies.[115] The primary purpose is to secure that in the long term, noise levels are not increased from industrial premises. Once the zone is designated, the local authority is required to measure the noise emanating from the classified premises within the zone and to keep a public record of the levels.[116] Regulations under the Act specify the method of taking sound levels. The levels recorded become the maximum levels permitted unless the local authority consent otherwise in writing. Exceeding the recorded levels is an offence. Where the local authority consider the noise level from premises is unacceptable and that a reduction would be practicable at reasonable cost and would benefit the public, it may serve a notice requiring reduction of noise.

(iii) Noise in streets

The use of loudspeakers in a street is prohibited between 9.00 p.m. and 8.00 a.m. for any purpose and at any other time for advertising any entertainment, trade or business.[117] Exemptions include police, fire or ambulance purposes, in case of emergencies; and loudspeakers in vehicles for warning purposes, communication with the driver or entertainment. Advertising perishable foods is permitted between noon and 7.00 p.m. providing no reasonable cause for annoyance is given.

3. REGULATION BY STATUTE

There are three major forms of statutory regulation of landowners and property owners which should be noted—building control,

---

[114] *Ibid.*
[115] s. 63.
[116] s. 64.
[117] s. 62, re-enacting the provisions of s. 2 of the Noise Abatement Act 1960.

planning control and control of disrepair. These supplement restrictions which operated locally and privately, and are a major feature in determining whether or not operations on land or buildings are feasible.

(a) **Building Control**

The traditional Scottish requirement as far as control over the standard of construction of buildings is concerned was exercised through the local dean of guild court. This has been superseded by regulations introduced under the Building (Scotland) Acts of 1959 and 1970. These regulations cover such issues as resistance to moisture, fire resistance of material, minimum sizes and external access. Whilst neighbours must receive notice that alterations to buildings are proposed the building regulations only permit them to object on technical grounds that the building regulations are not being complied with. There is no place in building control for aesthetic or amenity considerations, which are the province of planning control. In addition, the local building authority duty of care is limited.[118]

(b) **Planning Control**

Since 1909 there has been some form of public planning control over new developments to land or buildings. Control is exercised by the elected local politicians—normally district councillors—on behalf of the community. This discretion is subject to the overriding control of the Secretary of State for Scotland. The major innovation in this area took place in the Town and Country Planning (Scotland) Act 1947 which forms the basis of the current Scottish legislation, the Town and Country Planning (Scotland) Act 1972. The legislation requires any person who has development proposals to obtain planning permission for these proposals. Development covers broadly new building, extensions of existing buildings and material change of use of property from, say, residential to office or commercial purposes. Planning permission is a matter for the discretion of the local planning authority, taking into account such matters as their local development plan and any representations made to them by affected parties. There is no requirement for planning proposals

---

[118] W. Stewart, "Liability of Building Control Departments", *Scottish Housing Law News* (1988), 7/63.

to be made public except for certain "bad neighbour" activities. These include some specified developments such as hot-food shops, zoos or Turkish baths. There must also be publicity where a proposed construction will affect the neighbourhood by reason of fumes, noise or vibration or which will attract crowds into a generally quiet area or cause activity and noise at night. However, there is a register of planning applications for consultation by the public. Planning permission can be granted unconditionally or subject to such conditions as the planning authority choose to impose.[119]

(c) **Control of Disrepair**

Local authorities have wide powers under the Building (Scotland) Act 1959, the Civic Government (Scotland) Act 1982 and the Housing (Scotland) Act 1987 to deal with housing which is in disrepair. The powers cover actions in relation to individual houses as well as whole areas. As far as individual houses are concerned the 1987 Act provides powers exercisable through the environmental health department ranging from the power to require repairs or improvements to be carried out, to the closure of houses or even their demolition. Dangerous buildings are dealt with by the local authority building control department using powers under the Building (Scotland) Act 1959. Mandatory and discretionary loans are available from the local authority to owners in certain circumstances where either voluntarily or at the behest of the local authority their property is being repaired or improved.

As far as housing in general is concerned the local authority has an obligation to ensure that the housing in its area meets the "tolerable standard."[120] This allows the district council to assess the housing needs of their area as required under the 1987 Act. To meet the "tolerable standard" a building requires to be structurally stable, free from rising or penetrating damp, satisfactorily lit, ventilated and have a hot and cold water supply to a sink, an internal w.c. for exclusive use of occupants, an effective drainage system, satisfactory cooking facilities and satisfactory access to all external doors and outbuildings. On the basis of this assessment local authorities will draw up their housing plans including the designation of housing action areas. An authority may designate an

[119] See Eric Young and Jeremy Rowan-Robinson, *Scottish Planning Law and Procedure* (1986).
[120] Pt. IV.

area as an H.A.A. for either improvement or demolition or a combination of both. The approval of the Secretary of State is required for such proposals. Local authorities also have powers to control the numbers of individuals who may live in housing under the terms of the Housing (Scotland) Act 1987.[121]

---

[121] For further details see Chris Himsworth, *Public Sector Housing Law in Scotland* (3rd ed., 1989). Paul Watchman, Housing (Scotland) Act 1987 (1991).

CHAPTER 9

NATURE AND FORMATION OF LEASES

1. INTRODUCTION

A LEASE involves the hiring of land or heritage for a definite period of time. There is a body of law which affects all leases and we will examine this initially. Thereafter there are a number of issues on which the different kinds of leases have distinct provisions. We will look at the major areas of significance and concentrate on conditions, rent levels and security of tenure. There are three major codes of law governing leases in Scotland. Firstly, as far as the renting of dwelling-houses is concerned there are controls over what conditions they must reach to be tenantable, as well as restrictions on the rent recoverable by the landlord and limitations on when a landlord can recover possession of the subjects. Similarly in leases of agricultural property tenants are provided with protections in relation to rental levels and security of tenure, but in broad terms there is no guarantee as to the viability or suitability of land or fishings rented out. Finally there are the provisions covering commercial or industrial property. These are regulated by the general rules of the common law of leases and contractual variation is permitted in relation to the terms of such leases examined here. Minimal protection for commercial tenants exists in Scotland.

Common features of all leases

Where there is a lease, whether or not it be of agricultural land, commercial premises or a dwelling-house, the rules are the same as to the creation of the lease. The rights and obligations of landlord and tenant are broadly similar at common law. The capacity of the parties to make and take leases is largely covered by the normal rules of contractual capacity.[1] However, there are distinctive and

---

[1] S. E. Woolman, *An Introduction to the Scots Law of Contract* (1987); W. W. McBryde, *The Law of Contract in Scotland* (1987); W. M. Gordon, *Scottish Land Law* (1989).

different rules for the fixing of rent, security of tenure and fitness obligations in leases of agricultural land and dwelling-houses. One common feature of leases in Scotland is the concept of tacit relocation. This provides that where an agreement reaches its technical termination date it is assumed to be continued on the same terms and conditions unless one of the parties formally terminates the agreement with notice.

At common law there were very few limitations on what individuals could agree. Statute has limited the formal length of leases of dwelling-houses, as well as providing that individuals can stay on beyond the term of the agreement. In addition, in some situations members of the family of the occupier may be entitled to stay on in the property on the death of the original occupier.

A lease (formerly known as a "tack") is a contract of hire, sometimes termed a "location." Under it the use of land or some other heritable subject is granted by one party to another for a period of time in return for money, commodities or even services. The grantor is known as the "landlord" or "lessor." The grantee is the "tenant" or "lessee." Formerly the words "tack" and "tacksman" were used in Scotland, and they will be encountered in older cases and texts. Where the grantor is a tenant of the subjects under another lease, this is known as the principal or head lease and the second grantee as the "sublessee" or "subtenant."

Rankine's classical definition of a lease is as follows:

"A lease or tack is a contract of location (letting to hire) by which one person grants and another accepts certain uses, current or definitive, or the entire control, of lands or other heritages for a period or periods, definite or indefinite or even in perpetuity, in consideration of the delivery by the grantee of money or commodities or both, periodically or in lump, or in both of these ways. The grantor is known as the lessor, landlord or overlessee, or if he holds immediately under the landlord, the principal lessee. The grantee is known as lessee, tenant, tacksman, sublessee or subtenant. The periodical payment is rent, royalty or lordship: the lump sum is grassum or foregift. The contract is in its essence purely personal: in certain circumstances it gives rise to what is substantially a real right." (*The Law of Leases in Scotland* (3rd ed., 1916).)

There are crucial differences between leases and other occupancy rights in land.[2] A grant of a feu, adding a new link in the feudal chain

---

[2] See Chap. 11 on service occupancies and licences.

[see above at p. 37] or simple sale of heritage confer rights in perpetuity, whilst the rights conferred on the tenant by a lease are generally limited to a specified duration. Would-be purchasers may withdraw or resile (*i.e.* back out) from a bargain if, unknown to them, the subjects are leasehold as opposed to feudal. Compared with a sale of heritage, the property, in the case of a lease never becomes that of the tenant under a lease—although under modern rent legislation certain tenants may have almost complete security of tenure during their own lifetime and for the lives of other members of the family. The landlord remains the owner, and if the conditions of the lease are broken the tenant may be evicted. Purchasers of property, on the other hand, under a valid contract of sale, once title has been recorded in the General Register of Sasints on Land Register for Scotland may do what they wish with the property (subject, of course, to planning, nuisance, servitude restrictions and any restrictions imposed by the feudal superior, etc.).

A tenant has a right to the limited use of the subjects, whilst an owner has full rights to use and dispose. A clear exception is the mineral lease where, by its very nature, the minerals which are the subject of the lease are used up by the lessee. Purchasers of land by instalments will generally have their rights and duties determined by the sale agreement. In such cases it is usual for the title to be given on the completion of the payments. However, until this time the purchaser, provided there is compliance with the terms of the agreement, has the rights of an owner as contrasted with the more limited rights of a tenant. A method of avoiding the obligations of a landlord as to repair has also been the use of a purported sale agreement. In these devices the seller agrees to an inflated sale figure. For the first year or six months the buyer must pay instalments towards the price, and then the final balance. If the final balance is not paid then all the purchaser's rights are lost. This means that in reality "sellers" are able to rent out for a year or six months knowing that the property will revert to them and that in the meantime the buyer/tenant is responsible for any intervening repairs.

2. LEASE AS A PERSONAL CONTRACT

At common law a lease is a personal contract and governed by the general rules applicable to contracts. There are, in particular, four cardinal elements on which there must be agreement so that a contract may be a lease at common law. If one of these elements is missing then the contract may well be binding but will not be a lease. It might be a valid personal contract of hire, but the rights and duties of lease would not apply to such a validly made contract.[3]

(a) Consent

There must be complete agreement between the parties not only to enter into a contract but also as to the terms. This is termed *consensus in idem*. There must be an agreement to enter, otherwise there can be no contract. Problems usually occur after there have been negotiations but followed by a failure by one party or other to sign. If there is failure to agree to one or more of the conditions then there is no agreement, no consensus. Similarly where there is an informal contract followed by some actings amounting to *rei interventus* these must disclose agreement on the terms. If there are informal documents involved these must show consensus.

There must be more than mere negotiations and the parties must agree on the topics of subjects, consideration and period. There are certain occasions where one of these matters may be inferred from the circumstances or from the parties' negotiations, but failing this the courts are not keen to fix a rent or supply a duration for the "lease." In one instance after protracted negotiation, though it was found that a tenant was willing to pay a reasonable or fair market rent, this did not amount to consensus on the rent.[4]

Not only must there be consensus, but it must not have been obtained as a result of fraud, misrepresentation, force or fear. Where there have been, for example, false statements made by one party to induce the others to enter into the lease, these will render the lease voidable, and the "cheated" party may have the contract set aside,[5] subject to the plea of personal bar.

---

[3] See comment in *Shetland Islands Council* v. *British Petroleum Development Ltd.*, 1989 S.C.L.R. 48 at p. 69.

[4] *Gray* v. *Edinburgh University*, 1962 S.C. 157; but see *Glen* v. *Roy* (1882) 10 R. 239 for circumstances where the court was prepared to supply a rent.

[5] This now has a statutory version in the Housing (Scotland) Act 1987, s. 40, in relation to false statements made by applicants to secure accommodation for homeless people.

(b) **Rent**

There must be provision for rent although the court has been willing to read into certain situations the intention that the rent shall be the annual value (*i.e.* the sum which the valuation officer puts on the house for rating purposes). This sum used to be set under statute and was the notional rent given equal supply of and demand for the property, or at the market rent (*i.e.* the rent which is paid in the open market for comparable premises). The parties in such a situation must, however, have clearly entered into a relationship of landlord and tenant. The distinction between this situation and the *Gray* case is in that case there was actual disagreement about what such a sum was.

The rent may be in money or in kind, *e.g.* in the form of fruits (grain, minerals, timber or services). The rent may be purely nominal or elusory. So, provided that a sum is fixed as rent, it may be a sum like one penny per annum or a white feather annually. If there is no provision for rent there is no contract of lease. In one instance a garage owner permitted a person to occupy a garage for a period of 10 years in return for a lump sum of £200. The owner was to repay to this occupier in the event of termination of the agreement the sum of £20 for each unexpired year of the 10-year period. Here the agreement provided that no rent should be payable and the contention that the £200 was rent was rejected.[6] Thus as there was no rent provision there was no lease.

(c) **Heritable Subjects**

Leases are only operative over heritable subjects and unless subjects are in law heritable then a contract will be one of hire only and will be governed by the rules relating to hire.

(d) **Period**

There must be a time specified or capable of inference from the parties having entered into the relationship of landlord and tenant.[7] The length of the lease which the circumstances imply will depend on all the facts surrounding the lease. The general guiding principle

[6] *Mann* v. *Houston*, 1957 S.L.T. 89; see also *Shetland Islands Council* v. *British Petroleum Development Ltd.*, 1990 S.L.T. 83.
[7] *Cinema Bingo Club* v. *Ward*, 1976 S.L.T.(Sh.Ct.) 90.

is that the least time suggested by the words is to be taken as the duration. Parole evidence will be admitted to prove the intention of the parties as to the duration of the lease.

Although a lease may be granted at common law for any period including an indefinite one—as where a lease was accepted which was to last "perpetually and continually as long as the grass groweth up and the water runneth down"[8] nevertheless the absence of any kind of date of termination—may indicate that the parties intended that the agreement was to be merely a revocable licence or even an outright disposal and not a lease at all. Thus where there was an agreement for a family to live in an estate cottage and the agent stated that there could be no guarantee as to the length of time the cottage could be made available,[9] this was held to be no lease, as a termination date (or "ish" as it is called) was lacking and the contract was revocable by the grantor. The lack of an ish was discussed in the *Gray* case. In addition to the problem of determination of the rent, there was no agreement reached as to the length of the "lease." No term or date for the end of the agreement could be inferred as the university did not take possession, though it was suggested that the implication of negotiations was that the lease should last for a period of one year. The court held that this could only be inferred when the parties had entered the relationship of landlord and tenant. In this case there were merely protracted negotiations and never agreement on anything other than the principle of some sort of lease, at a rent not settled and for a time not settled. Had there been a clear sign of the relationship, such as possession, it might have been possible for the court to infer the matters not agreed on specifically. It is interesting to contrast this situation with that in the *B.P.* case where the company took possession.[10]

3. Lease as a Real Right

If a lease complies with the requirements mentioned then it will be a valid lease at common law, provided too that the requirements as to formality and capacity of the parties are also observed. At common law, though, the rights which a tenant has are severely limited in

---

[8] *Carruthers* v. *Irvine* (1717) Mor. 15195.

[9] *Scottish Residential Estates Development Co. Ltd.* v. *Henderson*, Court of Session, May 17, 1990.

[10] *Shetland Islands Council* v. *British Petroleum Development Ltd.*, 1990 S.L.T. 83.

being personal only. This means that a valid lease between parties with both power and capacity so to contract will bind the landlord only and personal representatives. What this meant was that if a tenant and landlord entered into a lease contract for five years and the landlord died after three years, then the heirs of the landlord were bound to abide by the terms of the lease. If, on the other hand the subjects became the property of persons other than personal representatives of the landlord then such persons were not bound. The lease at common law was a personal contract which did not bind *singular* successors of the lessor. The term "singular successors" applies to persons who derive a right from the grantor other than through succession, either through purchase or in the process of insolvency.

The problem was dealt with by statute in the Leases Act 1449. This provided that a lease should be enforceable against singular successors by the tenant, provided that certain conditions were fulfilled. Although this Act was originally designed to protect "the puir pepil that labouris the grunde," it was soon applied to urban property and is the basis of the modern law of leases today.

The statute reads (in translation)

> "It is ordained for the safety and favour of the poor people that work the land, that they, and all others that have leased or shall lease property in future from any landlord, and have time to run on the lease that if the landlord sells or disposes of that property the tenants shall continue in their leases until their dates of termination on the same terms and conditions."[11]

The requisites under the 1449 Act for a lease to confer a real right as interpreted by the courts are as follows.

(a) **Writing**

A lease for more than one year must be in writing though if for a lesser period this would be unnecessary. Although a verbal agreement for more than one year may be established as a valid binding

---

[11] The original 15th-century version was: "It is ordanit for the sauftie and favour of the puir pepil that labouris the grunde that thai and al utheris that hes takyn or sal tak landis in tym to cum fra lordis and has termes and yeris thereof that suppose the lordis sel or analy thai landis that the takaris sall remayn with thare takis on to the ische of thare termes quhais handis at euir thai landis cum to for sic lik male as thai tuk thaim of befoir" (2nd ed., 1966). The word "tak" or "tack" for lease will still be found in relatively modern documents.

lease on the grantor where there is *rei interventus* on such verbal agreement this does not bind singular successors of the landlord. Apart from this, however, if writing is enough to bind the original landlord then it will bind the singular successor and writings need not be probative if supported by *rei interventus*. Thus the exception only occurs in matters relating to the actual constitution of a verbal lease.

(b) Subjects

The subjects must be land. The statute refers to "landes," though this has been interpreted as all adjuncts of land which are capable of separate ownership—mills, minerals, salmon fishing, quarries, ferries, harbours and houses as well as the land itself. Although fishing and shooting are not separate rights in land but incidents of land-ownership leases of them have been recognised.

(c) Definite "Ish" or Termination Date

Although at common law a lease may be perpetual in order to be afforded the protection of the 1449 Act a lease must have a definite ish. This does not mean that it needs to be fixed. A lease may be given for an uncertain period of time provided the date of its ending is bound to happen. Thus a lease may be given for the successive lives of certain persons X, Y and Z. Now although it is impossible to say when these three people are finally going to die it is absolutely certain (in legal terms) that they are all going to die at some date in the future. While it is possible for a lease to be perpetual at common law, and therefore to be enforceable as between the original parties and their representatives, this will not confer a real right and bind singular successors. It seems possible, though not certain, that a lease for a definite yet extremely long duration may fall under this heading. In one instance a lease of 2400 years (with an elusory rent) was held to be outwith the 1449 Act though the rent element may well have been conclusive here.[12] However a lease of 1140 years has been held to be within the terms of the Act,[13] and many leases have been granted for 99 and 999 years.[14]

---

[12] *Alison* v. *Ritchie* (1730) Mor. 15196.

[13] *L.A.* v. *Fraser* (1762) 2 Pat. 66.

[14] *Spook Erection (Northern) Ltd.* v. *Kayer*, 1990 G.W.D. 16–892, which involved a lease for 99 years which one party thought was for 990 years.

Some of the problems of long leases were dealt with in the Long Leases (Scotland) Act 1954 and the White Paper, *Land Tenure in Scotland—A Plan for Reform*, Cmnd. 4099 (1969) proposed that the leasing of land for the purpose of building dwelling-houses should only be allowed in special circumstances and subject to the most stringent safeguards, and in the commercial field a limit of 60 years was suggested. This bore fruit in the Land Tenure Reform (Scotland) Act 1974 which limits leases to 20 years in residential cases.[15]

(d) Rent

The 1449 Act does not apply if there is no rent. The statute allows tenants to remain "at such rent as they took them for," and this implies there must be a definite rent and that this must not be elusory nor merely nominal. As indicated in *Alison* v. *Ritchie*,[16] the fact that there was rent which was elusory as well as a duration of 2400 years meant that this lease was ineffectual against singular successors. The problem is that the Act gives no indication of what is satisfactory to form rent. There is no need for the rent to be fair or reasonable. There may be a lump sum or grassum in addition to the continuing rent, but a grassum alone will not form a satisfactory rent.[17]

The kinds of transaction which will be accepted as rent in addition to the normal money payment are a certain amount of minerals, grain or other goods or services to be rendered by the tenant to the landlord, such as mending machinery or gathering a crop. The amounts of articles like minerals or grain may be expressed in quantity, percentage or value. If the latter is involved and the lease is silent on the method of determining the value of the articles, then a system like "fiars prices" will be used (this is an officially recognised method of stating the sums paid on average at any given time for grain, etc., in the markets). The percentage may be that of the yield of a crop or of the landlord's expenditure on improvements or any calculation which is both definite and not elusory.

---

[15] See above at pp. 42–43.
[16] *Loc. cit.*
[17] *Mann* v. *Houston*, 1957 S.L.T. 89.

(e) Possession

There must be possession for the rights in the lease to operate in favour of the tenant. Possession involves both a mental and physical side. Though more usually possession is a problem in connection with corporeal moveables, such as banknotes or golf balls, it must be present for a real right to be conferred in heritable property both corporeal and incorporeal, *i.e.* to leases which are only a bundle of rights in the land in question as opposed to ownership which is a right in the land itself. Thus a tenant has a limited right over the land in the same way as a hirer of a car. The hirer may use the car in accordance with the agreement to hire whereas the owners, if they wish to, may strip the car down and throw pieces on an officially approved rubbish tip.

It is similar with a tenant and landlord, the tenancy being an incorporeal right and the ownership a corporeal right. With appropriate planning permission owners may knock their houses down or alter them substantially, for better or worse. The tenant on the other hand is prohibited from altering or destroying the substance of the premises.

The physical aspect of possession is less complex, clearly where heritable property is concerned and is a matter of fact. The right may be exercised either personally, through servants (natural possession) or through another person such as a sub-tenant (civil possession). The need for possession is in order that a singular successor or creditor of the landlord or a competing lessee can learn of the existence of the lease. The need for possession prevents collusive (*i.e.* fraudulent) agreements. It is equivalent to registration of titles to land. Thus if A agreed to buy a house from B where C was the sitting tenant this would greatly diminish the value of the property to a purchaser. Unless there is a requirement of possession for a real right then the purchaser would have no clear means of knowing about the sitting tenant. Where there are competing leases, the later lease with possession will be preferred to an earlier lease without possession, although the latter are rare. Where there is, on the other hand, a singular successor there must be possession before the singular successor becomes a proprietor, *i.e.* when the written title of ownership is registered in the Register thereby converting the personal right against the seller into a right against the world. In one case a lease was arranged with entry at Whitsunday (May 15) but before that date the "landlord" sold the property. The purchaser recorded his title on April 21. It was here impossible for the tenant to take possession and convert his own personal right into a real right against the singular successor and this person could validly repudiate the lease.[18] Here also the fact that the tenant had even entered before the lease came into force to carry out improvements on the subjects could not constitute possession, as his rights under the lease did not commence till Whitsunday, and these actings were only a limited personal licence allowed by the "landlord." The general principle is that "possession" must refer to the lease in question as in *rei interventus*.

4. Restrictions on the Contract of Lease

The major restriction of note is the limitation of parties to make long leases of residential property. The Land Tenure Reform (Scotland) Act 1974, Part II, states that any long lease executed after August 31, 1974 may not apply to property used wholly or in part as a dwelling-house. The term "dwelling-house" includes any garden, yard, garage, outhouse or pertinent used along with any dwelling-house. Use as a site for a caravan is not included within the term use as a dwelling-house. Where use as a dwelling-house is ancillary to the use of the rest of the property leased, and where exclusion of the dwelling-house use would be detrimental to the efficient exercise of the non-dwellinghouse use, then this is not struck at in the Act. Examples suggested for this are the caretaker's house in a block of commercial offices or possibly houses for resident staff within an industrial complex. Agricultural holdings, holdings under the Small Landholder (Scotland) Acts and crofts are specifically excluded.

A "long lease" is defined as any lease or right of occupancy granted for payment (other than running costs) which has a duration of more than 20 years (including the option to renew if this takes the period of the lease beyond 20 years). For leases created before 1974 which contain a provision for renewal in excess of 20 years the Law Reform (Miscellaneous Provisions) (Scotland) Act 1985 indicates that such renewals may still be granted. Houses under the Rents Acts are not struck at in any way here, so that a tenant may exercise security of tenure rights to remain in the house for as long as the Rent Acts provide.

5. Constitution of a Lease

As a contract involving heritable property a lease requires to be in probative writing. However, where a lease is for not more than a year, this will not be required (see below).

---

[18] *Millar* v. *McRobbie*, 1949 S.C. 1.

There is no particular form of writing required, provided that the intention of the parties can readily be found out from the writing used, nor does it matter what the contract is called. By the same token, simply calling an agreement a "licence" does not mean that it cannot in fact be a lease. The fact that a more formal form of agreement was envisaged by the parties and this does not materialise does not have the effect of a condition preventing a valid lease coming into being. Typically it may be agreed to lease a property "subject to lease drawn out in due form." What this does is to require a formal lease to be prepared to give effect to binding missives.[19] There is no objection to having standard conditions contained in a document which is then adopted in whole or in part by the parties to the agreement, though this will be done expressly if this is the intention.

Negotiations create no obligation on either side and either party may withdraw until there is a probative writing by both parties or its equivalent.[20] This is the general rule required for any binding contract where heritage is involved—*i.e.* it covers selling or leasing land and/or houses. The source of the rule was the medieval economic importance of land.

(a) Leases for More than One Year

If the parties intend that the lease should be binding on them for a period exceeding a year, then they must conclude a formal lease in probative form. Although leases for more than one year should be constituted by probative writing only, there may well be situations where the formalities are not complied with but where there is either possession or some other actings which take place on the faith of the bargain without any formally authenticated lease. Where, for example, there is a probative offer by the landlord but no probative acceptance by the "tenant" but instead possession on the agreement by the "tenant," an otherwise defective lease is validated and rendered binding by *rei interventus*, or a combination of this and homologation. Thus a lease for a number of years may be constituted by a verbal or improbative written agreement followed by such actings.

If an agreement is proved or admitted, subsequent actings may perfect any informality. Where the subsequent actings of the parties are both known to and permitted by the other party and clearly

---

[19] *Erskine* v. *Glendinning* (1871) 9 M. 656.
[20] *Errol* v. *Walker*, 1966 S.L.T. 159; *Goldston* v. *Young* (1868) 7 M. 188.

relate to the agreement set up, then, if these are such as to produce an alteration of circumstances, loss or inconvenience, a verbal or improbative agreement can be perfected and made as binding as if it were a properly constituted probative agreement. It means that the person who has permitted such actings to take place cannot turn round and claim that, because there is a technical defect in the agreement, there is no binding lease.

The actings must be clearly related to the prior agreement. This means that they must be consistent with, and unable to be explained except by, the prior agreement. Mere possession itself with no other *rei interventus* will not have the effect of perfecting an informal lease, but if this possession can be shown to follow on and be attributable to improbative documents this would perfect them. One year's possession on a lease for 14 years, signed by the tenant and retained but not signed by the landlord, bound the landlord.[21] Similarly where the landlord had signed a lease for 15 years but the tenants had not, then here the possession by the tenants for two years bound them for the full term.[22] In one instance a landlord failed to establish by *rei interventus* the constitution of a written lease, never signed, whilst the tenant was able to show that his possession could equally well be ascribed to a prior verbal lease.[23] The most typical example of *rei interventus* is where possession is followed by improvements. Thus where a tenant, after agreeing to a draft lease for 19 years but not signing any contract, took down ruined cottages for the landlord to use the materials as agreed in the draft as well as constructing drains and bringing in lime and manure, such actings constituted *rei interventus*.[24] Lesser acts may amount to *rei interventus* too, such as sub-letting with the landlord's knowledge, the tenant ceasing to look for other accommodation, or on the landlord's part ceasing to look for a tenant (such as removing a "To let" sign).

As a contract in writing, a lease cannot generally be contradicted or qualified by parole evidence. So, if a contract validly entered into and completed showed that subjects were included in the letting "by mistake," the objector could not prove this by parole evidence. There are a number of exceptions—where there is an obvious omission which must be supplied. Thus, where a two-year lease of property for use as a bulb-growing establishment was concluded by informal letters without specifying a date of commencement for the

[21] *Ballantine* v. *Stevenson* (1881) 8 R. 959.
[22] *Macpherson* v. *Macpherson* (1815) May 12, F.C.
[23] *Pollock* v. *Whitford*, 1936 S.C. 402.
[24] *Bathie* v. *Wharncliffe* (1873) 11 M. 490.

lease, here parole evidence was admitted to establish the commencement date.[25]

For leases not less than 20 years in duration the Registration of Leases (Scotland) Act 1857 introduced an equivalent to possession, substituting for it the requirement of registration.

(b) Leases for Not More than One Year

Leases for not more than one year may be constituted either verbally or by writings which are not probative, and are an exception to the general rule requiring probative writings. The existence of such a lease may be proved *prout de jure*.[26]

6. GENERAL RULES APPLICABLE IN LEASES

(a) Tenant's Obligations

Tenants must take and retain possession. The landlord will want the subjects to be possessed as this will prevent the condition of the subjects deteriorating through want of occupation. If there is no possession the landlord may bring the lease to an end, sue for resumption of possession in an action of implement, or alternatively bring an action of damages for loss occasioned by the tenant's failure. The obligation to possess does not require the tenant to reside personally on the subjects, although this may be specifically agreed between the landlord and tenant in the contract of lease. The obligation to retain possession will not in the case of a shop extend to carry on business at the premises let, though the premises must be kept furnished sufficiently for the purposes of hypothec (to make the rent secure), kept heated and aired.[27] This stems from the need to prevent damp from non-use and can be seen in a case involving a dwelling-house. The tenant was sued for damages in respect of deterioration of the subjects from exposure to damp, frost and dirt, damage from burst waterpipes and the breakage of windows from outside as a result of the deserted appearance of the

[25] *Watters* v. *Hunter*, 1927 S.C. 310.

[26] There is no limitation on the evidence which may be brought. There may be writings produced, or the parole evidence of witnesses, or both, as well as reference to the oaths of the parties.

[27] *Whitelaw* v. *Fulton* (1871) 10 M. 27.

house.[28] A tenant of an inn was also successfully sued when there was loss of goodwill after the premises were shut for months.[29]

Tenants must not "invert possession." Subjects are let with a particular sort of possession in mind and the tenant may only possess the subjects for that purpose. This may be expressly stated in the contract, making it easy to discover whether there has been a breach or not. Alternatively it may be inferred from the subjects—a dwelling-house for residence; garden for horticulture or shop for trading, etc. Where the tenant uses the subjects for purposes outwith those either expressed or implied, this amounts to inversion of possession. This is, in effect, a course of conduct inconsistent with the objects of the lease. The landlord may lose the right to complain on inversion either where this is expressly renounced or where this occurs through acquiescence, as where a tenant used a paper mill as an oil mill for six years and then his assignee used it as a grist mill for one year with the knowledge of the landlord. Here the landlord could not have the original use restored on the basis of inversion.[30]

The tenant must use reasonable care in the management of the subjects and will be liable to make good any damage caused by negligence such as burst pipes resulting from non-occupation of premises. In addition the tenant must abide by any specific rules as to management. There may be restrictions on the tenant on building on the subjects let or a prohibition of any trade or business on the premises. Such a typical restriction limiting premises to use as "residential dwelling-house only" will be breached by use of such subjects as a school or even a charitable institution where no money was taken, such as a hospital.

The existence of rent is an essential for the existence of a contract of lease and is generally covered by an express stipulation. Where this is not the case, a tenant who has entered into possession is by implication bound to pay to the landlord the real worth of the subjects.[31] Rent may take various forms and may be paid at either the legal or conventional term. This is of importance where arable and pastoral farms are concerned. In arable farms the crop here is separated before Martinmas and the new tenant's possession is deemed to start then. Where there is a right of hypothec in existence in the landlord's favour the tenant must stock the premises to such

---

[28] *Smith* v. *Henderson* (1899) 24 R. 1102.
[29] *Graham* v. *Stevenson* (1792) Hume 781.
[30] *Young & Co.* v. *Ramsey* (1824) 2 S. 793.
[31] *Glen* v. *Roy, supra*; but see *Shetland Islands Council* v. *BP Development Ltd.*, *supra*.

an extent as will make the full right of hypothec practically available.

The tenant must not assign or sub-let unless there is either an express or implied power to do so. An assignation of a lease is a transfer by the tenant of an interest in the lease to another person called the assignee, who becomes the new tenant in place of the tenant. The assignor (sometimes known as the grantor or cedent) ceases to have any further interest in the lease and as indicated the assignee steps into the previous tenant's shoes. Here there is just one contract, the parties changing. A sub-lease is a lease granted by a tenant of all or part of the subjects leased so that the original tenant becomes the landlord of the sub-tenant whilst still remaining the tenant of the original landlord. Where in a lease the tenant is given a clear right to assign or sub-let (as where the contract is granted to the tenant "his assignees and sub-lessees whomsoever") then this will displace any common law presumption against either assignation or sub-letting. Where the lease is not express then the tenant may sub-let or assign only as far as the particular kind of lease gives the power and this is determined by the common law as well as statute.

In urban unfurnished premises there is a common law presumption in favour of assignation and sub-letting. The basis of the rule is the lack of "solidarity" between landlord and tenant in such leases as compared with agricultural leases where the element of personal choice of the tenant ("*delectus personae*") was strong. The common law position has been eroded since the introduction of secure tenancies and assured tenancies in the 1980s for certain kinds of dwelling-house lease. For secure tenancies in the public sector[32] it is an implied term in every such tenancy that the tenant shall not assign, sub-let or otherwise give up to another person possession of the house or any part of it or take in a lodger without the consent in writing of the landlord. This consent must not be unreasonably withheld. In private sector assured tenancies (*i.e.* those entered into after January 2, 1989) under the Housing (Scotland) Act 1988 it is an implied term of every such tenancy that the tenant must not assign the tenancy, nor sub-let nor part with possession of the whole nor any part of the premises let.[33] There is no condition as to unreasonable withholding of consent modifying the assured tenancy prohibition.

Furnished lets have no implied power as the "rent" consists of two distinct parts—the rent for the premises and the sum for hire of

---

[32] Housing (Scotland) Act 1987, s. 55.
[33] Housing (Scotland) Act 1988, s. 23.

the furniture. This latter contract of hire is purely personal and does not carry the power to assign or sub-let the furniture. As the two contracts of hire of premises and furniture are so closely bound together as to be inseparable, it follows that the personal nature of the furniture hire prevents assignation or sub-letting of the subjects without express consent. Leases for the tenant's life and leases for the duration of the tenant's term of office implicitly include the powers to assign or sub-let as being deemed of unusual duration as do agricultural leases of extraordinary duration.

Such subjects as agricultural leases of ordinary duration do not carry an implied right to assign or sub-let as indicated above. In addition, in mineral leases the significant factor is the duration of the lease. Where the lease of minerals is for an extraordinary duration then this will carry power to assign and sub-let. Sporting leases more than any other kind of lease are subject to the limiting effects of *delectus personae*, and are accordingly not capable of assignation or sub-let without express approval. The reason is that much depends on the way these rights of fishing and shooting are exercised as this affects the comfort of the landlord, relations with farm tenants and the preservation of sufficient stock. Thus these leases have strong elements of the agricultural lease about them, so may not be assigned and sub-let without approval. Where there is no implied power to assign and sub-let then unless the landlord consents, there can be no such alienation. Even where the power is implied at common law the right may be excluded by a clause in the lease. One reason is to keep out impecunious "tenants" who may not be able to meet their debts.

Where relevant the landlord may modify the wording of the clause by adding that there may not be assignation without "consent in writing" or "unless specifically approved of by the landlord." This still gives the landlord an arbitrary power of veto, and it is not thought that he would be required to give reasons. There must, however, not be oppression in the landlord's exercise of his right. This is a familiar notion in English landlord and tenant law, and was considered in *Dorchester Studios (Glasgow) Ltd.* v. *Stone*.[34]

The court will not permit any covert assignation or sub-lease which is cloaked by another name, but in fact is a breach of the prohibition on assignation or sub-letting. Thus, an arrangement where the tenant of a shop removed his goods and gave occupation to a person alleged to be his "shopman," who in fact carried on a

---

[34] 1975 S.L.T.(H.L.) 56.

different trade, was held to be a mere transparent device to evade the operation of the restriction.[35]

(b) Landlord's Obligations

The primary right of the tenant is to be put into possession of the subjects let and to be maintained in such possession and it is obligatory on the landlord to fulfil this obligation. This right to possession means that landlords transfer to tenants their own rights in law to remove and eject third parties or tenants may alternatively demand that the landlord exercise this right on the tenant's behalf. Possession must be given timeously.[36]

Although in most cases possession will be given of the whole of the subjects there are certain circumstances where there may be certain parts of the subjects reserved. Typically in a lease of a country house the landlord without notice reserved possession of a charter-room, store-room, observatory and spare furniture room, and here the tenant was not entitled to abandon the lease.[37] This will be a matter of degree.

Although in the case of land and houses generally the very nature of the grant implies full possession, in other leases the rights granted are of a more limited character. Thus a lease of fishings does not prevent the landlord using the water where this does not interfere with the fishing, and a letting of woods gives no right to interfere with the surface of the subjects except in so far as necessary for the profitable exercise of the right.

The tenant's right to possession is of limited value unless it is a continuing right. Thus the landlord guarantees to do nothing adversely to affect the tenant's possession throughout the lease or any part of it. This "guarantee" is called a warrandice and is often, though not always, expressly included in the terms of the contract. It is always implied. This guarantee on the continuing possession of the tenant is the basis of any action by the tenant against the landlord for total or partial eviction. Before the tenant can establish breach of the obligation of maintenance in possession there must be either total or partial eviction. If there is partial eviction then an action for damages usually in the form of a reduction of rent (referred to as an abatement of rent) is appropriate. Where there is

---

[35] *Hatton* v. *Clay and McLuckie* (1865) 4 M. 263.
[36] *Drummond* v. *Hunter* (1869) 7 M. 347.
[37] *Webster* v. *Lyell* (1860) 22 D. 1423.

total eviction the tenant will normally be entitled to restitution or to damages.

Where the "eviction" is not directly at the hands of the landlord but comes about as a result of destruction of the subjects, different considerations apply. If there is no fault of the landlord then the landlord will not be liable for damages. The doctrine of *rei interitus* (*i.e.* destruction of the thing) applies. This means that where, without fault of either landlord or tenant, the subjects are destroyed either directly (*e.g.* by fire or flood) or indirectly (*e.g.* through being requisitioned) the relationship of landlord and tenant will come to an end. The tenant will be entitled to abandon the lease and again claim an abatement of rent but not claim damages if the landlord is in no way to blame. Clearly if the subjects were destroyed by the landlord's negligent or reckless actings the tenant would have a civil claim for damages here (as well as there being possible criminal proceedings).[38]

The Court of Session decided[39] that a lease came to an end when the subjects or the lease were destroyed by fire. Any obligations arising under the lease were thus extinguished as a result of the total destruction of the subjects. However the tenant cannot abandon the lease merely where the purpose of the lease is prevented, as where the licence of a wine and spirit merchant's shop let to a tenant was revoked.[40] Similarly before the lease can be abandoned there must be more than "considerable inconvenience" where the tenant must give the landlord an opportunity to have the damage repaired. The landlords' obligations where they are carrying out works on property adjoining the property let is higher than the usual duty of care of a neighbour.[41]

The obligation of the landlord not to derogate from his own grant by actings in breach of the implied duty of peaceable possession does not extend to omissions as well as acts. Here the landlord was not doing anything which substantially impaired the tenant's use of the premises adjacent to a previously defective drain on his own property.[42] This is distinct from the normal obligation on owners to their neighbours in buildings, which we see in the case where the proprietor of an upper flat was unsuccessful in his action of damages against the lower proprietor who had caused damage to the lower

---

[38] Rent (Scotland) Act 1984, Pt. III, deals with unlawful eviction.
[39] *Cantors Properties (Scotland) Ltd.* v. *Swears & Wells Ltd.*, 1980 S.L.T. 165.
[40] *Hart's Trs.* v. *Arrol* (1903) 6 F. 36.
[41] *Huber* v. *Ross*, 1912 S.C. 898.
[42] *Golden Casket (Greenock) Ltd.* v. *BRS (Pickfords)* 1972 S.L.T. 146.

flat in the course of structural alterations where there was no specific negligence proved.[43]

There are exceptions to the contention of eviction where the subjects are not covered or where there was knowledge of the risk or where the problem stems from the tenant's fault or carelessness. Also excepted are actings outwith the control of the lessor whether this is the result of supervening legislation which made it impossible to possess a lease of salmon fishings on the subjects though the practice only took place for four days per week,[44] or natural disaster. In such circumstances the tenant can give up the lease. The appropriate source of any compensation would be the authorities who in effect "destroy" the lease.

Where the loss results from illegal actings of a third party to which the landlord is not party, such as vandalism, then again there is no recourse to the landlord except as indicated to require proceedings to be taken against the third party (although the tenant may take this action personally). There may be a contractual alteration of this right so that the tenant is liable for restoration of only those items which have been harmed through his fault. Property damage by vandals such as broken windows might well not be the contractual responsibility of the tenant.[45]

At common law landlords renting out land or commercial premises are not obliged to guarantee the quality of the crops or the profitability of commercial locations. As to buildings, commercial leases normally impose obligations on the tenant as far as repair of the premises is concerned. The position in dwelling-houses is markedly different. At common law there is an obligation that premises must be tenantable and habitable. In case landlords should opt to exclude the common law obligation, legislation imposes two distinct obligations on landlords of dwelling-houses. In any residential lease contract it is implied that the contract must include a condition that the house is at the commencement of the tenancy and during the tenancy kept by the landlord in all respects reasonably fit for human habitation.[46] In addition in leases for periods of less than seven years there is an implied obligation that the landlord will keep in repair the structure and exterior of the house (including drains, gutters and external pipes) as well as keep in repair and working order the installations in the house for the

---

[43] See above at pp. 9–10—*Kerr* v. *McGreevy*, 1970 S.L.T.(Sh.Ct.) 7; but see also *MacNab* v. *McDevitt*, 1971 S.L.T.(Sh.Ct.) 41.

[44] *Tay Salmon Fisheries* v. *Speedie*, 1929 S.C. 593.

[45] *Laurie* v. *Edinburgh D.C.*, 1982 S.L.T.(Sh.Ct.) 83.

[46] Housing (Scotland) Act 1987, Sched. 10, para. 1.

supply of water, gas and electricity and for sanitation and for space heating or heating water. Landlords are expressly prohibited from putting a provision in the lease that the tenant will repair the premises including painting, pointing or rendering the premises or paying money in lieu of repairs.[47]

(c) **Remedies of Landlord and Tenant**

Where the other party breaches the implied and express obligation of the lease, then the remedies available to the aggrieved party are as follows:

Landlord's Remedies

Rent

The landlord has all the normal remedies of a creditor, such as an action in the sheriff court for the sum due; diligence such as an arrestment (where the property is in the hands of a third party); poinding (where the property is in the hands of a debtor); adjudication (where there is attachment of heritable property for debts preventing voluntary alienation by the debtor); inhibition (a personal prohibition on debtors alienating their interests in the property to the prejudice of the creditor). If there is a cautioner (guarantor) then the landlord may proceed against that person in the ordinary way and take the above action if there is no response to requests for payments of the guaranteed rent.

In addition to the normal remedies as a creditor for rent, the landlord of certain premises has the special remedy of hypothec available by implication. It is a right in security without possession of the subjects over which it extends in favour of landlords to ensure they get the rent.[48] The right was an implied term of all leases, but legislation has now taken most non-urban subjects outside the operation of hypothec.

There must of course be a *bona fide* landlord/tenant relationship and not simply a device to create a security over moveables which is not recognised in Scotland (except by means of a "floating charge" over a company's assets).[49] The right operates over subjects known as *invecta et illata* (things brought in and carried into the property).

---

[47] *Ibid.*, para. 3.
[48] G. Maher and D. Cusine, *The Law and Practice of Diligence* (1990).
[49] *Heritable Securities Investment Association* v. *Wingate's Tr.* (1880) 7 R. 1094.

They include furniture, books, pictures, plate and other moveable property brought on to the property by the tenant which do not already belong to the landlord.

In *Scottish & Newcastle Breweries Ltd.* v. *Edinburgh District Council*[50] the landlord sought hypothec for rent due. One of the items over which the landlord acquired a right of sale was a collection of beer kegs which were on the premises but which were the property of a brewery company. The brewery company sought interdict to prevent the sale of the kegs. It claimed that the kegs were excluded from the landlord's hypothec. The judge held, however, that the kegs were part of the *invecta et illata* of the tenant. He considered that the kegs were part of the ordinary equipment and stock-in-trade of someone leasing a public house.

Certain articles are excluded: cash, bonds, bills and other documents of debt (as these do not increase the tenant's visible wealth in the house), as well as necessary wearing apparel and tools of the trade which are absolutely necessary to enable the tenant to gain a living. There are special rules covering business premises, mines and quarries, fisheries, agricultural and pastoral subjects and horticultural subjects.[51]

Generally it can be taken from possession by tenants that they own the articles on the premises,[52] but there are problems when the articles belong to others. Goods owned by the tenant's children, guests, servants and lodgers are excluded, as people cannot pledge property which does not belong to them. There are, however, exceptions where property not belonging to the tenant comes under the landlord's right of hypothec.[53] As for goods on hire, it is presumed that the hirer was aware of the risk that the subjects might form part of the landlord's hypothec and that had the landlord realised that the plenishings were not available to him for hypothec he would have demanded more furnishing of the premises. Single articles on hire-purchase are also included—the owners of a juke box hired to a café owner claimed that even without intimation to the landlord single articles were not covered by hypothec, but their argument was rejected and the view expressed that the hirers accepted the possibility of the goods being sequestrated by the landlord and made allowances in the rent charged.[54] However, where the hiring is occasional and transient (as where china was

---

[50] 1979 S.L.T. (Notes) 11.
[51] See G. Maher and D. Cusine, *op. cit.* (1990).
[52] *Rossleigh Ltd.* v. *Leader Cars Ltd.*, 1987 S.L.T. 355.
[53] *D. H. Industries* v. *R. E. Spence & Co. Ltd.*, 1973 S.L.T.(Sh.Ct.) 26.
[54] *Ditchburn Organisation (Sales)* v. *Dundee Corpn.*, 1971 S.C. 96.

hired for a dinner party) then these do not come within the landlord's rights.[55] Goods deposited or gratuitously lent are the same as hired articles, in that in these circumstances there may still be hypothec over such goods even if it is only a single article. Goods for repair, in the custody of the tenant for this purpose, are exempt; but not where the buyer of goods merely leaves them with the tenant for convenience.

Hypothec covers not only rent under the lease but also any capital sum or interest on a capital sum laid out by the landlord. One year's rent due or current is covered. Each year's rent is secured successively and arrears are not included. Sequestration must be within three months from the last term of payment—otherwise the hypothec falls. If this is done the landlord will get full preference. The sale may take place after the three months, but provided that there is no undue delay that amounts to abandonment this does not matter. Thus it has been said that it is wise to apply the sequestration to the rent actually due and in security of the rent to become due at the next term where this is possible (*i.e.* not for crops).[56]

Certain rights are preferred to the landlord's hypothec—Crown rights such as taxes and duties though not exactions of a public nature, merely declared to be preferable to private debts, superior's hypothec, wages of employees, deathbed and funeral expenses. The landlord's right of hypothec is preferable to the rights of other creditors.

Other obligations

The landlord may raise an action of implement to compel performance of an obligation or of interdict to prevent the tenant committing some breach of the lease's conditions as by failing to occupy the subjects or by, say, selling goods which are outwith the goods permitted in the lease. The landlord may alternatively bring the lease to an end and claim damages.[57]

Tenant's Remedies

General

Again the equitable remedies of interdict and implement are available to a tenant to prevent a landlord from acting outwith the provisions of the lease or to compel performance. Where there has

[55] *Adam* v. *Sutherland* (1863) 2 M. 6.
[56] G. C. Paton and J. G. S. Cameron, *Leases* (1967), pp. 215ff.
[57] See below at pp. 133–135 for irritancies.

been a breach, then the tenant may seek damages or an abatement of rent where possession is given of only part of the subjects in the lease, or where the landlord fails to keep the subjects in a fit state of repair. Where the breach by the landlord is sufficiently material then the tenant may abandon the lease, as where defective drains resulted in the death of the tenant's daughter.[58] Lesser failures by the landlord may lead only to the right of the abatement of rent rather than abandonment as where a landlord failed to provide gas fittings in a shop as promised at his own expense.[59] In these cases, of course, each situation is judged on its own merits as to whether in a particular set of circumstances the breach is material enough to permit the tenant to throw up the lease (resile). As indicated, the effect of destruction of the subjects (*rei interitus*) is to allow such abandonment of the lease, though the fact of *damnum fatale* will preclude an action of damages by the tenant.

Retention of rent

Retention of rent is a device permitted to tenants whose landlords fail to comply with their tenancy obligations. This right allows the tenant to withhold rent to force the landlord to carry out the obligations in question. When that purpose is achieved the withheld rent is due in full. If the tenant seeks damages or an abatement of rent a separate action must be raised.

It has been held that a tenant who attempted to retain rent and at the same time continue in possession under the provision of the Rent Acts was not able to do this. The reason given was that basically the provision in the Rent Act for suspension of statutory increases was more or less equivalent to the right of retention. This right in fact allowed the increases in controlled tenancies to be suspended—under the old statute the landlord lost all right to the rent increase until the defect was put right.[60] This seems a doubtful proposition nowadays.

(d) Termination of Leases

Tacit Relocation

Strictly, this is in fact an exception to the rule that contracts for a certain period of time cease upon the expiry of that time: *i.e.* at the

---

[58] *Scottish Heritable Security Co.* v. *Granger* (1881) 8 R. 459.
[59] *Davie* v. *Stark* (1876) 3 R. 1114.
[60] *Stobbs & Son* v. *Hislop*, 1948 S.C. 216.

end of a year a one-year agreement to supply fruit to a grocer would lapse and neither party could complain when the other party treated the contract as ended. However, in certain contracts (lease; partnership; service), there requires to be notice to end a contract. Failing this the contract is continued either for the length of the previous contractual period or a year (whichever is the shorter). This constructive renewal of the contract operates under the doctrine of tacit relocation (literally "implied rehiring"). This means that by not giving notice of termination of the contract the parties tacitly or impliedly agree to continue the contract. The lease will continue on the same terms and conditions as before, except that the maximum duration of a lease continued under tacit relocation is one year. If at the end of this further year there is again no notice of termination from either party, then the lease is tacitly continued for yet a further year and so on, until finally there is notice or some other form of termination.

The doctrine can operate for shorter leases too, and the majority of tenement flats were traditionally let on either a monthly or weekly basis and continued by tacit relocation (theoretically every month or week), often for many years. In effect there is a fresh contract every time the doctrine operates, although the period of let is looked upon as one whole when it comes to matters of accepting the risk of dangerous premises, damages for unhealthy conditions, etc. From the tenant's point of view the requisite notice to terminate must still be given even if the tenant does not continue in possession of the subjects, as the new contract is equally binding as regards such notice.

Subjects

Tacit relocation applies to all kinds of leases, though there are minor exceptions dictated for the most part by common sense. There are certain exceptions—leases for less than one year for grazing or mowing (uses here being seasonal), fishings and shootings merely for a season, holiday house lettings for a season or less and service occupancies.[61] It is no bar to tacit relocation that the party having an interest to prevent it is incapacitated by insanity, minority or death. On the other hand, the right to plead tacit relocation is not lost by the death of the person entitled to claim, as the successor takes over such a right. Where there is a sub-tenancy, then it is not enough for the landlord to warn the sub-tenant if the latter is not recognised as having the direct responsibility to the landlord.

[61] See below at p. 172.

Notice

Due notice must be given to exclude the operation of tacit relocation even where the lease provides that the tenant is to remove at the date of termination without warning or process of removing. Houses with or without land not exceeding two acres, let for more than a year, are covered by the Sheriff Courts (Scotland) Act 1907 as to notice—"notice of termination of tenancy shall be given in writing to the tenant."

Formality of notice

It seems that a technically invalid notice could equally well exclude the operation of tacit relocation, as the essence of the doctrine is consent. There are problems where there are joint landlords or tenants and the notice to exclude comes from one or more of such a group but not all. Here though, it appears that notice given by such person or persons would be equally effective to exclude tacit relocation as if it had come from all the tenants/landlords.[62] In some situations it may well be that continued possession by the tenant is not a result of tacit relocation but on an entirely new lease. Thus, where a landlord intimated an increase in rent and the tenant replied that he would not pay it but did not give notice to terminate the lease and remained in possession, it was held that he had consented to the new terms and was in the position of a tenant under the new lease and its new terms, not on tacit relocation of the old lease.[63]

Tacit relocation will operate where the parties seeking to exclude it bar themselves, as where the landlord gives notice to quit but takes no further steps and allows the tenant to remain in possession, and similarly with a tenant who gives notice to quit and remains. Mere delay in taking steps to remove the tenant will not itself set up tacit relocation, but it will be inferred where this delay is beyond a reasonable time.

Termination During the Lease

A lease may be brought to an end before the stipulated date of termination in several ways, where the parties agree to this. In a renunciation the tenant gives up the lease where there is agreement or acquiescence by the landlord. Renunciation may be express and may be in either a bilateral form or unilateral with an acceptance by

---

[62] *City of Glasgow* v. *Brown*, 1989 S.C.L.R. 439 and 679.
[63] *McFarlane* v. *Mitchell* (1900) 2 F. 901.

the landlord, though apart from the need for the renunciation to be clear and explicit there are no formal requirements. Rescission applies where there is some failure by the landlord to adhere to the implied or express obligations of the lease and may be accompanied by an action for damages. Also the lease may make provision for breaks. This means that at some specified time during its currency the lease may be terminated. The break may be in favour of either party or both and it will give a landlord the power of total resumption of the subjects and a tenant the option to renounce the lease. Unlike an irritancy there need be no reason such as a breach of conditions. Usually breaks occur at one or more specified times, although power may be given to break the lease at any time with suitable notice. Notice of intention to exercise the right to break the lease must be given in the manner and within the period of notice laid down in the lease. If no time is stated and the right is exercised by the landlord, then a reasonable time must be given to the tenant. If a tenant fails to leave, then the landlord has a right to an action of removing.

Irritancies

The lease may be brought to an end at the behest of the landlord if the tenant fails to comply with the terms of the contract. Such a provision is termed an irritancy. Irritancies may be either legal or conventional. Normally this will prevent the landlord also claiming damages for premature termination of the lease, unless this right is expressly reserved. The right of irritating the lease rests solely with the landlord and a tenant who is contravening the lease's conditions subject to irritancy does not have the right to abandon the lease— where in a 19-year lease there was a conventional irritancy in the case of the tenant's bankruptcy, it was held that this gave the landlord the option to put an end to the lease when the tenant became bankrupt, but did not allow the tenant the privilege of ending his obligations when this occurred.[64]

Legal irritancies exist both at common law and under statute. At common law the irritancy covers non-payment of rent for a period of two years. When the rent has not been paid for at least two years then the landlord could have the irritancy declared by the sheriff and insist on a summary removing.

As far as legal irritancies for agricultural subjects are concerned these are now dealt with under the Agricultural Holdings (Scot-

[64] *Bidoulac* v. *Sinclair's Tr.* (1889) 17 R. 144.

land) Act 1949, which provides that if six months rent is due and unpaid the landlord may raise an action in the sheriff court for removal of the tenant at the next term of Martinmas or Whitsunday unless the arrears are paid or caution found for the arrears and a further year's rent. A legal irritancy may be purged (*i.e.* satisfied) by payment of the arrears before decree is extracted in an action to enforce payment. After this it is too late.

Conventional irritancies cover such matters as non-payment of rent. Typically the period of irritancy may be changed either by shortening or even lengthening the permitted time for arrears. Also the procedure may be simplified and purging may be excluded. Hypothec gives urban landlords strong rights, and the 1949 Act provides remedies for the agricultural landlord though the irritancy clause will still be included. It is very important where there is no hypothec, as in sporting leases.

Irritancies are also frequently centred on the prohibition of assignation or sub-letting. Where permitted at common law this right may be excluded and fenced with an irritancy, so that not only is the right of the assignee null but also the original tenants lose the rights they had under the lease: in effect as a punishment for attempting to assign the lease against the wishes of the landlord. Similarly for unauthorised sub-tenants, any breach of the conditions of the lease may under an irritancy result in the tenant receiving notice to quit— failure to possess or stock the subjects, or even where the tenant commits a breach of any other term or condition of the lease such as using the subjects as a shop or public house.

There must be a court action unless the tenants quit voluntarily. Landlords must exercise their rights within a reasonable time but will be regarded as kept in reserve during negotiations with the tenant on the breach.[65] The breach must be proved unless admitted by the tenant by means generally of an action of declarator of irritancy. Once incurred, unlike a legal irritancy, a conventional irritancy could not be purged. The principle was strictly applied. A tenant was due to pay rent at Whitsunday and failed to do so. There was a conventional irritancy if the rent remained unpaid for three months and the landlord, after giving notice of his intention, raised an action for declarator of irritancy and an order ordering him to remove. The tenant paid the arrears before the court case was heard. It was held that this was not good enough and the landlord was entitled to decree.[66] The court has prevented the oppressive use of the irritancy, as where several tenants were due parts of rent for

[65] *Penman* v. *Mackay*, 1922 S.C. 385.
[66] *McDougall's Trs.* v. *MacLeod*, 1940 S.C. 593.

subjects and one tenant offered to pay the whole and the landlord had refused and insisted on irritancy.[67] However, the strictness of irritancy can be seen where an irritancy on tenant's insolvency was still held enforceable where the tenant settled with his creditors,[68] and where the landlord was able to evict a tenant who was 11 days late in proffering the rent.[69]

There has been a change introduced following concern at the harsh way in which the conventional irritancy was being used by some commercial landlords whose tenants did not enjoy the rights of security of tenure of dwelling-house tenants[70] (see below). As far as dwelling-house leases are concerned there is usually the need for the court to be satisfied that it is reasonable to allow the landlord to repossess the property.[71]

Termination at the End of the Lease (ish)

At the normal end of a lease the tenant is required to remove from the subjects let. Under Scots law, as indicated, unless there is notice given to a tenant by the landlord or vice-versa then tacit relocation will have the effect of continuing the lease. Thus there must be a notice of removing. The process of the tenant relinquishing the lease is known as "removing." Where this takes place at the normal ish of the contract this is termed "ordinary removing" whilst where this is premature to the date of ish it is known as "extraordinary removing."

7. STATUTORY RESTRICTIONS ON THE LEASE CONTRACT

Over the past century various special rules have been introduced in relation to a wide range of leases covering residential property and agricultural land, as well as (to a limited extent) commercial subjects. These cover both the terms of the tenancy on such matters as rent and payment for improvements, and also the right of tenants to continue in their property beyond the term of their contract.

---

[67] *Old College, Aberdeen* v. *Earl of Northesk* (1678) Mor. 230.
[68] *Tennent* v. *McDonald* (1836) 14 S. 976.
[69] *Dorchester Studios (Glasgow) Ltd.* v. *Stone*, 1975 S.C.(H.L.) 56.
[70] Law Reform (Miscellaneous Provisions) (Scotland) Act 1985, ss. 5 and 6.
[71] Rent (Scotland) Act 1984, Sched. 2 (protected tenancies); Housing (Scotland) Act 1987, Sched. 3 (secure tenancies); Housing (Scotland) Act 1988, Sched. 5 (assured tenancies).

(a) **Residential Property**

Private Rented Housing

Traditionally the lease was a contract where the rent as fixed by the parties was conclusive and there was no body to whom one could appeal. Similarly when the tenancy came to an end the tenant had no right to remain, provided that notice to quit had been served preventing tacit relocation operating. Throughout Europe from 1914 onwards protection was given to residential tenants against arbitrary eviction and rent rises. These protections were broadly retained until the attempt to end rent control and security of tenure in the Rent Act 1957. This controversial legislation was abused by landlords who sought to persuade their tenants to leave by a variety of unsavoury methods. The response of the Labour administration—the Rent Act 1965—provided a new means of dealing with the question of rents for private rented housing. In place of the policy of "freezing" rents, the 1965 legislation provided for fixing rents in accordance with specified criteria as well as reviewing these after three years. The Rent Act 1974 provided that leases of furnished property should be treated in the same way as of unfurnished as to both rent fixing and security of tenure.

The subsequent apparent disappearance of many properties from the letting market led to concern from some quarters that the amalgamation of the two codes, giving full protection to furnished tenants, had dried up the supply of furnished property. However, at the same time there was an extension of renting by landlords using arrangements which avoided the protection of the Rent Acts. There was an attempt by the Tory government to stimulate the traditional private rented sector in the Tenants' Rights Etc. (Scotland) Act 1980 with the introduction of the short tenancy. In order to qualify as a short tenancy a tenancy had to be for not less than one year and not more than five years as well as have a fair rent registered and notification to the tenant that the tenancy was a security-free short tenancy. They were not a success, and the final stealthy return to market principles occurred in the Housing (Scotland) Act 1988. Henceforth tenants entering contracts on or after January 2, 1989 would have restricted rights as to rent levels and security of tenure. However, learning from the unfortunate post-1957 experience, those with rights under the older legislation retained those rights. It is therefore necessary to decide which of the private sector codes apply to any particular tenancy. This will normally be decided by the date of the contract.[72]

---

[72] s. 42 deals with transitional situations.

Regulated Tenancies under the Rent (Scotland) Act 1984

For privately-owned housing rented prior to January 2, 1989 the 1984 Act applies provided that there is no specific exclusion. Such tenancies are termed protected or regulated. In order to qualify for the benefits of the legislation it is necessary that the tenancy satisfy both the positive requirements laid down for a protected tenancy as well as not come within the category of excluded tenancies. It must satisfy the statutory conditions laid down in the Rent (Scotland) Act 1984.[73] It must be let as a dwelling-house (which may be a house or part of a house); let as a separate dwelling; the rateable value on the appropriate day must not exceed a specified sum; a rent must be payable under the tenancy and it must be not less than two-thirds of the rateable value on the appropriate day; the rent must not include *bona fide* payments in respect of board or attendance.

Part I of the Rent (Scotland) Act 1984 specifically excludes certain tenancies from coverage of the protected tenancy régime. Certain types of property do not receive the full measure of protection enjoyed by most unfurnished and furnished leases of housing (although some of them are afforded a degree of security). Some of the excluded areas have their own codes of protection (such as local authority housing), whilst others are less contentious because full protection is obviously less appropriate—licensed premises—or totally inappropriate—like holiday homes. These exclusions are stated in the 1984 Rent (Scotland) Act,[74] and cover agricultural land exceeding two acres; public sector tenancies—where the landlord is a local authority, New Town Development Corporation, Scottish Homes or any housing trust, housing association or housing co-operative; licensed premises; Crown tenancies; student tenancies granted by specified educational institutions; holiday lets; tenancies granted by resident landlords; properties released by the Secretary of State from rent regulation.

The impact of the protected tenancy régime

Two central rights emerge from a tenancy covered by the Rent (Scotland) Act 1984. The first relates to the level of rent payable and the second is the right to remain in the property after the formal termination of the tenancy.

Rents

The system of fair rents set up in the original 1965 reforms does

[73] s. 1.
[74] s. 2.

not apply automatically. Even where a tenant lives in a property below the appropriate rateable value level, and pays sufficient rent for the Acts to apply and where the landlord is not exempted for some reason (like a local authority), then there is still no obligation on either landlord or tenant to apply to have a fair rent fixed. There is nothing to prevent the landlord asking any rent and the tenant paying it. Ignorance of rights, fear or satisfaction with the level of rent mean that there is no automatic guarantee that property which comes within the jurisdiction of the Rent Acts will ever have a fair rent registered. This is to some extent consistent with the original aims of Richard Crossman in setting up the "fair rent" system as a long-stop to prevent blatant exploitation.

A rent may be registered voluntarily at the behest of landlord or tenant, or both. This involved applying to the machinery for rent-fixing set up under the 1965 Act. This comprised two tiers—Rent Officers, who dealt with initial rent fixing; and Rent Assessment Committees (RACs), who were available to reconsider any rents where either or both parties were not happy with the Rent Officer's decision. Rent Officers are full-time officials, whilst those who deal with the querying of their decisions are part-time professionals and lay persons drawn by the Secretary of State for Scotland from a panel of lawyers, valuers and lay people. There is also a President of the Rent Assessment Committees, who along with a Vice-President exercises overall supervision of RACs. Rent Assessment Committees sit in panels of three, and deliver their decisions without dissenting notes. The procedure involves visiting the property as well as oral and written representations.[75]

The formula for determining rents introduced in the Rent Act 1965 remains almost unchanged in the current legislation.[76] Rent Officers and RACs must have regard to certain factors and ignore others in coming to a fair-rent figure as well as making one crucial assumption. In determining a fair rent the rent fixers—the Rent Officers or Rent Assessment Committees—must specifically have regard to all the circumstances and, in particular, they must apply their knowledge and experience of current rents of comparable property in the area. In addition they are required to have regard to the age, character and locality of the dwelling-house and its state of repair. Where there is furniture involved the state of this furniture as regards its quantity, quality and condition must be looked at. They must disregard the personal circumstances of the parties, any

---

[75] J. A. M. Inglis, "*The Fair Rents System*" in *A Scots Conveyancing Miscellany* (1990).
[76] Rent (Scotland) Act 1984, s. 48.

disrepair which stems from the tenant failing to abide by the terms of the lease, tenants' improvements, and any deterioration in the condition of furniture. There are certain assumptions that supply and demand are in balance. This involves in practice making a "scarcity deduction." A percentage of the rent is deducted from the market rent as representing the impact of scarcity on the level of rents. Two main methods have dominated the rent fixing process— use of comparables[77] or return on capital investment.[78]

Security of tenure and protection from eviction

The security of tenure provisions attempt to ensure that the landlord is barred from evicting arbitrarily or merely on whim. The principle which is incorporated in the legislation is that a landlord can get rid of a tenant only for an approved reason. Again, as in the rent-fixing process, these protections are voluntary. There is no obligation on a landlord to obtain a court order for possession if the tenant is compliant. Similarly there is no compulsion on the tenant to exercise the rights of security. The provisions will only come into play if the tenant is unwilling to leave when the landlord purports to put the contract of lease to an end.

The Scottish rule in the law of leases of tacit relocation means that, even where a contract of lease reaches its end, it is automatically continued until one of the parties gives notice of termination. If tenants give notice of termination they cannot be compelled to continue in the tenancy. If, however, one were to attempt to leave before the term of the lease there would be liability for the contractual obligations. Normally landlords cover themselves for this eventuality by taking both rent in advance and a deposit—although this is often actually taken to cover breakages, it is typically applied to cover other forms of loss to the landlord.

Where the landlord gives the appropriate notice to quit then, despite the compulsive wording of such notices, the tenant in a protected tenancy does not need to leave. They can stay on in the property, relying on the Rent Acts. Their occupancy is known as a statutory tenancy. The onus is on the landlord to show that the tenant should leave for one of the approved reasons. Such reasons may be of two kinds—discretionary or mandatory—depending on whether the sheriff may or must terminate the tenancy.[79]

The sheriff has discretionary powers in many of the eviction

---

[77] *Tormes Property Co.* v. *Landau* [1971] 1 Q.B. 261.
[78] *Learmonth Property Investment Co.* v. *Aitken*, 1970 S.C. 223; *Western Heritable Investment Co. Ltd.*, 1978 S.C. 304.
[79] Rent (Scotland) Act 1984, Sched. 2.

situations which come up before the court. This means that a Sheriff must normally be satisfied not only that the situation falls within the terms of the specific ground of possession, but also that to grant the order for possession would be reasonable. The specific approved reasons are that the landlord is ending the tenancy but offering suitable alternative accommodation[80]; or that there is a recognised reason for terminating—rent arrears or the tenant in breach of the tenancy; nuisance or annoyance; condition of dwelling-house deteriorated; condition of furniture deteriorated; tenant withdraws a notice to quit; assignation/sub-let of whole house; house reasonably required by the landlord for occupation by a full-time employee; house reasonably required by landlord for occupation as a residence for self or close family member[81]; excessive rent charged for sub-let; overcrowded house.

In addition there are a number of reasons for repossession where the sheriff must make an order for repossession if the ground is satisfied—owner-occupier who gave tenant notice when renting; landlord's retirement home; off-season holiday let; educational body student let; short tenancy; minister/lay missionary property; ex-agricultural worker; amalgamation of farms; farm occupation; adapted for special needs; landlord in Armed Forces.

After 1965 and the introduction of the Rent Act into unfurnished property, there was a shift of investment by landlords into providing furnished accommodation with its limited rights of security. Similarly, after the amalgamation of the furnished and unfurnished codes in 1974, there were a number of moves by landlords to avoid allowing their tenants rights.[82] Some of the avoidance devices were quite transparent, such as holiday lettings which were not really for such a purpose. Others offended against the prohibition on contracting out of the Rent Acts rather less obviously—bed and breakfast where some food was made available or the deferred purchase agreement which could be both a genuine and a fake transaction. The simplest avoidance mechanism was the licence—all the signs of a lease but the name changed. In England the licence has given rise to extensive litigation between 1978 and 1988 and the position is still far from clear.[83] While the Housing (Scotland) Act 1988 provides a

---

[80] *Redspring* v. *Francis* [1973] 1 All E.R. 740; *Siddiqui* v. *Rashid* [1980] 3 All E.R. 184.

[81] There is an additional requirement for this specific head that the court must not make an order for possession if it is satisfied that greater hardship would be caused by granting the order than refusing it—Sched. 2, Part III.

[82] See A. McAllister, *Scottish Law of Leases* (1989), at p. 208.

[83] *Street* v. *Mountford* [1985] A.C. 809; *Antoniades* v. *Villiers* [1988] 3 W.L.R. 1205; *A.G. Securities* v. *Vaughan* [1988] 3 All E.R. 1058.

mechanism giving landlords market rents and tenants no security beyond the term, some landlords may still choose to use these mechanisms in certain circumstances. The most obvious will be where they wish to rent out for a very short period—the short assured tenancy has a minimum initial term of six months.

Apart from being able to take civil action to enforce a contract, the Rent Acts have provided a criminal sanction against landlords who attempt to deprive tenants of their rights. Protection against this was given in the original Rent Act 1965. This was retained in the Rent (Scotland) Act 1984 and has been strengthened by the Housing (Scotland) Act 1988. It is a criminal offence under Part III of the Rent (Scotland) Act 1984 for any person unlawfully to deprive the residential occupier of any premises or attempt to do so, unless they prove they believed or had reasonable cause to believe that the residential occupier had ceased to reside in the premises.

If any person with intent or likely to cause the residential occupier (a) to give up occupation of the premises, (b) to refrain from exercising any right or pursuing any remedy in respect of the premises does acts calculated or likely to interfere with the peace or comfort of the residential occupier or members of his household or persistently withdraws or withholds services reasonably required for the occupation of the premises as a residence, they shall be guilty of an offence. The person guilty is liable to a fine or imprisonment or both.

In order to avoid tenancies having their rents restricted but these rents being inflated by "hidden" charges, the Rent Acts have always prohibited premiums. The interpretation of when a payment is a premium has been the scene of quite extensive litigation, mainly in England. The statutory control is found in Part VIII of the Rent (Scotland) Act 1984.

Assured Tenancies under the Housing (Scotland) Act 1988

Any contracts entered into after the commencement of Part II of the Housing (Scotland) Act 1988 (January 2, 1989) can no longer be regulated tenancies. Most private sector tenancies are likely to be assured tenancies. The key features of the Scottish assured tenancy are that it lessens the degree of security of tenure whilst also abolishing any direct method of regulating the rents landlords charge, other than the operation of supply and demand.

The definition of an "assured tenancy" requires that there be four elements as well as requiring that it does not come within the category of one of the excluded tenancies laid down in the Act. The specified elements are that there should be a tenancy; the property must be let as a separate dwelling; the tenant or at least one of the tenants must be an individual; and the property must be the tenant's only or principal home.

Certain kinds of tenancies are excluded from coming within the assured tenancy framework—tenancies entered into before January 2, 1989, low rent premises, shops, licensed premises, agricultural land, agricultural holdings, student lettings by specified educational institutions, holiday lettings, resident landlords, Crown tenancies, public sector landlords, shared ownership agreements, protected tenancies, housing association tenancies and secure tenancies, and temporary accommodation for homeless persons.[84]

Rents and other conditions

There are more limited rights for tenants of assured tenancies as to rent fixing and security of tenure than with protected tenancies. Although there is no equivalent for a tenant applying to have fair rent fixed, there is a procedure where the Rent Assessment Committee can be involved where no provision has been made for rent increases in the tenancy agreement.

Where the negotiated rent period comes to an end and the landlord seeks to increase the rent, the tenant may apply to the Rent Assessment Committee for a determination of the rent.[85] A landlord seeking an increase of rent at this time must serve a notice on the tenant in the form prescribed by the Secretary of State. Tenants cannot initiate the referral procedures themselves as with the fair rent system. It is assumed that they find the initial rent level acceptable. The fact that the rent level may not be accepted by the local authority for housing benefit purposes was drawn to the Government's attention. As alternatives to the proposed increase the landlord and tenant can agree to a change in the rent different from that in the notice, or they may agree that there should be no change in the rent.

Landlords in assured tenancies can avoid the rent assessment committee having a rôle by providing for a rent increase either by a specified sum or by a percentage of the rent. There appears to be no reason why the specified sum cannot be related to some external method of measurement such as changes in the Retail Price Index

---

[84] Detailed in Sched. 4.
[85] s. 24.

or a similar factor, provided that such a mechanism is ascertainable by the tenant without undue difficulty.[86]

Where a tenant refers a notice of increase to a Rent Assessment Committee they must fix a rent which they consider the house would let for in the open market by a willing landlord. There are no detailed criteria as found in the fair rent formula. Relevant issues could include the capital value of the property, the extent of past and likely capital appreciation, levels of alternative investments and their capital growth potential. In addition the state of repair of the property and its age, character and locality should provide guidance as to what rent it is reasonable to ask for the property in question. Once a body of rents exists, these will also be available as "comparables" as under the Rent (Scotland) Act 1984.

The Rent Assessment Committee are also to disregard the effect of certain factors, such as the fact that the tenancy was granted to an individual who was already a sitting tenant. In addition, tenant's "voluntary" improvements are not to be counted against tenants in their rent although repairs would not be relevant. If tenants have expended money on improving the landlord's property they are not expected to pay for the privilege. On the same lines the Rent Assessment Committee must disregard tenant's damage or harm to the landlord's property. Just as tenants do not have to pay for their improvements, so it is reasonable that they should not benefit from their misdeeds. If tenants have caused the property to deteriorate they cannot expect to obtain a lower rent as a result of their failing to abide by the conditions of the tenancy.[87]

In addition, there is provision for the fixing of rental and non-rental terms in a statutory assured tenancy, *i.e.* where an assured tenant takes advantage of the rights of security of tenure[88] and remains in the property after the termination date of the original contract, then provision is made for the adjustment of the terms both of rent and terms other than rent. The variation does not affect specific rights given in the Act covering the prohibition on assignation without consent and the requirement that there be access for repairs.

Where a notice of proposed changes is duly served, then the recipient—whether landlord or tenant—has three months from the date of service to refer this proposal to the Rent Assessment Com-

---

[86] s. 24 as amended by Sched. 11, para. 99, to Local Government and Housing Act 1989.

[87] See also s. 48(3)(*a*) of the Rent (Scotland) Act 1984 for equivalent in regulated tenancies.

[88] s. 16.

mittee. If there is no referral to a Rent Assessment Committee then the terms proposed become the terms of the agreement.[89] Where there is a reference to a Rent Assessment Committee then their task is to assess the terms in terms of what terms might reasonably be expected to be found in a contractual assured tenancy granted by a willing landlord to a willing tenant. The Rent Assessment Committee have discretion to adjust the rent where they approve proposals to change the tenancy conditions. This includes changes proposed by the committee themselves.[90]

Security of Tenure

Often a rental agreement contains a clause or clauses purporting to take away the rights of the assured tenant in relation to security of tenure and requiring the tenant to quit the premises without any further order at the end of the contract. Such statements are of no effect and are overridden by the express requirement in the legislation that a tenancy cannot be brought to an end except through an order by the sheriff.[91]

The current statute retains the concept of security of tenure, but extends those situations where landlords can have tenants evicted. Under the assured tenancy régime—as with regulated tenancies under the Rent (Scotland) Act 1984 and secure tenancies under the Housing (Scotland) Act 1987—there is a requirement that possession orders only be given on one or more of the grounds specified in the legislation. The grounds for repossession must be established as well as proper notice given.

The sheriff has no power to make an assured tenancy possession order except in specified circumstances.[92] One or more of the grounds for possession must be established. There are two situations which can exist when a possession order is sought—in certain instances the sheriff has discretion and must be satisfied, not only that the conditions in the ground are met but also that it is reasonable to grant the order for possession. In other situations if the ground is satisfied there is no element of discretion and the order must be granted. As well as giving a notice to quit, proper notice of

---

[89] s. 24.
[90] s. 25.
[91] s. 18 and Sched. 5.
[92] Specified in Sched. 5.

proceedings must be observed before there can be an order for possession.[93]

Where a mandatory ground such as rent three months in arrears is established[94] then the sheriff must grant a possession order. In addition some of the grounds may only be available if additional use requirements are satisfied—off-season holiday lets and out of term lettings of students accommodation by specified educational institutions.[95] There are also grounds which are within the discretion of the sheriff.[96] These cover suitable alternative accommodation being offered; the tenant withdrawing a notice to quit; persistent delay in rent payment; rent arrears; breach of tenancy obligations; condition of house or furniture deteriorated; nuisance annoyance and illegal/immoral use of premises and property occupied by an ex-employee. The sheriff must be satisfied as to the overall reasonableness of making the order. It involves taking into account every relevant circumstance affecting the interests of the parties, such as their conduct and any possible hardship which might result if the order were to be made, as well as the interests of the public. The question of the possibility of the tenant obtaining other accommodation, as well as any rights under statute such as legislation for homeless persons, is relevant.

The Housing (Scotland) Act 1988 makes provision for the sheriff to adjourn, sist (temporarily halt), suspend or postpone possession.[97] Where the landlord is seeking possession under one of the discretionary grounds the action can be postponed or sisted. Even where a possession order is granted it is possible for the sheriff to postpone the date when the eviction is to take place. Alternatively conditions can be set concerning payment of rent arrears or about any other conditions.

The sheriff may not exercise these provisions in relation to halt-

---

[93] s. 19, which lays down the time limits, *i.e.*
   1. *Two months*:
      i. landlord's former home (ground 1).
      ii. mortgage repossession (ground 2).
      iii. minister/lay missionary (ground 5).
      iv. H.A. demolition/reconstruction (ground 6).
      v. inherited tenancy (ground 7).
      vi. suitable alternative accommodation (ground 9).
      vii. ex-employee tenancy (ground 17).
   2. *Two weeks*:
      in any other case.
[94] Sched. 5, Pt. I.
[95] Pt. I.
[96] Sched. 5, Pt. II.
[97] s. 20.

ing or postponing possession actions for short assured tenancies and tenancies where the mandatory grounds are used. The mandatory grounds cover situations where the landlord wants the property for his own home or if it was formerly his own home; mortgage default; off-season holiday lets; student tenancies; property tenanted by a minister/lay missionary; demolition or reconstruction work to go ahead and needing vacant possession; tenancies inherited under a will or on intestacy or where there are three months of rent arrears.

The criteria for landlords regaining their property when they provide the sitting tenant with suitable alternative accommodation are on the same lines as those provided in the Rent (Scotland) Act 1984 and the Housing (Scotland) Act 1987. They can stem from either a local authority certificate of suitability or from being deemed by the sheriff to be suitable looking to whether the accommodation is reasonably suitable to the needs of the tenant and family. They are determined by looking to proximity to work and whether the property is similar as regards rental to equivalent public sector housing or reasonably suitable to the means and needs of the tenant.

Short Assured Tenancies

This is a quite distinct form of assured tenancy whose main distinction is that there is no provision for a right to a continuation of the term of the tenancy beyond the term of the original minimum of six months. A short assured tenancy requires that there be a minimum period of six months and notice must be served to the effect that the tenancy is a short assured tenancy.[98] The landlord can regain possession of a short assured tenancy either automatically on giving notice or on any of the assured tenancy repossession grounds.[99] This notice establishing that the tenancy is a short assured tenancy must be served on the prospective tenant before the creation of the tenancy. The notice indicates to a prospective tenant that the landlord will be allowed to evict provided that the proper notice is given as well as that there is a right to apply to a Rent Assessment Committee for a rent determination. There can be no valid short assured tenancy unless this notice is served, and in such cases a tenancy would be an assured tenancy. Where at the end of the short assured tenancy it continues by tacit relocation or there is a new contractual tenancy of the same or substantially the same premises,

[98] s. 32.
[99] Sched. 5, Pt. I.

then such a tenancy is a short assured tenancy. This applies whether or not the requirements as to length of time of the tenancy and notice apply to the renewed tenancy.

Rent determination

There is a limited rôle for the Rent Assessment Committee, provided that certain criteria are satisfied.[100] The tenant can have the rent decided by a Rent Assessment Committee. The criterion they must apply is what rent the landlord might reasonably be expected to obtain under a short assured tenancy. There is an element of circularity in this, except that it is expected that those occupying under less secure shorthold assured tenancies will have to pay lower rents than the market assured tenancy rents. Before the R.A.C. can make a determination they must be satisfied that there is a sufficient number of similar houses in the district let on either kind of assured tenancy. In addition they are not to fix a rent even where there are sufficient comparables unless the rent paid by the tenant is significantly higher than the rent which the landlord might reasonably expect to be able to obtain judging by rents charged locally. The rent determination lasts for one year from the date when it comes into operation. The previous private sector rents fixed under the Rent (Scotland) Act 1984 lasted for three years although the English legislation since 1980 provided for two-year intervals.

Security of tenure

The tenant of a short assured tenancy has no defence to a properly-based possession action.[101] As mentioned, the landlord has this ground as an addition to those mandatory and discretionary grounds available.[102] Where there is a short assured tenancy the sheriff must grant an order for possession if satisfied that the tenancy has reached its termination date, that tacit relocation is not operating, that no further contractual tenancy is in existence, and that the landlord has given notice that possession of the house is required. This is rather different from the question of whether the landlord "reasonably requires" the house "for occupation as a residence," as occurs under the Rent (Scotland) Act 1984.[103] Here the requirement is formal and does not involve the landlord satisfying any test of necessity. It is for the landlord to decide if possession

[100] s. 34.
[101] s. 33.
[102] Sched. 5.
[103] Sched. 2, ground 8.

is required of the property and does not seem to be open to the sheriff to consider whether the landlord has an objective need for the property. In addition to a notice to quit, the legislation requires that a notice of proceedings for possession be served on the tenant. The period of the notice that the landlord requires possession must be either two weeks, two months or such period in excess of two months as the tenancy agreement provides.

Public Sector Rented Housing

Proposals for introducing tenants' security were well under way before the General Election of 1979 under the Labour government and these were adopted by the incoming Tory government. These rights were introduced in the Tenants' Rights Etc. (Scotland) Act 1980 (for Scotland) and the very similar English equivalent (the Housing Act 1980). Both the public sector codes have been consolidated, and the law for Scotland is contained in the Housing (Scotland) Act 1987.

Secure tenancies

Part III of the Housing (Scotland) Act 1987 makes provision for security of tenure for public sector tenants. These are termed secure tenancies and are satisfied if the dwelling-house is let as a separate dwelling; the tenant is an individual and the dwelling-house is his only or principal home; and the landlord is a public body.[104] Housing association tenancies entered into prior to January 2, 1989 are also covered, but where these landlords enter tenancies after the introduction of the Housing (Scotland) Act 1988 assured tenancies are created (see above at pp. 141–144).

Certain tenancies are specifically excluded from the ambit of secure tenancies under Schedule 2 to the Housing (Scotland) Act 1987—premises occupied under contract of employment where the contract of employment requires the tenant to occupy the house for the better performance of duties; temporary letting to persons taking up employment in area and seeking accommodation; temporary letting pending development; decant property let

---

[104] *i.e.* 1. an islands or district council; 2. a regional council; 3. a new town development corporation; 4. Scottish homes; 5. a police authority; or 6. a fire authority.

temporarily; homeless person's temporary accommodation; agricultural and business premises.

Rents for local authority accommodation

These are a matter for the discretion of the local authority. They may "charge such reasonable rents as they may determine for the tenancy or occupation of houses provided by them." The local authority must review its rents from time to time and make such charges as circumstances may require. When deciding the standard rents to which their housing revenue account relates, they must take no account of the personal circumstances of the tenants.

In relation to the operation of the general discretion, there is the overall restriction of *ultra vires*. One local authority tried to avoid the impact of the Housing Finance Act 1972. The Act imposed mandatory rent increases which one authority attempted to avoid by raising the rent of one house from £7·71 a week to £18,000 a week (the property was empty, so that the figure was notional rather than actual). In this case, *Backhouse* v. *Lambeth Borough Council*[105] the court said that the figure was one which no reasonable authority could have arrived at, and was not a valid exercise of the authority's powers under the English obligation corresponding to the Scottish 1987 Act.

Apart from this it is up to the local authority, whether they operate rent pooling or differential rents, provided they do not offend the unreasonableness test, which would make the decision *ultra vires* the local authority's power.

Security of tenure

A secure tenancy may not be brought to an end except in the following circumstances which may not be varied by the tenancy agreement—death of the tenant where there is no qualified person to succeed[106]; declining of tenancy by qualified person; death of succeeding qualified person; written agreement between the landlord and tenant; abandonment of the tenancy; possession order from the sheriff court; four weeks' notice by tenant to the landlord.

Abandonment of tenancy

If a landlord considers that the tenant may have ceased to be resident in the house tenanted, the authority may repossess. The landlord must have reasonable grounds for believing that the dwelling is unoccupied and the tenant does not intend to occupy it as his

---

[105] *The Times*, Oct. 14, 1972.
[106] s. 52.

home. Apart from entering to secure the dwelling against vandalism the landlord may take possession of the house with notice stating that the landlord has reasons to believe that the house is unoccupied and that the tenant does not intend to occupy it as his home; requiring the tenant to inform the landlord within four weeks of service of the notice if he intends to occupy the house as his home; and informing the tenant that if it appears to the landlord at the end of the four-week period that the tenant does not intend so to occupy the house that the tenancy will be terminated forthwith. When the notice has been served and when the landlord has made such inquiries as may be necessary to be satisfied that the dwelling is unoccupied and that the tenant does not intend to occupy it as his home, then at the end of the four-week period a further notice is served bringing the tenancy to an end. Where these requirements have been complied with there may be repossession without further proceedings.[107]

Possession order from sheriff

The landlord must serve a notice on the tenant of proceedings for possession.[108] This notice must be served in prescribed form. This is provided by the Secretary of State in statutory instrument and includes the ground on which the landlord's action is being raised. In addition to the notice of proceedings the landlord must serve a notice to quit bringing the tenancy to an end. In the ensuing summary cause the sheriff may adjourn proceedings for repossession for a period or periods with or without imposing conditions as to payment of outstanding rent or other conditions. There is no precise equivalent to the private sector split between discretionary and mandatory grounds, except that under certain grounds an order must be made where other suitable accommodation will be made available for the tenant when the order takes effect.[109]

The grounds or heads for possession resemble those grounds available in the private sector where the tenant's conduct makes it appropriate that there be eviction—rent unpaid or any other obligation broken; using the house or allowing it to be so used for immoral or illegal purposes; deterioration of the house or common parts owing to acts of waste or neglect or default by the tenant or any resident or lodger; condition of furniture has deteriorated due to ill-treatment by tenant or lodger or sub-tenant; absence from the dwelling-house by tenant and spouse without reasonable cause for a

---

[107] s. 49.
[108] s. 47.
[109] Grounds 8–15 of Sched. 3 (s. 48(2)(*b*)).

continuous period exceeding six months or ceasing to occupy house as principal home; conduct which is a nuisance or annoyance in or in the vicinity of the house and it is not reasonable in all the circumstances that the landlord should be required to make other accommodation available to the tenant. For these grounds the sheriff must be satisfied that it is reasonable to make an order.

The remaining grounds cover situations where by and large the house is inappropriate and hence the court must be satisfied that suitable accommodation is available for the tenant—conduct which is a nuisance or annoyance in or in the vicinity of the house and in the opinion of the landlord it is appropriate in the circumstances to require the tenant to move to other accommodation; overcrowding in terms of the Housing (Scotland) Act 1987; demolition or substantial work on the building intended by the landlord within a reasonable time and this work cannot reasonably be done without obtaining possession of the house; house designed or adapted for occupation by a person with special needs and there is no longer such a person occupying the house and the landlord requires the house for occupation by another person with special needs; house part of group designed or provided with or located near facilities for persons in need of special social support and no longer a person with such a need occupying the house and landlord requires it for another person with such needs; housing association landlord whose objects are or include housing persons who are in a special category by reason of age, infirmity, disability or social circumstances and tenant no longer in such circumstances or house no longer suitable for tenant's needs and accommodation required for someone who is in a special category; landlord's rights have either ended or will do so within six months from raising of possession action.

Where the landlord is repossessing property and providing alternative accommodation its suitability is determined as to whether the security is equivalent as well as whether it is reasonably suitable. In deciding whether a house is reasonably suitable to the needs of the tenant and the family, the sheriff must have regard to specific factors.[110] These are proximity to the place of work of the tenant and other members of the family compared with existing dwelling-house (also includes attendance at an educational establishment); the extent of the accommodation required by the tenant and his family; the character of the accommodation offered compared with existing house; terms on which accommodation offered compared with existing house; where furniture provided compare with pre-

---

[110] Housing (Scotland) Act 1987, Sched. 3, Pt. II.

viously provided furniture; any special needs of the tenant or family.

(b) Agricultural Land

From the first legislation on agricultural holdings in 1883 there has been legislation to ensure that tenants are not deprived of their improvements on leaving the land. The freedom of contract of the parties has been modified considerably over the years and the legislation confers on tenants substantial rights of security, an arbitrated rent, and compensation for improvements and disturbance.

The Agricultural Holdings legislation[111] applies to leases of "land used for agriculture which is so used for the purpose of a trade or business." Agriculture covers every sort of farming activity including horticulture, fruit growing and market gardening.

Rent and Other Conditions

Tenants of agricultural holdings have statutory rights, which include the right to a written lease of at least a year and the right to have the question of their rent referred to arbitration. This is to be fixed at the rent at which the holding might reasonably be expected to be let in the open market by a willing landlord to a willing tenant, disregarding the tenant's right to security. The landlord has the right to automatic rent increases for certain improvements provided that the tenant is given timeous notice.

Apart from rent, the tenant has the right of freedom of cropping subject to the obligation to exercise good husbandry, the right to remove fixtures and the right to have a record of the holding and its fixed equipment.[112] This record is required for any claims for continuous good farming and for deterioration or dilapidation. The parties are expressly prohibited from contracting out of such obligations as freedom of cropping and compensation,[113] whilst some rights in the legislation are subject to contractual variation.[114] Com-

---

[111] The major statute continues to be the Agricultural Holdings (Scotland) Act 1949 (as amended).

[112] Specified in s. 93 of the Agriculture (Scotland) Act 1949, and including buildings, fences, ditches, drains, fanks, farm roads, water and sewerage systems.

[113] *e.g.* s. 16 prohibits the landlord's right to penal rent or liquidate damages.

[114] See B. Gill, *The Law of Agricultural Holdings in Scotland* (2nd ed., 1990); s. 13, prohibiting the removal of manure after notice to terminate the tenancy, may be varied by agreement.

pensation is available for disturbance and improvements. Game damage is covered by the common law. The question of improvements is based on the value to an incoming tenant and in the event of failure to agree there is provision for arbitration.

Security of Tenure

The tenancy can be terminated for non-payment of rent, but this does not affect the compensation rights available for improvements. Apart from this, where a landlord serves a notice to quit the tenant may serve a written counter-notice and require the matter to be dealt with by the Land Court. Their consent must be given before there can be termination. They must be satisfied on one or more of the following grounds—that the landlord's purpose in seeking recovery is in the interests of good husbandry; in the interests of sound estate management; desirable for the purposes of agricultural research, education, experiment, demonstration, smallholdings, allotments; that greater hardship would be caused by refusal than consenting; that the landlord proposes to terminate the tenancy for the purpose of the land being used for a non-agricultural use. In addition the Land Court must withhold consent to the operation of the notice to quit if it appears to them that a fair and reasonable landlord would not insist on possession.[115]

Recourse to the Land Court is excluded in certain circumstances and the landlord will be able to recover possession[116]—for instance when the tenant is bankrupt, where within the last nine months a certificate of bad husbandry has been issued by the Land Court; or where the tenant is in breach not capable of being remedied in reasonable time and at economic cost.

(c) Crofters and Cottars

Statutory control over the position of crofts was introduced in 1886 to cover those holding from year to year who lacked security of tenure, suffered high rents, and had no rights as to compensation for improvement.[117] The code was introduced in the crofting coun-

[115] *Altyre Estate Trs.* v. *McLay*, 1975 S.L.T. (Land Ct.) 12, where a unit was not viable on its own and the landlord sought to recover it for amalgamation. The tenant had farmed it along with a holding one mile away for 30 years.

[116] s. 25(2) (as amended by the Agriculture Act 1958, s. 3 and Scheds. 1 and 3, and the Agriculture (Misc. Provs.) Act 1976, ss. 13 and 14).

[117] D. MacCuish and D. Flyn, *Crofting Law* (1990).

ties—Argyll, Caithness, Inverness, Orkney, Ross and Cromarty, Shetland and Sutherland. In 1911 the protections were extended to those in the rest of Scotland, and landholders were classified as either small landholders or statutory small tenants.

A distinct crofting code was reintroduced by the Crofters (Scotland) Act 1955 to cover holdings within the crofting region. They cover the holdings occupied by small landholders and statutory small tenants prior to the introduction of the 1955 legislation.[118] The legislation provided for the application of the legislation to new crofts provided they did not exceed a certain size or rental[119] to be determined by the Secretary of State. There is provision for enlargement of existing crofts by the addition of non-crofting land provided that the total extent and rental do not exceed the specified limits.[120] The Crofters Commission have a duty to maintain a Register of Crofts, although this is not conclusive as to any holding being a croft.[121] In 1976 the crofting code was significantly amended to introduce the right to acquire ownership of the croft house as well as croft land.[122]

The crofting code lays down statutory conditions which must be complied with, including the requirement of the crofter to pay rent, to cultivate the croft, not to subdivide it, not to sell intoxicating liquors, and to permit the landlord access to take minerals, timber and fishing.[123]

The rent payable may be altered by agreement in writing between landlord and crofter. There is a specific right for crofters to apply for a fair rent.[124] Either the crofter or the landlord can apply to the Land Court for such a determination. The parties must be heard and the Land Court must take into consideration all the circumstances of the case, of the croft and of the district, and in particular must take into consideration any permanent or unexhausted improvements on the croft and suitable thereto which have been executed or paid for by the crofter or any predecessors in the tenancy.

---

[118] As to the very limited compensation rights of cottars, see MacCuish and Flyn, *op. cit.*, Chap. 11. Cottars are those paying no rent for a dwelling-house or tenants from year to year paying rent not exceeding £6, in the crofting counties, but whose presence and status are recognised by the landowner.

[119] Under the 1955 legislation this was either 50 acres or £50 annual rental. The Crofters (Scotland) Act 1961 increased the acreage limit to 75 acres.

[120] 30 hectares and £100: Crofters (Scotland) Act 1961, s. 2(1) as amended by Sched. 2, para. 17 to the Crofting Reform (Scotland) Act 1976.

[121] Crofters (Scotland) Act 1961, s. 3.

[122] Crofting Reform (Scotland) Act 1976.

[123] Crofters (Scotland) Act 1955, Second Sched. (as amended).

[124] Crofters (Scotland) Act 1955, s. 5.

As to security of tenure, a crofter must not be removed from the croft unless one year's rent is unpaid or there is breach of one or more of the statutory conditions. No contracting out is permitted. If there is a breach of conditions the landlord can apply to the Land Court. They must consider any objections raised by the crofter and may make an order for removal. In addition there is a procedure for resumption of the whole or part of the croft by the landlord "for some reasonable purpose[125] having relation to the good of the croft or the estate or to the public interest." The Land Court may, if satisfied as to these matters, authorise the resumption and require the crofter to surrender the whole or part of the croft. Adequate compensation either by letting other land of equivalent value or money or rent adjustment is provided for. Provision is also made for termination of crofting tenancies where there are "absentee" crofters. This involves the Crofter's Commission taking action where it is in the general interest of the crofting community in the district that the tenancy of the croft be terminated and let to some other person.[126] Where there is termination, whether voluntary or involuntary, there is entitlement to compensation for improvements based on the amount which the landlord might reasonably be expected to receive from an incoming tenant if the croft were offered for letting on a crofting tenancy on the open market.[127]

(d) Commercial Premises

In Scotland there is no developed body of law providing rent control or security of tenure for the tenants of commercial premises. In the event that a tenant of commercial premises finds the terms offered by a landlord unacceptable, there is no body of law which provides for such a disagreement to be arbitrated to which the tenant may have recourse.

Rents in all commercial premises—offices, shops or industrial premises—are determined by the market. Inability to pay or exorbitance of the rent is not a concern of any forum of appeal or

---

[125] Crofters (Scotland) Act 1955, s. 12—reasonable purpose includes use of land for building houses, small allotments, harbours, piers, boat shelters, churches, schools, halls or community centres, planting, roads for vehicular access from croft to public road or seashore or any other purpose likely to provide employment for crofters and others in the locality or protection of any object of historical or archaeological interest.

[126] Crofters (Scotland) Act 1955, s. 17—currently a crofter is absent if not ordinarily resident on or within 16 km. of the croft, measured in a straight line.

[127] Crofters (Scotland) Act 1961, s. 6(2).

adjudication. There may be provision for arbitration in the tenancy agreement.[128]

There is provision for a limited right to renew a tenancy of a shop covered by the Tenancy of Shops (Scotland) Act 1949. This applies to any premises where any retail trade or business is carried on. The statute specifically covers: "the business of a barber or hairdresser, the sale of refreshments or intoxicating liquors, the business of lending books or periodicals when carried on for the purpose of gain, and retail sales, but does not include the sale of programmes and catalogues and other similar sales at theatres and places of amusement." The legislation has been held to cover a garage selling second-hand cars and selling accessories, a sub-post office selling stamps, and an optician's where dispensing and sale of spectacles was the sole business. Where a tenant is unable to obtain a renewal of the tenancy from the landlord on satisfactory terms there may be application to the sheriff. The sheriff may decide that there should be a renewal, but is limited to the period of one year on such terms as thought in all the circumstances reasonable. There may be refusal to renew if the sheriff considers it reasonable to do so. The sheriff must refuse to renew if there has been a material breach of the tenancy conditions, or the tenant is bankrupt, or if the landlord has offered to sell to the tenant at an arbitrated price, or if alternative accommodation has been offered, or if the tenant gave notice to terminate on the strength of which the landlord has contracted to sell or lease the premises and there would be serious prejudice if possession could not be obtained or if in all the circumstances of the case greater hardship would be caused by renewing the tenancy than by refusing to renew. The sheriff's decision is not subject to appeal.

Commercial tenancies of subjects other than shops are covered by the normal rules as to termination of the tenancy. There is no guarantee that a tenant will be provided with a renewal. It will depend on the contract. The protection that does exist for commercial tenants is to be found in the Law Reform (Miscellaneous Provisions) (Scotland) Act 1986 which introduced a formal requirement when a landlord was seeking to enforce a conventional irritancy. To prevent what was seen as a harshness of tenants being evicted for trivial lateness in rent payment,[129] it is now provided that after monetary irritancies have been incurred the tenant must be given a further 14 days' written notice to pay the arrears. Only after

---

[128] See McAllister, *op. cit.*, Chap. 10.

[129] *Dorchester Studios (Glasgow) Ltd.* v. *Stone*, 1975 S.C.(H.L.) 56; *HMV Fields Properties Ltd.* v. *Tandem Shoes Ltd.*, 1983 S.L.T. 114.

the lapse of this period without payment may the landlord go ahead and enforce the irritancy.[130] At the same time statutory protection was provided for tenants where landlords are seeking to enforce other irritancies. The court may only enforce the irritancy in cases where it considers that a fair and reasonable landlord would do so.[131] There may be no contracting out of this provision.

[130] Law Reform (Misc. Provs.) (Scotland) Act 1985, s. 4.
[131] s. 5.

CHAPTER 10

RIGHTS IN SECURITY

1. INTRODUCTION

THE most familiar symbols of rights in security are the pawnshop on the one hand and the building society on the other. The essence of a security is that it is a property right in a specific item of property. This property acts as security for a debt, and in the event of the debtor becoming insolvent then the holder of the security has a preferential right in the secured property before other unsecured creditors. Typically a building society lends the purchase price to the buyer and takes out a security right over the house being purchased. If there is another lender who also lends on the security of the house, then this person would rank over the first lender but ahead of unsecured creditors. When one creditor has a security over two subjects belonging to the debtor and another creditor has a postponed security over one of these subjects, the first creditor is termed the catholic creditor and the other the secondary creditor. Catholic creditors may choose which of the subjects the debt will be met from, and may disregard the interests of the secondary creditor in pursuit of any legitimate interests of their own. In the event that the catholic creditor chooses to meet the debt from the subjects covered by the secondary creditor, there must be an assignation to the secondary creditor of any remaining security rights. As between catholic bonds and several subjects in which there are secondary creditors, then apportionment must be done rateably according to the value of each subject and irrespective of the date of the secondary bonds involved.[1] The property right in a security does not convert to a full property right and there must be no clog or obstacle to redemption of the security, such as by postponing the period of redemption so as to prevent the return of any subject given in security where payment is made.[2]

[1] *Ferrier* v. *Cowan* (1896) 23 R. 703; *Earl of Moray* v. *Mansfield* (1836) 14 S. 886.
[2] *Fairclough* v. *Swan Brewery Co.* [1912] A.C. 565.

Security rights have three sources. They may be provided for by statute. The statutory form may be the only one recognised, and in order to qualify as a security right it will be crucial to abide by the terms laid down in the statute. An example would be a mortgage over a house in Scotland and the requirement to use the standard security mechanism as laid down in the Conveyancing and Feudal Reform (Scotland) Act 1970. The Companies Act lays down specific requirements where floating charges are used. In addition various bodies are granted rights at common law without possession of the property through hypothec, lien and diligence.[3] Finally, parties may grant security rights through agreement.[4]

Distinctions exist depending on whether the property involved is moveable or heritable. The difference noted in Roman law was between pledge and mortgage.[5] The former involves delivery, whilst this is not available in the latter. Since possession is the badge of ownership as far as moveables are concerned, it is important that potential purchasers or lenders be made aware of the prior debtor's rights. This is effected through delivery. As far as heritable rights are concerned the existence of a public property register protects a purchaser or subsequent lender from undisclosed debts over the property concerned. Any mortgage over the property would emerge on consultation of the Register of Sasines or Land Register.[6] Finally there are special arrangements in existence for securities over ships. A ship may be mortgaged in a statutory form which must be entered by the registrar in the register book.[7] Entry in the register book determines preference between creditors[8] but is secondary to the bond of bottomry, a maritime lien[9] or a lien for repairs.[10] The holder of a mortgage over a ship has a variety of powers including interdict where the security might be imperilled,[11] as well as the power of sale.[12] This latter includes the taking of possession.[13]

---

[3] Now supplemented by statute as in the case of the solicitors' hypothec.

[4] Examples might include the arrangements where money is lent in exchange for delivery of family credit or other social security books of vouchers.

[5] Justinian's *Institutes*, IV.4.6.7.

[6] See Chap. 6 and D. J. Cusine, *Standard Securities* (1991).

[7] Merchant Shipping Act 1894, s. 31 and Sched. 1, Pt. I, Form B.

[8] s. 33.

[9] See below.

[10] *Tyne Dock Engineering Co.* v. *Royal Bank of Scotland*, 1974 S.L.T. 57.

[11] *Laming* v. *Seater* (1889) 16 R. 828.

[12] s. 35.

[13] Bell, *Prin.*, § 1382A.

2. SECURITIES OVER MOVEABLES

The basic principle which underlay Scots law on security rights over
moveables is the requirement for delivery. Although there are now
significant exceptions to this notion, it is a useful baseline from
which to start consideration of the nature and operation of security
rights. The doctrine derives from Roman law, that it is by delivery
that the ownership of things passes—not mere agreements.[14]

The traditional pawnshop transaction typifies securities rights in
relation to moveables. Here the borrower pledges the goods and
delivers them to the lender. The pledge may be redeemed by
repayment of the capital and interest. If goods are not subject to the
security rights of the creditor, then in a bankruptcy the creditor has
no preferred position and stands alongside other creditors. Delivery may be satisfied, not only by the physical transfer of the goods in
question but also where there is symbolic delivery or constructive
delivery. Physical delivery has included enclosure of goods within a
fence and the delivery of the key to the lender[15] and is not required
in situations where delivery is impossible.[16] Symbolic delivery is
acceptable for goods which are shipped and for which a bill of lading
is taken. The bill of lading is regarded as a symbol of the goods, and
its transfer has the same effect as the physical delivery of the goods
themselves.[17] Other forms of symbolic delivery have not found
favour in the courts.[18] Where, however, goods are in a store there
may be effective delivery where the delivery order is addressed to
the storekeeper or by the indorsation of the storekeeper's warrant.
This requires the intimation of the transfer to be made to a
storekeeper who is an independent third party, as well as that the
goods must be ascertainable.[19] This process is known as constructive
delivery.

However, even so it is not always easy or convenient to deliver
goods which are alleged to be the security for the transaction. To
avoid the inconvenience of delivery, a variety of mechanisms have
been used with a varying degree of success. A genuine sale, even

---

[14] "*Traditionibus non nudis pactis dominia rerum transferuntur.*"

[15] *West Lothian Oil Co.* v. *Mair* (1892) 20 R. 64.

[16] *Darling* v. *Wilson's Tr.* (1887) 15 R. 180.

[17] Bell, *Prin.*, § 417.

[18] *Paul* v. *Cuthbertson* (1840) 2 D. 1286 (part cutting of standing trees); *Stiven* v.
Cowan (1878) 15 S.L.R. 422 (sasine ceremony aimed to affect machinery as well as
heritage).

[19] *Rhind's Tr.* v. *Robertson & Baxter* (1891) 18 R. 623; *Anderson* v. *McCall* (1866)
4 M. 765; *Hayman* v. *McLintock*, 1907 S.C. 936.

where the aim is to provide security, has been accepted,[20] but not a fictitious lease[21] nor placing a label on goods.[22]

These problems of delivery were particularly felt by commercial concerns and the floating charge was introduced into Scots law in 1961 to allow a security over both moveables and heritage without the need for delivery. It is available where granted by an incorporated company[23] or by an industrial or provident society.[24] To be operative it must be registered with the Registrar of Companies. There is no need for transference of possession or the giving of intimation.[25] The charge crystallises or attaches only at the start of the winding up of the company,[26] or upon appointment of a receiver by a creditor.[27] It does not attach to any particular item of property. When the charge crystallises the holder ranks alongside holders of similar charges but ahead of ordinary creditors.

3. HERITABLE SECURITIES

There are statutory limitations on the kinds of securities which may be created over heritage. The older pre-1970 forms of securities[28] will continue to be found, but new ones are not recognised and have not been created since the introduction of the Conveyancing and Feudal Reform (Scotland) Act 1970. These may be either the normal mortgage—standard security[29] or a floating charge.[30] As indicated the latter are only available where granted by an incorporated company or by an industrial or provident society,[31] whilst there are no equivalent restrictions on who may grant a standard security.

There are two prescribed forms in which a standard security may be granted, and to be effectual this must be followed by recording in

---

[20] *Duncanson* v. *Jeffrey's Tr.* (1881) 8 R. 563.
[21] *Heritable Securities Investment Assn.* v. *Wingate's Tr.* (1880) 7 R. 1094.
[22] *Orr's Tr.* v. *Tullis* (1870) 8 M. 935.
[23] Companies Act 1985 Pt. XVIII.
[24] Industrial and Provident Societies Act 1967, s. 3(1).
[25] Companies Act 1985, s. 462(5).
[26] Companies Act 1985, s. 463(1).
[27] Insolvency Act 1986, s. 53(7).
[28] Bond and disposition in security; cash credit bond and disposition in security; *ex facie* absolute disposition—discussed at some length in W. M. Gordon, *Scottish Land Law*, Chap. 20.
[29] In terms of the Conveyancing and Feudal Reform (Scotland) Act 1970.
[30] See above.
[31] Industrial and Provident Societies Act 1967, s. 3(1).

the Register.[32] It vests the interest in the creditor as security for the debtor meeting their obligations—normally this would involve making mortgage payments promptly.[33] The conditions which attach to standard securities are specified in the 1970 legislation.[34] The ranking of competing creditors is determined by the date of recording of any properly-executed standard security,[35] although this may be altered by the parties.[36] The debtor may redeem the debt by giving two months' notice.[37] Where the debtor fails to pay there may be a calling-up notice issued.[38] If debtors fail to discharge their debts as requested, creditors may exercise their rights, which include the right to take possession of and to sell the subjects.[39] If the creditor is unable to sell the subjects or part of them, a decree of foreclosure may be sought giving the right to the unsold portion of the property.[40]

4. Securities over Incorporeal Property

As far as incorporeal property is concerned it is not possible to effect delivery of such items by their very nature. They may be transferred in security by a written assignation followed by intimation to the debtor. Both these elements must be included. Thus there would be no preferential right created by the transfer of a policy of insurance without intimation to the insurance company.[41] The position as regards shares in a company is a little more complex. Whilst these may be used as a security, through transferring them to the creditor subject to an obligation to retransfer, this is a cumbersome and expensive process. Simply depositing the share certificates effects no security.[42] A duly-executed transfer of the shares may be given to the creditor with the certificates, and this would allow the creditor to compete, provided that the transfer is sent in for registration within six months of the debtor's sequestra-

---

[32] Formerly Register of Sasines and now (under Land Registration (Scotland) Act 1979) the Land Register.

[33] Conveyancing and Feudal Reform (Scotland) Act 1970, s. 11(1).

[34] See Sched. 3.

[35] s. 13(1).

[36] s. 13(3)(*b*) and Sched. 5, Note 2.

[37] s. 18.

[38] s. 19.

[39] s. 20.

[40] s. 28.

[41] *Wylie's* v. *McJannet* (1901) 4 F. 195.

[42] *Gourlay* v. *Mackie* (1887) 14 R. 403.

tion.[43] This would be effectual even where the transfer is registered after the petition for sequestration of the debtor had been presented, provided that this was done before the trustee had taken steps to register as owner of the shares.[44] The effectiveness of the practice of depositing the share certificates with blank transfers is untested in the Scottish courts, and could run up against problems in terms of the Blank Bonds and Trusts Act 1696 which declares that instruments which are blank in the name of the creditor are void.[45]

5. HYPOTHEC

Hypothec provides a security without transfer of possession. Hypothecs may be legal or conventional. There are a number of specific situations where a legal hypothec is available—superior, landlord, solicitor and certain maritime forms. Superiors have rights of hypothec for feuduty over the goods brought on to the property by their vassals. The landlord's hypothec applies in the same way over tenants' property for rent. These rights are subject to the limitations on the subjects which may form part of the hypothec under legislation.[46] Solicitors have, both at common law and under statute, rights to have the expenses of an action met out of any expenses the client may be entitled to, as well as out of most property recovered in the action.[47] There are certain maritime hypothecs which give creditors the right in security over the ship without possession on a variety of questions, including to seamen for wages, to salvors for any sum due for salvage, to anyone for damages caused directly by the ship, and for repairers to cover repairs executed or necessaries supplied in a foreign port. These rights may be enforced by sale, and they rank before mortgage holders. The only recognised conventional hypothecs relate to bonds available in maritime dealings. Bottomry is available to creditors over a ship without possession, whilst *respondentia* is available for the cargo. Their rôle has been displaced by the introduction of the floating charge.[48]

---

[43] Bankruptcy (Scotland) Act 1985, s. 36; *Guild* v. *Young* (1884) 22 S.L.R. 520.
[44] *Morrison* v. *Harrison* (1876) 3 R. 406.
[45] *Shaw* v. *Caledonian Ry.* (1890) 17 R. 466.
[46] Hypothec Abolition (Scotland) Act 1880 on leases of rural subjects.
[47] Solicitors (Scotland) Act 1980.
[48] See above.

6. Lien

Related to hypothec is the notion of the lien. This provides a right to retain goods in settlement of a debt. Here, perhaps, the best-known is that of the innkeeper for unpaid bills. The lien gives a right to remain in possession of a subject which belongs to another party who is failing to meet some obligation. The right extends to holding the subjects on limited title and to reconvey the property. Typically under statute is the right of the repairer to dispose of uncollected goods after a certain period of time.[49] There is a general lien which is a right to retain until some balance arising on a contract is discharged. No lien founded on possession can be asserted if it would conflict with the express or implied terms of the contract under which possession is obtained. The courts exercise an equitable control over liens.[50] The primary purpose of lien is to act as lever on the debtor, but if this fails then the items may be sold.

Special liens exists in a variety of situations, most notably in the employer/employee relationship and in certain relationships of agency like bankers, factors and solicitors. Since there is a mutual relationship, in contracts of employment employees, who are in possession of articles belonging to the employer, are entitled to retain them until they have been paid for their work on that contract. It does not require there to be proof of a particular custom of trade. It is not material that no work has been done on the article in question.[51] Bankers have a general lien over all bills, notes and negotiable securities lodged in their capacity as a monetary agent rather than merely for safe keeping. The lien covers any balance due by the customer.[52] Express notice or previous knowledge of the true ownership of negotiable instruments lodged by stockbrokers alters the reasonable assumption that these belonged to the stockbroker.[53] Factors or mercantile agents[54] have a general lien over all goods, bills money or documents belonging to the employer which have come into their possession in the course of their employment.[55] It covers all advances made to the principal, the factor's salary or commission and any liabilities incurred on the principal's

---

[49] Disposal of Uncollected Goods Act 1952, which provides for the sale of goods which are uncollected.

[50] *Garscadden* v. *Ardrossan Dry Dock Co.*, 1910 S.C. 178.

[51] *Meikle & Wilson* v. *Pollard* (1880) 8 R. 69.

[52] Bell, *Prin.*, § 1451.

[53] *National Bank* v. *Dickie's Tr.* (1895) 22 R. 740.

[54] See Factors Act 1889, s. 1(1), but note that the term has been held to extend, as far as lien is concerned, to auctioneers and stockbrokers.

[55] Bell, *op. cit.*, § 1451.

behalf.[56] It does not cover debts due to the factor on another account, in the event of the bankruptcy of the principal.[57]

Solicitors have a general lien over all papers placed by clients in their hands. This includes title-deeds and wills. Solicitors may not obstruct the course of justice by refusing to produce papers for an action,[58] except where these relate to cases against them for alleged professional negligence.[59] The lien covers business accounts and advances made in the ordinary course of business such as to counsel or witnesses.[60] A similar general lien is not enjoyed by parallel professionals like accountants, whose lien over papers only relates to work done in connection with those particular papers rather than the whole professional account.[61] The lien operates against clients rather than against third parties. The solicitor must give up all papers to a company liquidator or trustee in sequestration, subject to an implied reservation of the lien. The solicitor's expenses will be postponed to those of the liquidation or sequestration.[62] The lien only gives a right of retention and does not permit disposal and is of limited value when there is no estate from which the expenses can be taken.[63]

Innkeepers have a lien over the ordinary items of luggage of their guests for the amount of the bill,[64] but this does not cover the clothes of the guest.[65] It does not cover articles not brought as luggage but hired during the stay,[66] nor items delivered by a third party for the use of the guest.[67] The Hotel Proprietors Act 1956 makes certain modifications to the common law excluding vehicles or property therein as well as horse, harness and other equipment.[68] The fact that an item belonged to another person and the hotel proprietor knew of this does not prevent the sale of the item.[69] An innkeeper is entitled by statute, after advertisement to sell by auction goods

---

[56] *Glendinning* v. *Hope*, 1911 S.C.(H.L.) 73.
[57] *Miller* v. *McNair* (1852) 14 D. 955.
[58] *Callmen* v. *Bell* (1793) Mor. 6255.
[59] *Yau* v. *Ogilvie & Co.*, 1985 S.L.T. 91.
[60] *Richardson* v. *Merry* (1863) 1 M. 940.
[61] *Findlay* v. *Waddell*, 1910 S.C. 670.
[62] *Miln's Factor* v. *Spence's Trs.*, 1927 S.L.T. 425.
[63] *Garden, Haig Scott & Wallace* v. *Stevenson's Tr.*, 1962 S.C. 51.
[64] Bell, *Prin.*, § 1428.
[65] *Sunbolf* v. *Alford* (1838) 3 Mees. & W. 248.
[66] *Broadwood* v. *Granara* (1854) 10 Ex. 417.
[67] *Bermans and Nathans Ltd.* v. *Weibye*, 1983 S.L.T. 299.
[68] s. 2(2).
[69] *Bermans and Nathans Ltd.*, above.

brought to or left in the inn, provided that the debt for board and lodging is outstanding for at least six weeks. Any surplus is to be accounted for to the guest.[70]

---

[70] Innkeepers Act 1878, s. 1.

Chapter 11

SUBSIDIARY PROPERTY RIGHTS

THERE are certain categories of property rights which provide benefits to those who enjoy them which are more restricted than full ownership. *Liferents* are a creature of Scots common law. The status of *licences*, especially where residential accommodation is concerned, is less well-defined. *Occupancy rights* can be created by wills and trusts, as well as existing in a slightly different form as the creation of statute. There is an extensive case law on liferents, although the other two categories have been discussed less in the courts.

1. LIFERENTS

Property may be enjoyed by individuals during their lifetime only. Their status is similar to that of a tenant. They may enjoy the fruits of the property, as well as being responsible for the annual costs which an owner would have to meet. The rights of the liferenter are determined by the document creating the liferent. However, the common law has established various rules which are to operate where the document is silent. A liferent has been defined as "the right to enjoy the use or the fruits of a subject without destroying or encroaching upon the substance."[1]

The liferenter receives the fruits and income yielded up during the occupancy. The fiar receives the capital or the property itself. This arrangement generally operates where a person wishes to pass ownership of some item of property into the hands of another but reserve the use of the property to a third person during that person's lifetime. Thus a regular arrangement in Scots law has been for a father to leave the family home in fee to the children but to reserve a liferent over the property to his wife. The wife is given occupancy and use of the house during her lifetime. The children are, however, left the ownership of the house. Their rights of occupancy only attach on the death of the mother. A different example of a liferent

---

[1] W. Dobie, *Manual of the Law of Liferent and Fee in Scotland* (1941) at p. 1.

and fee relationship is that of the mother receiving the right to use the property or receive the income in the case of a liferent over investments, the offspring receiving the property or the capital invested on her death.

Liferents can be created in favour of any person, and the right to the fee can go to any person or organisation. As its name suggests, a liferent comes to an end at the death of the liferenter. Other dates, however, can be set for the dissolution of the liferent, such as the liferenter attaining the age of majority or upon his marriage. A liferent must be distinguished from other types of limited property rights.

Right of occupancy

A liferent is more than a right of occupancy, since a liferenter is entitled to use the rents from the property for his own purpose and has a corresponding obligation to pay the burdens of the property such as feuduty.[2]

Annuity

An annuity can be defined as a limited right to a periodical payment of money which comes as an equal share each year. Since an annuitant has to receive a fixed sum each year, it may be that in times of recession some of the capital will have to be realised in order to pay annuitants their income. This is the single most important distinguishing feature between an annuity and a liferent, the fact that an annuity may encroach upon the capital.[3]

Classification of Liferents

The law recognises three distinctive groups of liferents:

(a) *Liferents implied by law and conventional liferents*

The liferents terse and courtsy[4] were implied by the common law until 1964. A conventional liferent is one created by some person's express wish. An obvious example of this type would be a testator creating a liferent-and-fee situation in a will.

(b) *Liferent by constitution and by reservation*

The former, often called simple liferent, is created where the

---

[2] *Clark and Others* (1871) 9 M. 435.
[3] *Colquhoun's Trs.* v. *Colquhoun*, 1922 S.C. 32.
[4] W. M. Gordon, *Scottish Land Law*, on p. 474.

owner of property grants to someone else a liferent over it. In such a case the fee can either be retained by the grantor or sold to a third party. The latter occurs where owners of property sell the fee but retain the liferent for themselves.

(c) *Proper liferent and beneficiary liferent*

The former is created by direct grant (*e.g.* in a will). In the latter the relationship of liferenter and fiar is created through the operation of a trust. In such a case the property is actually vested in trustees, with the liferenter receiving a right to benefit termed a *jus crediti*.

Since a liferent is supposed to exist in a way which means that the property or the capital itself cannot be destroyed, a liferent cannot be created over a "fungible"—*i.e.* something destroyed in its use.

The Rights of the Liferenter

The liferenter is entitled to the fruits of the property but not to anything which is part of the corpus of the property or the capital. The costs of repair over the property will be borne by either liferenter or fiar depending on whether the repair is exigible out of interest or out of capital. Whether the cost of repair is exigible out of capital or interest depends on a complicated test as to whether the repair is a once-and-for-all payment or something which is likely to recur annually. The liferenter is entitled to ordinary windfalls of timber on the property. The fiar, on the other hand, is entitled to the wood growing on the estate and to any trees blown down in an exceptional storm. The liferenter is permitted to cut wood which has reached maturity.[5]

(a) *Alimentary liferents*

An alimentary liferent is one which is intended for the support of the liferenter. An alimentary liferent is one which has been declared to be so by its creator. It cannot, therefore, be assigned by the liferenter, nor can it be attached by that person's creditors nor, once accepted, can it be renounced.[6]

(b) *Extinction of liferents*

A liferent is extinguished generally upon the death of the liferenter. It can also be discharged because of some other event, or upon

---

[5] Dobie, *op. cit.*, Pt. III, Chap. 4.
[6] *Dewar's Trs.* v. *Dewar*, 1910 S.C. 730.

the liferenter renouncing it, or upon the liferent and fee becoming vested in the same person.[7]

(c) *Apportionment of income*

At common law income accrues on a daily basis. The apportionment of income can create problems:

(i) where during the lifetime of the liferenter stocks and shares are actually sold off. In this case the liferenter is entitled to a compensatory payment of a sum equivalent to the dividend which is likely to have been paid on the shares at the next date a dividend was payable.

(ii) where the liferenter dies during the financial year. In this case apportionment will be necessary in order to determine how much of the dividend will go to the representatives of the liferenter and how much to the fiar. This apportionment is done on a time basis, and under the provisions of the Apportionment Act 1870 dividends accrue day-to-day and must be calculated on that basis.

2. LICENCES AND SERVICE OCCUPANCY

Provided certain requirements are satisfied a lease confers rights against the whole world, rather than simply providing personal rights enforceable against the original landlord. These requirements are that there must be agreement, heritable subjects, rent, a termination date and possession. In England and Wales the law has recognised since the seventeenth century a lesser form of right called a licence. This involves the landlord in providing less than the full range of rights to the occupier. This has occurred where the relationship between the parties is close and the intention is assumed not to be to create a landlord-and-tenant contract. This has occurred typically where the parties are related or are friends.

Where a person is allowed to occupy property rent-free and where there is no rent and none contemplated, then this will not amount to a lease. There has in the past been a willingness of the courts to say that parties in the relationship of landlord and tenant, without any rent agreed, intend that the annual value or market rent of the premises shall be taken as the rent.[8] In this instance the company occupied subjects for a proposed oil terminal from July 1974 whilst negotiations on the terms of the lease were conducted.

---

[7] *Martin* v. *Bannatyne* (1861) 23 D. 705.
[8] *Glen* v. *Roy* (1882) 10 R. 239.

The oil terminal became operational in September 1978 but no lease had been agreed.

In situations where a contract does not consist of a grant of heritage but rather of the right to use a particular part of it or to put a particular part of it to some use, then there is a line of opinion that suggests that such occupancy should not be regarded as a lease. The alternative is to treat it on the same lines as the "licence" known in English law. This operates in commercial transactions extensively. An important factor in determining if commercial contracts for occupancy of land were leases was the question of exclusivity of the possession. If possession was exclusive, then the agreement could be a lease. If, however, possession was only partial, then it could not be a lease. This was illustrated by two garage cases. In *Broomhill Motor Co.* v. *Assessor for Glasgow*[9] a number of lock-ups were let for rents which included water, heating, light and washing facilities and each occupant had a key. The garage company, though, had a right of access to the lock-ups to inspect and clean and the occupants were expected to, and in most cases did, obtain supplies from the garage. It was held that, as there was no independent occupation by the occupants, this contract was only a right to use defined portions of the premises for a limited purpose. By contrast, in *Chaplin* v. *Assessor for Perth*[10] the proprietor of a piece of ground erected a number of wooden lock-ups each with its own key, which were occupied by car owners under verbal agreements whereby he received a weekly or daily payment and whereby either party could terminate the agreement at a week's notice. Although no services were given, the occupiers were entitled to use free of charge a wash bed and a wooden shed. The agreements here gave the occupier exclusive possession during the period of occupation and so they were held to be leases.

The difficulty is that the limited case law in Scotland which is cited has been concerned essentially with what the status of an agreement is for the purposes of valuation and rating. The quite distinct issues raised by licences in the context of residential property have never been fully discussed in Scotland. The nearest which the courts have come to discussing this issue is in a case concerning an agreement to occupy a cottage for an unspecified period of time in exchange for certain estate management duties. In *Scottish Residential Estates Development Co. Ltd.* v. *Henderson*,[11] the approach adopted by the Inner House was that their task was to construe the intention of the

---

[9] 1927 S.C. 447.
[10] 1947 S.C. 373.
[11] Court of Session, May 17, 1990.

parties. Since the agreement of the parties specifically indicated that no relationship of landlord and tenant was to be entered by the parties and since there was no ish, their Lordships felt that with this crucial feature of the agreement missing there was no lease. However, such an approach contrasts with that taken by the House of Lords in looking at evasions of the Rent Acts.[12]

Whilst the valuation cases are cited as examples of how the distinction between leases and licences would be treated by the Scottish courts, there is no traditional recognition of such a second-class tenancy right in residential property prior to the introduction of notions of security of tenure. It would be strange if landlords were able to avoid the impact of security of tenure as it applies to tenancies by simply renaming their contracts licences. The fact that in reality full possession is given would even in England qualify for the agreement to operate as a tenancy.[13]

As far as occupancy by employees is concerned, this may involve a lease. If there are no express provisions this limited right, ceasing on the termination of the employment, may be inferred. Each case will be judged on its particular circumstances. A service occupancy (*i.e.* the limited right of occupancy) will be inferred only if the occupation of the house is necessary for the performance of the employee's duties. It is not enough that one is only eligible for the house if one is employed in certain jobs. Thus, for example, a company employee living in a company-owned house, where there was nothing expressly stated about the occupancy, might well on ceasing to work for the company be able to live on in the particular house, as it was not necessary for the performance of company duties. In such circumstances his occupancy might well in fact be a lease rather than a service occupancy.

The test as to the distinction between a lease and a service occupancy is whether the occupation itself is that of an employee. A baker occupied one of the three houses in Dingwall which his employer found for him and to whom he paid a small rent. He was told this "went with the job," but not that the occupation would cease with his employment. This was held to be a lease, as where he lived in no way related to his efficiency as a baker.[14] Where, however, a sum was deducted from a teacher's salary equal to the annual value of the Education Authority's house occupied by him, it was held that the contract was one of the service, not of lease.[15]

---

[12] *Antoniades* v. *Villiers* [1989] 3 W.L.R. 1205.
[13] *Street* v. *Mountford* [1985] A.C. 809.
[14] *MacGregor* v. *Dunnett*, 1949 S.C. 510.
[15] *Pollock* v *Assessor for Inverness-shire*, 1923 S.C. 693.

3. RIGHTS OF OCCUPANCY

These occur in both a common law and statutory form. Under Scots succession law it has been possible for individuals to provide that another individual shall have the right to occupy property in accordance with the wishes of the testator. The courts have recognised these wishes along with the various different restrictions which have accompanied such testamentary documents. These rights and the distinction between them and liferents were discussed in a series of cases in the nineteenth and early twentieth centuries.[16] The beneficiary who enjoys a mere right of occupancy thus may not let the premises and is only liable for tenant's burdens.

In addition the 1980s saw the introduction of statutory rights for spouses and cohabitees to prevent them being evicted from the matrimonial home and allowing them to prevent the sale or disposition of the said home. These rights are enshrined in the Matrimonial Homes (Family Protection) (Scotland) Act 1981. This legislation provides rights and remedies which are largely temporary pending a divorce settlement.

The Nature of Statutory Occupancy Rights

Where the spouse who is owner or tenant refuses to allow the other partner the right to enter and occupy, then this right may only be exercised with the leave of either the sheriff court or Court of Session, *i.e.* there should be no "self-help."[17]

These rights are exercisable not only by spouses but also by a man and woman living as man and wife.[18] In addition the law also allows such a partner to bring in any child of the family.[19]

The Property Covered by Occupancy Rights

Occupancy rights can be exercised over the matrimonial home. This is defined as:

---

[16] See above at p. 168; discussed by Dobie, *op. cit.*, Pt. III, Chap. 7.

[17] *Nimmo* v. *Nimmo*, Glasgow Sh.Ct., Aug. 12, 1983 (noted in (1984) 29 J.L.S. 4; see also D. I. Nichols and M. C. Meston, *The Matrimonial Homes (Family Protection) (Scotland) Act 1981* (1986), and A. Jackson, M. Robertson and P. Robson, *The Operation of the Matrimonial Homes (Family Protection) (Scotland) Act 1981* (1988).

[18] s. 18.

[19] Since the Law Reform (Misc. Provs.) (Scotland) Act 1985, s. 13(3) amended the 1981 Act.

"any house, caravan, houseboat or other structure which has been provided or has been made available by one or both of the spouses, or has become a family residence."[20]

Garden ground and other ground normally occupied with or required for the amenity and convenience of the dwelling in question is also included. In general terms, where a property is tenanted or owned by one of the partners prior to marriage/cohabitation then this would become the matrimonial home upon marriage or when the couple can be said to be a cohabiting couple. The relevant factors in deciding when a couple are cohabiting in terms of the 1981 Act are the length of time for which they have been living together and whether there are any children of the relationship.[21]

Property excluded from being a "matrimonial home"
Where a residence is provided or made available by one spouse for that spouse to reside in separately from the other spouse, then this does not amount to a matrimonial home.[22]

By the same token there is authority which indicates that where a property is provided for the other spouse to live, this is not a matrimonial home either. This interpretation of the 1981 Act was made by Lord Mayfield in the Outer House in *McRobbie* v. *McRobbie*.[23] Here the husband had purchased a house for the wife and child to live in after separation and never lived in the property himself. His Lordship was not satisfied that this was a matrimonial home in terms of the Act.

Regulation of Occupancy Rights

Apart from providing a guarantee that one spouse cannot simply turn the other one out into the street, there are elaborate provisions which provide that the courts may not only declare and order the enforcement of occupancy rights but also restrict, regulate and protect such rights.[24] The criteria for such restriction, regulation and protection, etc., are whether it is just and reasonable having regard to all the circumstances of the case including—

[20] s. 22.
[21] s. 18(2).
[22] Amendment introduced by Law Reform (Miscellaneous Provisions) (Scotland) Act 1985, s. 13(10).
[23] O.H., Aug. 3, 1983 (noted at (1984) 29 J.L.S. 5).
[24] s. 3(1).

(a) the conduct of the spouses in relation to each other and otherwise;

(b) the respective needs and financial resources of the spouses;

(c) the needs of any child of the family;

(d) the extent to which the matrimonial home is used in connection with a trade, business or profession; and

(e) whether there has been an offer of suitable alternative accommodation.[25]

In *Fyfe* v. *Fyfe*[26] Lord Mayfield dealt with a case involving a wife who had been hospitalised, who was suffering from multiple sclerosis, and who was initially successful in the sheriff court[27] in preventing her husband selling the matrimonial home. She then sought to have her occupancy rights declared, as she hoped to be able to return to the house. However, she was unsuccessful and in due course the sale was allowed to go ahead.[28] The issue of suspension of occupancy rights is dealt with elsewhere.[29]

---

[25] s. 3(3).

[26] O.H., Dec. 12, 1985 (noted in *Scottish Housing Law News* (1987) 2/29).

[27] See below at p. 196.

[28] See below at p. 196.

[29] See below at pp. 198–200.

CHAPTER 12

RIGHTS RELATED TO PROPERTY OCCUPATION

THERE are a number of rights which relate to the occupation of property which are the product of statutes. These are for the most part of recent origin and include *rights to be housed*, the *right to be rehoused*, the *right to purchase rented housing* and the *right to dispossess co-occupiers*.

1. RIGHTS TO BE HOUSED

There are two kinds of statutory obligation on local authorities to provide housing for individuals in their district. In the first place, since 1919 there has been a general obligation on local authorities to provide accommodation for certain people in their area.

However, this is a general right and as such is not directly enforceable by individuals through the courts. The view is taken that the authority have the discretion vested in them.[1] Under statute every local authority must consider the housing conditions in their area and the needs for further housing accommodation.[2] Local authorities must ensure that a reasonable preference is given to persons occupying houses which do not meet the tolerable standard, who are occupying overcrowded houses, who have large families or are living under unsatisfactory housing conditions, and homeless persons.[3]

Until 1919 there was no such general obligation, and what local authority housing existed came from local initiatives aimed at clearing away city-centre slums in such towns as Glasgow, Edinburgh and Greenock. In 1917 a Royal Commission into the housing conditions of the industrial and agricultural workforce (set up after disturbances over housing conditions in the Lanarkshire coalfield in 1912) found that investment in building housing for the working classes below the level of the prosperous artisan had all but dried

---

[1] *Cameron* v. *Inverness C.C.*, 1935 S.L.T. 281.
[2] Housing (Scotland) Act 1987, s. 1.
[3] s. 20(1).

up. This structural failure of the traditional means of supply of rented housing provided the impetus for imposing an obligation in place of the power to build.

Each local housing authority (*i.e.* the district—not the regional—council) must consider the housing conditions in their district and the needs of the district with respect to the provision of further housing accommodation.[4] In considering the needs of their area for further housing the local authority must have regard to the special needs of chronically sick or disabled persons. The authority may carry out its duty, after assessing the local need, by erecting, converting, acquiring or altering, enlarging, repairing or improving houses or other buildings (with the limitation that, where a garden is provided, it must not exceed one acre). Having provided such accommodation the authority may lease it or sell it.

(a) Selection of Tenants

There are various restrictions on how the local authority may go about the process of selecting tenants. The authority must, in addition to complying with the requirements of sex discrimination and race relations legislation, follow certain rules as laid down in the Housing (Scotland) Act 1987. Part 1 of the 1987 Act vests the general management, regulation and control of houses held for housing purposes in and to be exercised by the authority. There are two levels to the operation of this discretion.

(b) Admission to the Housing List

In considering whether an applicant is entitled to be admitted to a housing list, a local authority must take no account of the age of the applicant provided that person has attained the age of 16 years; or the income of the applicant and his family; or whether, or to what value, the applicant or any of his family owns or has owned heritable or moveable property; any outstanding liability (for payment of rent or otherwise); or whether the applicant is living with, or in the same house as his spouse or cohabitee.[5] In addition admission to the waiting list must not depend on residence where an applicant is employed in the area of the local authority, has been offered employment in the area of the local authority, wishes to move into

---

[4] Pt. I, s. 1.
[5] s. 19.

the area of the local authority and the local authority is satisfied that his purpose in doing so is to seek employment or has attained the age of 60 years and wishes to move into the area of the local authority to be nearer a younger relative; or has special social or medical reasons for requiring to be housed within the area of the local housing authority.[6]

Where the rules of the authority give priority to applicants on its waiting list, it shall apply these no less favourably to those groups noted above than it applies them to any tenant living in the area with similar housing needs who is seeking a transfer to another house belonging to the local authority.[7]

(i) **Priority on the housing list**

A local authority must secure, in relation to all houses held by them for housing purposes, that in the selection of their tenants a *reasonable preference* is given to various groups[8]—persons occupying housing which does not meet the tolerable standard; those in overcrowded houses; those with large families; those living under unsatisfactory housing conditions; homeless persons to whom they have a statutory duty (see below at pp. 179–187).

(ii) **Prohibitions in allocation**

No account must be taken, in allocating local authority housing, to the following matters—the length of time the applicant has resided in the area, any outstanding liability (for payment of rent or otherwise) attributable to the tenancy of any house of which the applicant is not and was not when the liability was incurred a tenant, age, income or value of any heritage/moveables. This is particularly important where there is a relationship breakdown. In addition there must be no requirement that an application must have been in force for a minimum period or that a divorce or separation be obtained or that the applicant no longer is living with or in the same house as some other person.

Specific enforceable obligations are also imposed by statute in respect of homeless persons, but are of a different kind. These involve securing that accommodation be made available to those homeless applicants who satisfy the local authority that they meet the tests imposed under the legislation.[9]

---

[6] *Ibid.*
[7] *Ibid.*
[8] s. 20.
[9] ss. 28, 31 and 32.

(iii) **Homeless individuals and families**

The legislation is unequivocal as to the existence of housing duties towards qualifying homeless applicants.[10] In order to qualify for direct assistance *i.e.* the provision of housing, a person must be homeless or threatened with homelessness. In addition to those who have no right to occupy accommodation, anyone occupying unsatisfactory accommodation may be entitled to be provided with accommodation. It includes those who have no accommodation in Scotland or England and Wales,[11] as well as someone living in temporary refuge accommodation such as night shelters[12] and women's refuges,[13] or who had accommodation outside Great Britain. Applicants are treated as having no accommodation where they do not have accommodation which they have the right or permission to occupy along with the members of the family unit.[14] The right or permission can be express or implied. It may stem from a rule of law or enactment such as the rights of occupancy of a non-entitled spouse or cohabitee under the Matrimonial Homes (Family Protection) (Scotland) Act 1981.[15]

In addition, a person who actually has accommodation is still regarded as homeless[16] where they cannot secure entry to the property, such as after forcible eviction by a landlord. The fact that one has a housing right which may not be put into effect is recognised as amounting to homelessness. It also covers housing which had been made the subject of a closing order thus rendering the right of ownership or tenancy inoperable. Accommodation is also unacceptable if it is probable that occupation will lead to violence from some other person residing in the property,[17] or if there are threats from another resident and that person is likely to carry out the threats. In addition the legislation since 1991 covers the situation of those who previously resided with the applicant whether in that accommodation or elsewhere and it is probable that occupation will lead to violence or threats of violence which are likely to be carried out. In addition the changes introduced in 1990[18] provide that a person is homeless if it is accommodation which it would not

[10] s. 31(2).

[11] s. 24.

[12] *R.* v. *Waveney B.C., ex p. Bowers, The Times,* May 25, 1982.

[13] *R.* v. *Ealing L.B.C., ex p. Sidhu* [1982] 2 H.L.R. 45.

[14] s. 24(2).

[15] ss. 1 (spouses) and 18 (cohabitees).

[16] s. 24(3).

[17] *R.* v. *Broxbourne B.C., ex p. Willmoth (No. 2)* [1989] 21 H.L.R. 415.

[18] Law Reform (Miscellaneous Provisions) (Scotland) Act 1990, s. 65, amending s. 24 of the Housing (Scotland) Act 1987.

be reasonable to continue to occupy. This would cover violence or threats of violence from neighbours as well as accommodation which is in poor physical condition but does not meet the specific tests as to overcrowding and being a threat to health. Applicants are also homeless if they have accommodation but it is statutorily overcrowded and may endanger the health of the occupants.

People are also entitled to assistance if they are threatened with homelessness, if it is likely that they will become homeless within 28 days.[19] This covers those who have tenancy rights but which are likely to be lost through a successful possession action in the courts. It also covers situations where permission to stay is withdrawn as by a parent from a child.

(c) **Priority Need**

There are two further hurdles which must be satisfied. The applicants for assistance as homeless persons must have a priority need. The following have a statutory priority need for accommodation— women who are pregnant, people with dependent children or who are vulnerable or are homeless as a result of an emergency. Within the category of vulnerability the legislation indicates four specific conditions—old age; mental illness; mental handicap; physical disability. In addition a person may be vulnerable as a result of any other special reason.[20] The general test of vulnerability according to the Court of Appeal depends on whether a person is "less able to fend [for himself] so that injury or detriment will result when a less vulnerable man will be able to cope without harmful effects."[21]

(d) **Intentional Homelessness**

Local authorities' obligations to provide accommodation to homeless applicants in priority need are restricted to providing temporary accommodation where the homelessness is deemed to be intentional. Applicants become homeless intentionally if they deliberately do or fail to do anything in consequence of which they cease to occupy accommodation which is available for their occupation and which it would have been reasonable for them to continue

---

[19] s. 24(4).
[20] s. 25(1)(c).
[21] *R.* v. *Waveney D.C., ex p. Bowers* [1982] 3 All E.R. 727.

to occupy.[22] The obligation is restricted to providing accommodation for such period as they consider will give a reasonable opportunity to secure that accommodation becomes available for occupation by the applicant.[23] Actions which have resulted in the loss of accommodation and a finding of intentionality include wilful non-payment of rent[24]; voluntarily terminating a tenancy[25]; giving up a job with "tied accommodation"[26]; failing to maintain a satisfactory tenancy[27]; moving from abroad without ensuring that there is accommodation available in Great Britain[28]; and moving from another part of the United Kingdom without ensuring that permanent accommodation is available.[29]

When looking at whether the applicant is intentionally homeless the authority must consider whether the applicant has given up accommodation which is sufficient for both the applicant and any other person who might reasonably be expected to live with him.[30] The fact that accommodation was previously available cannot displace the requirement to make inquiries at the time of application.[31] Accommodation offered but never accepted by the applicant is not available for occupation.[32]

The authority must have regard to the housing conditions which led the applicant to give up the accommodation.[33] Overcrowded conditions and damp unhealthy conditions may lead to a finding that it would not have been reasonable to continue to live in that accommodation.[34] In deciding whether or not it would have been reasonable to continue to occupy the available accommodation the authority may look at the general circumstances prevailing in rela-

---

[22] s. 26(1).

[23] s. 31(3).

[24] *Robinson* v. *Torbay B.C.* [1982] 1 All E.R. 726; *Hynds* v. *Midlothian D.C.*, 1986 S.L.T. 54.

[25] *Dyson* v. *Kerrier D.C.* [1980] 1 W.L.R. 1205; *Mazzaccherini* v. *Argyll and Bute D.C.*, 1987 S.C.L.R. 475.

[26] *R.* v. *North Devon D.C., ex p. Lewis* [1981] 1 All E.R. 27; but *cf. R.* v. *Kensington and Chelsea L.B.C., ex p. Minton, The Guardian,* Aug. 8, 1988.

[27] *Mackenzie* v. *West Lothian D.C.*, 1979 S.C. 433; *R.* v. *Salford City Council, ex p. Devenport* (1983) 82 L.G.R. 89.

[28] *R.* v. *Tower Hamlets L.B.C., ex p. Monaf* (1988) 20 H.L.R. 529.

[29] *R.* v. *Peterborough D.C., ex p. McKernan* (Q.B.D.) July 17, 1987; *R.* v. *Vale of White Horse D.C., ex p. Preen* (Q.B.D.) April 18, 1983.

[30] s. 41.

[31] *R.* v. *Westminster C.C., ex p. Ali* (1983) 11 H.L.R. 83.

[32] *R.* v. *Westminster C.C., ex p. Chambers* (1982) 81 L.G.R. 401; *R* v. *Ealing L.B.C., ex p. McBain* [1986] 1 All E.R. 13.

[33] *R.* v. *Eastleigh B.C., ex p. Beattie (No. 1)* (1983) 10 H.L.R. 134.

[34] *R.* v. *Westminster City Council, ex p. Ali, supra.*

tion to housing in the district of the local authority.[35] In addition to looking at the housing suitability, factors personal to the circumstances of the applicant are relevant.[36] These have included lack of employment prospects,[37] marital breakdown,[38] threats of violence from outwith the household,[39] medical problems of applicant,[40] unavailability of welfare benefits.[41]

There must be a direct link between the actions of the applicant and the loss of accommodation and the homelessness must be a consequence of these actions.[42] Authorities are entitled to look back to events in the past which triggered off the current state of homelessness.[43] The authority must look at the question of causation at the date the applicant became homeless rather than the date of application.[44] The disadvantages of intentional homelessness will not be avoided by an applicant giving up accommodation and obtaining other temporary accommodation.[45] Accommodation which has failed to break the chain of causation includes off-season holiday lets,[46] holiday lets,[47] staying with friends or relatives,[48] lodgings without security of tenure[49] and bed-and-breakfast accommodation.[50] The effect of obtaining one of the newer post-1980 tenancies without security of tenure is not fully settled.[51] If, however, another cause intervenes to result in the loss of accommodation where, but for this occurrence, the applicant would have been intentionally homeless the same principle applies. The applicant cannot be then deemed intentionally homeless.[52]

---

[35] s. 26(4).
[36] *R.* v. *Hammersmith and Fulham L.B.C., ex p. Duro Rama* (1983) 81 L.G.R. 702.
[37] *R.* v. *Kensington and Chelsea L.B.C., ex p. Cunha* (1989) 21 H.L.R. 16.
[38] *R.* v. *Basingstoke and Deane B.C., ex p. Bassett* (1983) 10 H.L.R. 125.
[39] *R.* v. *Hillingdon B.C., ex p. H.* (1988) 20 H.L.R. 544.
[40] *R.* v. *Wycombe D.C., ex p. Homes* (Q.B.D.) Dec. 1, 1988.
[41] *R.* v. *Hammersmith and Fulham L.B.C., ex p. Duro Rama* (1983) 81 L.G.R. 702.
[42] s. 26(1).
[43] *Hynds* v. *Midlothian D.C.*, 1986 S.L.T. 54; *Mazzaccherini* v. *Argyll and Bute D.C.*, 1987 S.C.L.R. 475.
[44] *Din* v. *Wandsworth L.B.C.* [1983] 1 A.C. 657.
[45] *Dyson* v. *Kerrier D.C.* [1980] 1 W.L.R. 1205.
[46] *Ibid.*
[47] *Lambert* v. *Ealing L.B.C.* [1982] 2 All E.R. 394.
[48] *De Falco* v. *Crawley B.C.* [1980] Q.B. 460.
[49] *Mazzaccherini* v. *Argyll and Bute D.C.*, 1987 S.C.L.R. 475; *R.* v. *Merton L.B.C., ex p. Ruffle* (1989) 21 H.L.R. 361.
[50] *R.* v. *Harrow L.B.C., ex p. Holland* (1982) L.A.G. 113.
[51] *R.* v. *Christchurch B.C., ex p. Conway* (1987) 19 H.L.R. 238.
[52] *Gloucester City Council* v. *Miles* (1985) 85 L.G.R. 607.

There is a difference between actions which are deliberate and those which are involuntary or largely attributable to external factors. The former include failure to keep up mortgage or rent payments because of real personal or financial difficulties, arrears of a partner, victims fleeing domestic violence, pregnant women deemed intentionally homeless on account of their pregnancy, people no longer able to afford rent or mortgage payments and living conditions which have degenerated to a point where they cannot reasonably be expected to live. Non-deliberate actions and omissions accepted by the courts have included failing to pay rent or mortgage payments through financial hardship,[53] leaving accommodation early where there is no effective defence to a possession action,[54] and fleeing violence and threats of violence from political opponents.[55]

Where acts or omissions are in good faith made by a person who was unaware of any relevant fact, they are not to be treated as deliberate.[56] Examples of persons who might be regarded as unaware of a relevant fact are those who get into rent arrears unaware of their entitlement to welfare benefits and those who leave rented accommodation on receipt of a notice to quit, unaware of their rights of security of tenure.[57] The courts have accepted as unaware of a relevant fact a young woman coming from abroad who assumed that availability of accommodation for her brothers meant that she would be treated the same by her father on her entry into Britain,[58] a tenant who failed to appreciate the need as indicated in correspondence to respond promptly in order to secure a tenancy renewal,[59] and a young woman who did not believe her father's threats to refuse her re-entry to the family home if she stayed with her mother while pursuing a higher education course away from home.[60] The acceptance of a mistaken belief is subject to the proviso that the belief must be intrinsically reasonable.[61]

Although it has been pointed out that the legislation refers to an

[53] *R.* v. *Wyre B.C., ex p. Joyce* (1983) 11 H.L.R. 72.
[54] *R.* v. *Portsmouth City Council, ex p. Knight* (1984) 82 L.G.R. 184 (tied accommodation and dismissal); *R.* v. *Surrey Heath B.C., ex p. Li* (1984) 16 H.L.R. 79 (licensees).
[55] *R.* v. *Westminster City Council, ex p. Iqbal* (Q.B.D.), Oct. 21, 1988.
[56] s. 26(3).
[57] *Code of Guidance* (S.O.E.D.) April 1991, para. 4.5.8.
[58] *R.* v. *Wandsworth L.B.C., ex p. Rose* (1984) 11 H.L.R. 105.
[59] *R.* v. *Christchurch B.C., ex p. Conway* (1987) 19 H.L.R. 287.
[60] *Wincentzen* v. *Monklands D.C.*, 1987 S.C.L.R. 712 (O.H.); 1988 S.L.T. 847 (I.H.).
[61] *Ibid., per* I.H.

applicant,[62] it has been suggested in the courts that the legislation, in practice, deals with the family unit.[63] This means that all members of the family unit are assumed to be party to the acts of one member. Accordingly if these acts lead to a finding of intentionality then this covers all the family unit.[64] There are some situations where it would be unreasonable to assume that, for example, one partner acquiesced in the actions or omissions amounting to intentionality.[65] The courts have recognised non-acquiescence in such situations as when the husband failed to heed the wife's urgings to pay the rent[66] or mortgage,[67] and the surrender of the tenancy by the wife when leaving her husband where there was a later reconciliation.[68] It is not enough to simply assert non-acquiescence.[69] However, this will be much easier to establish where there is some tangible evidence of non-acquiescence such as making payments towards paying off rent arrears.[70]

Local authorities must accept a different assessment by another authority on intentionality[71] where the applicant is referred back under the local connection provisions,[72] unless there is no sound basis for the rejection of the original decision.[73] This involves the second authority making full investigations, including getting the relevant information on which the first authority made its decision.[74] By the same token, where one authority makes a negative decision on intentionality and the unsuccessful homeless person applies elsewhere, the second authority normally must make its own investigations into the question of intentionality. It cannot simply assume the first authority's decision is correct without having grounds for such a belief.[75]

[62] *Hynds* v. *Midlothian D.C.*, 1986 S.L.T. 54.

[63] *Lewis* v. *North Devon D.C.* [1981] 1 All E.R. 27.

[64] *R.* v. *Swansea City Council, ex p. John* (1982) 9 H.L.R. 58.

[65] *Lewis, loc. cit.* at p. 31.

[66] *R.* v. *West Dorset D.C., ex p. Phillips* (1985) 17 H.L.R. 168; *R.* v. *East Northamptonshire D.C., ex p. Spruce* (1988) 20 H.L.R. 508.

[67] *R.* v. *Eastleigh B.C., ex p. Beattie* (1983) 10 H.L.R. 134.

[68] *R.* v. *Penwith D.C., ex p. Trevena* (1984) 17 H.L.R. 526.

[69] *Stewart* v. *Monklands D.C.*, 1987 S.L.T. 630; *R.* v. *East Hertfordshire D.C., ex p. Bannon* (1986) 18 H.L.R. 515.

[70] *R.* v. *Thanet D.C., ex p. Groves* (Q.B.D.) Dec. 19, 1988.

[71] *R.* v. *Slough B.C., ex p. Ealing L.B.C.* [1981] Q.B. 801.

[72] s. 33(2); see below at p. 00.

[73] *R.* v. *Tower Hamlets L.B.C., ex p. Camden L.B.C., The Times*, Dec. 12, 1988.

[74] *R.* v. *Newham L.B.C., ex p. Tower Hamlets Council, The Independent*, Oct. 26, 1990.

[75] *R.* v. *South Herefordshire D.C., ex p. Miles* (1983) 17 H.L.R. 82.

Local connection

In exercising their obligations towards homeless applicants local authorities have a power to investigate whether an applicant has a local connection with the district of another local authority in Scotland, England or Wales.[76] In determining what having a local connection with a district means, there are four issues to be considered[77]: past normal voluntary residence, employment, family associations or any special circumstances. Residence is not deemed to be of a person's choice where that person was serving in the regular armed forces of the Crown or was in prison or was detained under the mental health legislation.[78] The courts, including the House of Lords, have accepted decisions taken in strict conformity with the guidelines laid down in the *Agreement on Procedures for Referrals of the Homeless*[79] as lawful.[80] In addition the House of Lords have suggested that, whilst a local connection not founded upon one of the four grounds is irrelevant, an applicant does not have a local connection simply through satisfying one or more of the grounds. Local connection is established through either one or more of these factors being present. It is these which spell out a local connection in real terms.[81] It must be built up and established and this is done through either residence, employment, family connection or other special circumstances.[82]

Normal residence has been interpreted following strictly the guidelines in the *Agreement*,[83] which equates this phrase with six months' residence during the past 12 months or three years during the previous five years. Longer periods of residence have not been recognised where the character of the residence did not denote permanence.[84] The general category of special circumstances has not been accepted as covering the tenant's desire to stay in a particular area,[85] nor membership of local institutions or organisations.[86]

If the authority establish in their inquiries that there is a local

---

[76] s. 28(2).
[77] s. 27.
[78] s. 27(2).
[79] Association of District Councils, Association of Metropolitan Associations and the London Boroughs Association (1979); reproduced in Andrew Arden, *Housing Act 1985*, Pt. III (3rd ed., 1986).
[80] *R. v. Eastleigh B.C., ex p. Betts* [1983] 2 A.C. 613.
[81] *Ibid.*
[82] *Ibid.* at p. 627.
[83] *R. v. Eastleigh B.C., ex p. Betts* [1983] 2 A.C. 613.
[84] *Brooks v. Midlothian D.C.*, Dec. 12, 1985 (O.H.).
[85] *R. v. Islington L.B.C., ex p. Adigun* (1988) 20 H.L.R. 600.
[86] *R. v. Vale of White Horse D.C., ex p. Smith and Hay* (1984) 17 H.L.R. 160.

connection elsewhere and none in their own area, the question of referral arises.[87] Pending agreement or referral elsewhere, the responsibility for housing the applicant remains with the original authority.[88] The conditions of referral affect both the applicant and any person who might reasonably be expected to reside with him.[89] The referral can operate in respect of another local authority where the original authority are satisfied that there is no local connection with their authority and there is one with the other authority.[90] This is subject to the overall test that the applicant will not run the risk of domestic violence in the other authority's district.[91] A person runs the risk of domestic violence if she runs the risk of violence from a person with whom, but for the risk of violence, she might reasonably be expected to reside.[92] This includes a person with whom she formerly resided.[93] Alternatively a woman runs the risk of violence if she runs the risk of threats of violence from a partner or ex-partner and these threats are likely to be carried out.[94] It is lawful for an authority to refer an applicant to an authority with whom the applicant has no local connection, provided all parties find such an arrangement to be acceptable.[95] Where applicants are entering Britain from abroad they are to be treated as having a local connection with the authority to which they apply.[96] If there is a local connection outwith Great Britain the local authority may refer the applicant back, exercising its power of securing accommodation from some other person.[97] The local authority must be satisfied that such a reference would not cause the applicant to run the risk of domestic violence.[98]

Since local authorities are given discretion to operate the homeless persons legislation, the appropriate method of challenge is through the medium of judicial review. The standard rules for judicial review apply under Rule of Court 260(B) which came into effect on April 30, 1985. Damages may also be sought as part of the

---

[87] s. 33.
[88] *R.* v. *Beverley B.C., ex p. McPhee, The Times*, Oct. 27, 1978.
[89] s. 33(2).
[90] s. 33(2)(*a*) and (*b*).
[91] s. 33(2)(*c*).
[92] s. 33(3)(*a*).
[93] *Ibid.*
[94] s. 33(*b*); *R.* v. *Islington L.B.C., ex p. Adigun* (1988) 20 H.L.R. 600.
[95] *R.* v. *Wyre B.C., ex p. Parr* (1982) 2 H.L.R. 71.
[96] *R.* v. *Hillingdon L.B.C., ex p. Streeting* [1980] 1 W.L.R. 430.
[97] s. 35(1)(*b*).
[98] *R.* v. *Bristol City Council, ex p. Browne* [1979] 1 W.L.R. 1437.

review process.[99] Provided an authority accept that they are under a duty, it is also possible to seek damages in the sheriff court.[100]

2. RIGHTS TO BE REHOUSED

Where occupiers of property affected by public works lose their current housing they are entitled to be rehoused in certain circumstances. Where a person is displaced from residential accommodation on any land in consequence of compulsory purchase, redevelopment or notices affecting substandard housing then, if suitable alternative accommodation on reasonable terms is not otherwise available to that person, the local authority must secure that suitable alternative accommodation will be provided.[101] There can be displacement where the dwelling is being improved and the original dwelling loses its identity.[102] Where there is different accommodation, it must be within a reasonable distance from the locality of the house from which he has been displaced.[103] There is authority that this does not entail the provision of permanent accommodation and can be limited to securing temporary bed and breakfast accommodation pending discussion on permanent accommodation.[104]

3. RIGHT TO BUY RENTED HOUSING

There are two groups of individuals entitled to buy rented housing. Sitting tenants who have secure tenancies may exercise the right to buy whether or not the landlord wishes to sell. In addition approved bodics may buy public sector housing whether the landlord wishes to sell or not, provided that the tenant is willing for the transfer to go ahead.

---

[99] *Mallon* v. *Monklands D.C.*, 1986 S.L.T. 347.

[100] *Purves* v. *Midlothian D.C.*, 1986 SCOLAG 144.

[101] Land Compensation (Scotland) Act 1973, s. 36; Housing (Scotland) Act 1987, s. 98.

[102] *Casale* v. *Islington L.B.C.* (1985) 18 H.L.R. 146.

[103] Housing (Scotland) Act 1987, s. 98.

[104] *R.* v. *Bristol Corpn., ex p. Hendy* [1974] 1 All E.R. 1047; *R.* v. *Hertfordshire D.C., ex p. Smith, The Times*, Jan. 25, 1990 on the equivalent English legislation; *Glasgow D.C.* v. *Douglas*, (unreptd.), discussed in 1979 ScoLAG 76.

(a) Tenant's Right to Buy

From 1980 public sector tenants were given the right to purchase the properties they were renting in certain circumstances. The coverage was extended in 1986 to tenancies granted by regional councils and housing associations. The law was consolidated in the Housing (Scotland) Act 1987. In terms of the Housing (Scotland) Act 1988, housing association tenancies granted on or after January 2, 1989 are assured tenancies, and these do not carry the right to purchase.[105]

(i) Entitlement to buy

Immediately prior to the date of service of the application to purchase, the tenant must have been resident for not less than two years in occupation of a house or a series of houses rented out by a public sector landlord. The right is not available to other relatives of the tenant except spouses, children (over the age of 16), or spouse of a child. Other family members may be accepted as a matter of discretion.[106] In computing what amounts to occupation the legislation provides that in the discretion of the landlord this included occupation by a member of the family of a tenant to whose rights as child of the tenant the applicant had succeeded.

(ii) Property subject to the right to buy

The full list of landlords whose property qualifies for the right to buy is specified in the Housing (Scotland) Act 1987[107] and covers public sector bodies. The most significant have been district and regional councils and Scottish Homes (formerly the Scottish Special Housing Association).

The basic rule is that secure tenancies are covered. A secure tenancy involves three requirements.[108] The property must be let as a separate dwelling.[109] The tenant must be an individual and the property must be the applicant's only or principal home.[110] The landlord must be one of a specific list of public sector tenancies noted.

Some of the properties of these landlords are exempted as they

---

[105] s. 43.
[106] See s. 61(10)(*v*)—*McDonald* v. *Renfrew D.C.*, 1982 S.L.T. (Lands Tr.) 30; *Robb* v. *Kyle and Carrick D.C.*, 1989 S.L.T. (Lands Tr.) 78.
[107] s. 61(2); see also s. 61(11) for qualifying occupancy.
[108] Housing (Scotland) Act 1987, s. 44.
[109] *Thomson* v. *City of Glasgow D.C.*, 1986 S.L.T. (Lands Tr.) 6; *Hannan* v. *Falkirk D.C.*, 1987 S.L.T. (Lands Tr.) 18.
[110] *Jenkins* v. *Renfrew D.C.*, 1989 S.L.T. (Lands Tr.) 41.

are declared not to comprise a secure tenancy.[111] These cover premises occupied under a contract of employment; temporary letting to persons seeking accommodation; temporary letting pending development; temporary accommodation during works; temporary accommodation for homeless persons; agricultural and business premises; police and fire authorities; houses part of, or within curtilage of, certain other buildings not used for housing purposes.

Most of the case law in relation to the right to buy stems from disputes about whether or not property that a public authority has been renting out falls within these exemptions. The question as to whether accommodation is occupied for the better performance of the employee's tasks has yielded extensive case law. The Lands Tribunal have looked at the reality of tasks actually done rather than at the formal contractual position.[112] The question of whether a building is part of or within the curtilage of non-housing property has generally been concerned with former schoolhouses[113] or related properties.[114] As indicated, housing association tenancies were briefly covered by the right-to-buy provisions after 1986 and until January 2, 1989 under the Housing (Scotland) Act 1988, and for those tenants with a right to buy these rights continue. However they are also subject to certain exceptions for specialist housing provision and other housing associations where sale would be particularly inappropriate.[115]

The Secretary of State may authorise refusal to sell certain houses provided for persons of pensionable age where these have facilities[116] which are substantially different from those of an ordinary house and which have been designed or adapted for occupation by persons of pensionable age whose special needs require accommodation of the kind provided by the house.[117] Where the landlord's application for exempt status is refused, then the landlord must make an offer to the tenant in accordance with the standard sale procedure.

[111] Housing (Scotland) Act 1987, s. 2.
[112] *McKay* v. *Livingston Dev. Corpn.*, 1990 S.L.T. (Lands Tr.) 54; *MacDonald* v. *Strathclyde R.C.*, 1990 S.L.T. (Lands Tr.) 10; *Gilmour* v. *City of Glasgow D.C.*, 1989 S.L.T. (Lands Tr.) 74; but see *De Fontenay* v. *Strathclyde R.C.*, Lands Tr., July 24, 1989.
[113] *Walker* v. *Strathclyde R.C.*, 1990 S.L.T. (Lands Tr.) 17.
[114] *Fisher* v. *Fife R.C.*, 1989 S.L.T. (Lands Tr.) 26; *Shipman* v. *Lothian R.C.*, 1989 S.L.T. (Lands Tr.) 82.
[115] s. 61(4).
[116] s. 69.
[117] See S.D.D. Circular 38/1980 for guidance on how the Secretary of State would operate this exemption.

(iii) **The price for sales**

The price is to be the market value of the house less any discount for years of occupancy.[118] The market value of the house is to be decided by the district valuer or a qualified valuer nominated by the landlord and accepted by the tenant. It is up to the landlord which of these individuals is selected. In fixing the market value the assumption must be made that the house is available for sale on the open market with vacant possession at the date of service of the application to purchase. The discount varies as between flats and houses and depends on the extent of the occupation by the tenant. For houses the discount is 32 per cent of the market value together with an additional one per cent of the market value for every year beyond two of continuous occupation by the appropriate person immediately preceding the date of service of the application to purchase the house. The period for continuous occupation includes a succession of houses provided by any of the public sector bodies indicated,[119] as well as any armed services accommodation provided by the Crown. The maximum discount is 60 per cent. This would be reached after 30 years. The discount for flats starts at 44 per cent of the market, together with an additional two per cent of the market value for every year beyond two of continuous occupation by the appropriate person immediately preceding the date of service of the application to purchase the flat. Again succession of occupation is permitted. The maximum discount for flats is 70 per cent of the market value—this would be reached after 15 years. For discount purposes the tenant is the appropriate person unless there would be a higher discount by looking to the spouse—provided that they are cohabiting at the time of date of service of the application to purchase.

Where there is outstanding debt on a property incurred by a local authority in making improvements there is provision for the price to be adjusted to take account of this work. Where a debt is incurred by the local authority after a certain date on improvement work on a property, the price to be fixed in a right to buy must not be less than that outstanding debt or the market value of the house, whichever was the lesser.[120] The term "outstanding debt" is defined as meaning "any undischarged debt arising from the cost of works of improvement . . . together with the administrative costs attributable to these works."[121]

---

[118] s. 62.
[119] s. 61(11).
[120] s. 62(8).
[121] *Wingate* v. *Clydebank D.C.*, Lands Tr., Nov. 2, 1989.

In the event of the tenant selling the property before the expiry of three years from the date of service of a notice of acceptance by the tenant, the landlords may recover a proportion of the difference between the market value of the house and the discounted price at which the tenant purchased the property.[122] This does not apply where part only of the property is sold and the remainder continues to be the only or principal home of the purchasing tenant. It only applies on the first disposal during the period. The proportion of the difference varies from 100 per cent where the disposal occurs in the first year to 66 per cent during the second year and 33 per cent during the third year.

There is no recovery of discount where the disposal is by the executor of the deceased owner or as a result of a compulsory purchase order or the disposal is to a member of the owner's family who has lived with him for a period of 12 months before the disposal and there is no payment involved.

A specific procedure is laid down for the purchase of public sector housing under the Housing (Scotland) Act 1987.[123] A tenant who seeks to exercise a right to purchase a public sector house must serve an "application to purchase" notice on the landlord. This must contain a notice that the tenant seeks to exercise the right to purchase, a statement of any period of qualifying occupancy and the name of any joint purchaser.[124] The landlord must, unless disputing the application, within two months of receipt of the application to purchase serve an "offer to sell."[125] This must contain the market value of the house, the discount and the resulting price of the house, along with any conditions the landlord intends to impose and an actual offer to sell the house at the price and under the conditions mentioned. Where the tenant wishes to exercise the right to purchase and does not dispute the terms of the offer, then a "notice of acceptance" must be served on the landlord within two months of the offer to sell or of any date resolving a dispute on any aspect of the sale.[126] Reasonable conditions of sale may be included in the offer to sell, provided that the conditions allow the tenant to have as full enjoyment and use of the house as owner as he enjoyed as tenant.[127] In addition they must secure to the tenant such additional rights as are necessary for the reasonable enjoyment and use of the

[122] s. 72.
[123] s. 63.
[124] s. 63(1).
[125] s. 63(2).
[126] s. 66.
[127] s. 64.

house as owner as well as imposing on the tenant any necessary duties relative to rights so secured. The conditions must include such terms as are necessary to entitle the tenant to receive a good and marketable title to the house.

If there is a condition which imposes a new charge or an increase of an existing charge for the provision of a service in relation to the house, it must provide for the charge to be in reasonable proportion to the cost to the landlord of providing the service. No condition is to be imposed which has the effect of requiring the tenant to pay any expenses of the landlord. Option to purchase clauses in favour of the landlord are not permitted unless in relation to a house which has facilities substantially different from those of an ordinary house and which have been designed or adapted for occupation by a person of pensionable age or a disabled person with a special needs requirement. Where there is such a permitted option to purchase then the price is to be determined by the district valuer on a market value basis taking account of any early-sale recovered discount. The Lands Tribunal have the power to deal with objections about conditions, which they may strike out, vary or replace with new ones.[128] The market value does not constitute a condition which can be challenged.[129]

Where the landlord disputes the tenant's right to purchase it must serve a "notice of refusal" within a month of the service of the "application to purchase." A notice of refusal must specify the grounds on which the landlord disputes the tenant's right to purchase or the accuracy of the information upon which the purported right is founded. Where a landlord serves a notice of refusal the tenant may within a month of receipt of such notice apply to the Lands Tribunal for a finding that there is a right to purchase the house on such terms as it may determine.[130]

There is special provision, where an islands council is landlord of property held for the purposes of education and required for accommodation of a person who is or will be employed by the council for educational purposes, and where other suitable accommodation cannot be provided by the council, that the landlord may serve a notice of refusal within one month of service of the application to purchase.[131]

Where an offer to sell has been served on the tenant and a related

---

[128] s. 65.

[129] *MacLeod* v. *Ross and Cromarty D.C.*, 1983 S.L.T. (Lands Tr.) 5; see also *Pollock* v. *Dumbarton D.C.*, 1983 S.L.T. (Lands Tr.) 17.

[130] s. 68.

[131] s. 70.

notice of acceptance has been served on the landlord, a contract of sale of the house shall be constituted between the landlord and the tenant on the terms contained in the offer to sell. The question has arisen as to what happens to this agreement if the tenant dies after the contract has been concluded but before the conveyancing is completed. This has arisen in a Scottish case as well as under similar legislation covering England and Wales. The 1987 legislation provides a series of steps up to the making of a contract but is silent on the conveyance. The view taken by the Court of Session, confirmed in the House of Lords, was that the relatives of the deceased tenant were entitled to have the conveyance completed in their favour.[132]

(b) The Right to Buy for Potential Landlords

The Housing (Scotland) Act 1988 makes provision for certain approved landlords to make an approach to tenants of local authorities.[133] If the tenants are agreeable, then a procedure is laid down which the authority must follow. As in the tenant's right to buy, it is intended that the local authority will not be able to resist such a procedure on the grounds of housing policy. This procedure should be distinguished from voluntary transfers in terms of the Housing (Scotland) Act 1987.[134]

4. RIGHTS TO DISPOSSESS CO-OCCUPIERS

Statutory rights of occupancy have been provided since September 1, 1982 to spouses and certain cohabitees. The notion of occupancy rights for spouses and partners was a novel concept in Scots law when it was introduced in the Matrimonial Homes (Family Protection) (Scotland) Act 1981. It provided that where one spouse had a title to stay in a house, either as owner or tenant then the other spouse, who was neither tenant nor owner was given the right, if in occupation, to continue to occupy the matrimonial home and, if not in occupation, a right to enter and occupy the matrimonial home.[135]

Cohabitees have more limited occupancy rights. They may apply for the right to stay for six months (originally this was limited to

---

[132] *Cooper's Exrs.* v. *Edinburgh D.C.*, 1990 S.L.T. 621 (Court of Session); [1991] E.G.S.C. 34 (H.L.).

[133] Pt. III, ss. 56–64.

[134] ss. 13 and 14.

[135] s. 1(1).

three months). There is provision for extensions beyond this original period.[136]

(i) Termination of occupancy rights

Occupancy rights come to an end when the marriage ends; the owner/tenant loses his ownership/tenancy rights; the matrimonial home ceases to exist or when the rights are renounced in the form prescribed by the 1981 Act.

(ii) Treatment of property owned jointly

In the normal instance whilst joint owners are not relying on the existence of occupancy rights to remain in property if they are deserted the 1981 Act is involved. If a joint owner wishes to realise his or her share of a property there is a process open called an action of division and sale. This can be insisted upon by any joint owner.[137] Where a spouse brings an action for division and sale of the matrimonial home the court has a rôle in relation to the granting of such a request stemming from the 1981 Act. The court may refuse to grant such a request or postpone granting a decree for such period as it considers reasonable in the circumstances or may grant a decree subject to such conditions as it may prescribe.[138]

In deciding on such applications the court must have regard to all the circumstances of the cases along with the conduct of the spouses in relation to each other and otherwise; the respective needs and financial resources of the spouses; the needs of any child of the family and the extent to which the matrimonial home is used in connection with a trade, business or profession of either spouse and whether there has been an offer by the entitled spouse of suitable alternative accommodation.[139]

(iii) Protection of the non-owner if there are plans to sell the matrimonial home

The non-owner must give their consent to such an action. This consent must be given in a prescribed form in writing before a notary public.[140] There is provision where such consent is not given for the owner to ask the court to dispense with the consent. It must be established either that consent is unreasonably withheld; consent is not possible by reason of physical or mental disability; the

---

[136] s. 18.
[137] See above at pp. 195–196.
[138] s. 19.
[139] s. 3(3).
[140] s. 6(3)(*a*) and S.I. 1982 No. 971.

other spouse cannot be found after reasonable steps have been taken to trace him or her.[141] The criteria for deciding on such a request are the same set of criteria indicated above for declaring and regulation of occupancy rights and for actions of division and sale.[142]

The question of the unreasonable withholding of consent and the dispensation of consent to a sale was dealt with in *Hall* v. *Hall.*[143] Both the sheriff and sheriff principal refused a motion for division and sale because the husband had failed to establish that it was "fair and reasonably necessary to disturb" his wife's occupation of the five-room bungalow which they had bought with a view to retirement. They quarrelled and led separate lives within the house but shared a common social life. It was up to the party who was seeking to disturb occupancy rights to show that it was fair and reasonably necessary to cause this disturbance. In *O'Neill* v. *O'Neill*[144] the sheriff was not, however, prepared to allow a wife to withhold her consent to the sale of a second home used by the husband in his job some 85 miles from the original home. Here the wife had no intention of using the property but was using her right to withhold consent to the sale to obtain a better deal in the couple's divorce settlement.

The circumstances when a spouse can insist on an action of division and sale of the matrimonial home, and the interpretation of the relevant sections of the Matrimonial Homes (Family Protection) (Scotland) Act 1981, were discussed in *Berry* v. *Berry.*[145] The Berrys were seeking divorce from each other in separate cross-actions. They were joint owners of the matrimonial home. Mrs Berry wished to have the matrimonial home sold which Mr Berry was occupying. Mr Berry refused to agree to the sale of the house and Mrs Berry sought to obtain permission for an action of division and sale which was required from the court. Mr Berry's argument was that the questions of the conduct of the spouses and their financial resources were the subject of great dispute, and that it would be inappropriate to deal with such an important issue as the division and sale of the matrimonial home as a separate one. The value of the matrimonial home might well be a very relevant factor in determining what capital payment might be made between the parties. Mrs Berry successfully argued that the whole purpose of the

[141] s. 7.
[142] s. 3(3).
[143] 1987 S.L.T. (Sh.Ct.) 15.
[144] 1987 S.L.T. (Sh.Ct.) 26.
[145] 1988 S.L.T. 630.

Matrimonial Homes Act was to provide protection of occupancy rights as opposed to deciding on the ultimate division of the assets of the parties.

(iv) The nature of "dealings" which require consent

The 1981 Act protects non-owners against proposed sales by requiring various declarations by a seller concerning the existence of any other person who might have occupancy rights in the matrimonial home. There is no problem of course where there is a joint ownership, since the joint owner would not only need to consent to the sale but also to sign the relevant legal documents before witnesses.

Questions have arisen, however, as to what stage must be reached before it can be said that there is a proposed sale ("dealing" is the phrase used in the 1981 Act) to which the non-owner or joint owner can consider giving consent. In *Dunsmore* v. *Dunsmore*[146] the husband and wife reached an impasse over the sale of the house. They agreed that the husband would buy the wife's half-share but disagreed about the amount. The wife raised an action for division and sale and asked the court to dispense with the husband's consent to the proposed dealing. The court did not allow these difficulties to be overcome through dispensing with the consent of the husband to a proposed sale. There was no dealing here. That would require a third party to be involved. What was appropriate was an action of division and sale.

On a related theme the sheriff principal for South Strathclyde was unwilling to regard a plan to put the matrimonial home on the market at between £80,000 and £100,000 as a proposed sale or dealing in *Fyfe* v. *Fyfe*.[147] The husband here was trying to get the court to dispense with the consent of the wife when he wished to sell the matrimonial home. He sought sanction of the court to what he termed a "proposed dealing." The sheriff principal did not agree. If a spouse was considering the question of granting or withholding consent they were entitled to notice of what price and conditions of sale were proposed. A broad figure was not something one could apply one's mind to. Until the terms of such a dealing or proposed sale were known it was not possible to see whether the non-entitled spouse was withholding her consent unreasonably. In *Berry* v. *Berry (No. 2)*[148] Lord Cowie in the Outer House rejected the suggestion by Mr Berry that he should be able to buy out his wife's

---

[146] 1986 S.L.T. (Sh.Ct.) 9.
[147] 1987 S.L.T. (Sh.Ct.) 38.
[148] 1989 S.L.T. 292.

half-share at half the market price to be fixed by a reporter. He also rejected the alternative suggestion that the old method of public roup (auction) be used. His view was that the modern approach, following *Campbells* v. *Murray*,[149] was to prefer sale by private treaty, *i.e.* offers over a certain price, as is current in Scotland with the accepted written offer binding on the parties.

(a) Exclusion Orders and the Suspension of Occupancy Rights

In certain circumstances it is possible that a spouse or cohabitee can, in effect, lose their occupancy rights by having them suspended. The courts, if they are suspending occupancy rights, are required under the 1981 Act to grant a court order prohibiting the other party from entering the matrimonial home without the express permission of the applicant. To make this exclusion effective the court must also grant two other related orders—unless the other spouse can show the court that it is unnecessary to do so. These involve the granting of an order for summary ejection of the other party from the matrimonial home and an order prohibiting the removal by the other party of any furniture from the matrimonial home. The court may add such terms and conditions as it chooses to such orders.[150]

In addition the court may make an order prohibiting the other party from entering or remaining in the vicinity of the matrimonial home, adding such terms and conditions as it considers appropriate. There is also a discretion to give directions about the preservation of the other party's goods and effects remaining in the matrimonial home where an order has been granted for the summary ejection in the absence of the other party.[151]

Most of the legal controversy to date in this area centres around the swift procedure introduced in section 4(6) of the 1981 Act which provides for interim suspension of occupancy rights. Provision is made for a very early hearing on the question of exclusion, usually within a week of starting court proceedings. In legal terms this is extremely swift, since it is only a little longer than the time taken to serve the legal documents on the other party. Any decision to grant an exclusion order at this time has the same effect as a full hearing after all the legal procedures of a normal ordinary civil action have been completed. The area of interim exclusion orders is the one

[149] 1972 S.L.T. 249.
[150] s. 4(4).
[151] s. 4(5).

most often dealt with in applications under the 1981 Act, as these are usually part of an action for divorce. Since such orders as exclusion orders end on divorce there is little incentive to obtain a final order prior to the dissolution of the relationship. The legal tests are the same in any event for interim and final orders.

(b) General Principles for Suspension of Occupancy Rights

1. Exclusion cannot result from an order regulating occupancy rights.[152]
2. The general test for exclusion orders is whether or not the order is necessary.[153]
3. The court must not make an exclusion order if it appears that the making of the order would be unjustified or unreasonable.[154]
4. There can be no interim order suspending occupancy rights until the other party has had the opportunity of being heard by or represented before the court.[155]

The courts have indicated what sorts of issues are relevant in deciding whether or not it is necessary for an individual to lose his or her occupancy rights and in what circumstances it would be unjustified or unreasonable to grant an exclusion order. The statute provides for two stages in the process of deciding about exclusion orders.

(i) Is the exclusion order necessary?

The 1981 Act indicates that if the necessity test is satisfied the court must make an order (subject to the specific terms of section 4(3) on the question of whether such an order is unjustified or unreasonable):

> "the court shall make an exclusion order it if appears to the court that the making of the order is necessary for the protection of the applicant or any child of the family from any conduct or threatened or reasonably apprehended conduct of the non-applicant spouse which is or would be injurious to the physical or mental health of the applicant or child."[156]

---

[152] s. 3(5).
[153] s. 4(2) and *Bell* v. *Bell*, 1982 S.L.T. 224.
[154] s. 4(3).
[155] s. 4(6).
[156] s. 4(2).

This formulation is more limited than the law in England and Wales which talks simply in terms of whether or not an exclusion order is justified or reasonable. It is rather closer to the law in the Irish Republic which provides for equivalent "barring orders" where the court considers the "safety and welfare of the applicant spouse or of any child" if the family so requires.[157] The Law Reform (Miscellaneous Provisions) (Scotland) Act 1985 made it clear that an exclusion order is available to an applicant whether or not that spouse is in occupation at the time of the application.[158]

There was some evidence that in the early days of the operation of the 1981 Act some sheriffs were making decisions at the interim stage on the basis of how *ex parte* interdicts were decided. They were using the test of the "balance of convenience." This was explicitly rejected in *Smith* v. *Smith*.[159] The reason for this was simply the provisions of section 4(6) requiring the test to be whether the interim order is necessary rather than any question of balancing convenience. Essentially what some sheriffs' judgments indicated was that they seemed to be balancing the competing needs of the applicant and the other party rather than addressing the direct question of whether there was a necessity for the granting of the order. This was in practice a matter more often of the phraseology used by judges than a mistaken test. The most recent comprehensive test was put forward by Lord Dunpark in *McCafferty* v. *McCafferty*[160]:

(1) What is the nature and quality of the alleged conduct?

(2) Is the court satisfied that the conduct is likely to be repeated if cohabitation continues?

(3) Has the conduct been or, if repeated would it be, injurious to the physical or mental health of the applicant spouse or to any child of the family?

(4) If so, is the order sought necessary for the future protection of the physical or mental health of the applicant or child?

Establishing the need for the protection of an exclusion order was a practical problem which was also looked at in the *Bell* and *Smith* cases. Whilst it might be reasonably simple to obtain evidence in an ordinary action, the speed with which interim hearings reached court meant that problems could arise in getting satisfactory evidence to back up claims of harm or threats. The Court of Session made it clear that they were unhappy about sheriffs simply accept-

---

[157] Family Law (Protection of Spouses and Children) Act 1981.
[158] s. 13(5).
[159] 1983 S.L.T. 275.
[160] 1986 S.L.T. 650.

ing the *ex parte* statements of the applicant as opposed to their denial by the other party. Where possible, some external evidence was to be provided—convictions; medical certificates; or an independent report.

In addition, subsequently affidavits have been approved as a more reliable source than mere statements by the parties since, as Lord Wheatley pointed out when hearing the *Brown* appeal, they are made under oath. They are now frequently used and accepted as satisfactory evidence in applications at interim exclusion order hearings.

(ii) Would the making of the order be unjustified or unreasonable?

In terms of the 1981 Act the court must also consider a second question in their deliberations about making an exclusion order.[161] However, there are no reported cases where this aspect of the test has been fully discussed. The Scottish Law Commission in explaining its inclusion in the test for making an exclusion order had in mind that "exclusion of a husband may have serious economic consequences for the whole family unit which would render an exclusion order a quite inappropriate remedy."[162]

In *Cowie* v. *Cowie*,[163] Lord Grieve referred to "the peculiar exercise required by section 4(3)." In this particular case the matter which the husband had suggested should retain him in the house was his need to give mathematics tutorials from the home. Since this involved no specific apparatus it was no more than an inconvenience that he should be deprived of this possibility in the future. Beyond approving the sheriff's decision the Inner House provide no clue to the enigma of section 4(3). Perhaps it might be thought appropriate for a patient who has a dialysis machine or something similar installed in the matrimonial home but whose behaviour warrants the protection of an exclusion order. In addition, where a house has been specially adapted for a disabled person, it could be argued it would be a better use of housing stock to keep the disabled person in that house and require the able-bodied but abused spouse to move out. It has been suggested that the test would be required where both parties were able to establish necessity.[164]

---

[161] s. 4(3).
[162] Scot. Law Com., No. 60, para. 4.7.
[163] I.H., Nov. 4, 1986.
[164] Scot. Law Comm., *Family Law—Pre-Consolidation Reforms*, D.P. 85 (March 1990), at 6.34.

(c) **Exclusion Orders and Cohabitees**

Cohabitees' occupancy rights include the use of the exclusion order.[165] However, a problem has emerged which calls for attention. In *Clarke* v. *Hatten*[166] it was established that a cohabitee who was the tenant could not apply for an exclusion order where the other party did not seem to have his occupancy rights declared. The partner was not the tenant and assaulted the tenant, causing her to have to leave the house. For married couples the ceremony of marriage brings occupancy rights into existence. Cohabitation has no clear equivalent "starting point." For cohabitees the court may, on the application of the non-entitled partner, if it appears that the man and the woman are a cohabiting couple in that house, grant occupancy rights therein to the applicant. Until such an application a cohabitee has what could be called the "potential for a right." The tenant who seeks protection under the 1981 Act cannot, of their own volition, bring this section into force. The sheriff principal reviewed the question of whether an exclusion order could be properly granted if the non-tenant failed to make an application on his own behalf and decided that the pursuer might have a remedy in a common law action of ejection or interdict. The disadvantage with this is that this remedy would not carry with it a power of arrest.[167] The cohabitee therefore can be ejected and interdicted from returning, but with no powers of arrest attached.

[165] s. 18.
[166] 1987 S.C.L.R. 521.
[167] s. 15.

INDEX